START YOUR OWN
HAUL-AWAY BUSINESS

**EARN $50 TO $120 AN HOUR HAULING
JUNK WITH A PICKUP TRUCK OR VAN**

CRAIG WALLIN

Second Edition

**Start Your Own Haul-Away Business
Earn $50 to $120 an Hour Hauling
Junk with a Pickup Truck or Van**

Copyright © 2020 by Craig Wallin

www.headstartpublishing.com

All Rights Reserved. This guide may not be reproduced or transmitted in any form without the written permission of the publisher. Every effort has been made to make this guide as complete and accurate as possible. Although the author and publisher have prepared this guide with the greatest of care, and have made every effort to ensure the accuracy, we assume no responsibility or liability for errors, inaccuracies or omissions. Our liability is limited to the purchase price of this guide. Before you begin, check with the appropriate authorities to ensure compliance with all laws and regulations.

This guide is sold with the understanding that the author and publisher are not engaged in rendering legal, accounting or other professional services. If professional assistance is required, the services of a competent professional person should be sought. Any mention of a company or web site in this guide does not mean that the author or publisher endorse it. Readers should be aware that internet websites mentioned in this guide may have changed or disappeared between when the guide was written and when you read this book.

Dedication

If you've been downsized, outsourced, grown tired of the rat race or just need more income and a brighter future, this book is for you. If you're ready to take charge and become your own boss, this book is for you.

I'm proud of you! You're doing something that most of us only dream about but never begin - starting your own business. There are many steps that go into starting a business, and it can seem like an impossible task. Where do I start? What should I do first? Who can I turn to for help? Now, with this detailed guide you will have the help you need to start your own successful and profitable junk hauling business.

Since I published the first edition of this guidebook eight years ago, I've heard from many readers who have started their own profitable junk hauling businesses. I'm thankful they have shared their stories, because their contributions have made this second edition a bigger, better and more useful guide. Thank you all!

What was amazing to me is that many of these readers who started their own junk hauling business told me their sales were above $100,000!

Thanks for buying this guidebook and may your new business grow and prosper!

Craig Wallin

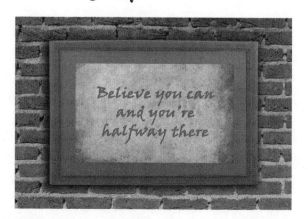

Table of Contents

Introduction - Hauling Trash for Cash   **1**
    How Much Can I Make?   4
    Success Factors   5

Chapter 1:   **Business Basics**   **7**
    Legal structure   7
    Licensing   9
    Solo or Employees?   9
    Naming your haul-away business   10
    Looking Good with a Logo   13
    Insurance   15

Chapter 2:   **Setting Up Your Business Office**   **16**
    Scheduling   17
    Business cards   19
    Magnetic signs.   19

	Taxes and Accounting	19
	Business Supplies	25
Chapter 3:	Services to Offer	30
	Foreclosure Cleanouts	34
	Sideline Business – Ikea Hauling	46

Chapter 4: How to Find Customers — 47

- Conventional marketing — 47
- How to Set Up Your Own Haul-Away Business Website — 52
- Let Google Help Your Customers Find You — 57
- Local S.E.O. — 59
- How to find the best keywords for local S.E.O. — 60
- How to Set Up Your "Google My Business" Profile — 61
- Google Reviews — 61
- How to Get More Google Reviews — 62
- Free Social Media Marketing — 62
- Is a Facebook Page Better Than a Web Site? — 65

Chapter 5: Pricing Haul-Away Services — 70

- Show Me the Money - Getting Paid — 73

TABLE OF CONTENTS

Chapter 6: Success Stories and Pro Tips		**76**
	Pro Tips	79
	Why You Should Love Complaints	81
Chapter 7:	**Setting Goals & Networking**	**83**
	Setting Realistic Goals	85
	Deadlines	85
	The 80/20 Rule	86
	Limiting Beliefs	88
	Visualize Your Success	88
	Networking - How to Do It Right	89
Chapter 8:	**Is a Franchise Right for You?**	**92**
Chapter 9: Forms & Safety Tips		**97**
	Haul-Away Log	98
	Safety Tips	103
Chapter 10: Growing Your Business		**105**
	Hiring Employees	105
	When is It Time to Hire Employees?	106
	How to Find Good Employees	107
	What to Pay Your Employees	107

Pre - Hiring Setup	108
Background Checks	108
Advertise Your Job	110
Employee Record Keeping and Taxes	110
Why Hire a Bookkeeper?	111

Introduction - Hauling Trash for Cash

Getting rid of junk can be a major problem for anyone unable to haul it away. Every time someone moves, they find things that don't work, don't fit or they simply don't need any more. Even if you stay in the same home, appliances break or die, furniture wears out or gets shredded by the cat and unwanted stuff piles up everywhere.

After a remodeling project, there is always a pile of debris. The old fence, deck or shed is too far gone to fix – more debris. Old exercise equipment, garden waste, busted lawn mower – more debris.

Most of us wish we could make it all disappear. Smart entrepreneurs can do just that, with a haul-away service. For a reasonable fee they will back up a truck or trailer, clean out all that debris and take it away.

Most haul-away services are green businesses as well. They don't just pick up your junk and dump it at the landfill. Any recyclable material, such as re-usable lumber or furniture, goes to local recyclers or to charities such as goodwill.

Because almost every home in America has too much junk, it fills up garages, closets, attics, basements and sheds. When the house and garage fill up, off it goes to a rented storage unit where even more junk piles up.

"Hauling – the World's Second Oldest Profession."

If you would like to earn an above-average income helping folks in your area get rid of their excess junk, consider starting a haul-away business. It's a business that is inexpensive to start, requiring only a pickup truck, van or utility trailer and a few hand tools. You can operate a haul-away business in your spare time, evenings and weekends, and make a few hundred dollars, or go full time for a higher income.

Most haul-away services make both "front-end" money from cleanup and haul-away fees from customers and "back-end" money from re- selling valuable items that your customers consider to be trash. Customers often say "Just get it out of here", even if they know an item, such as a piece of furniture, has value.

Of course, one person's junk is another's treasure. You'll be amazed at what gets discarded. People get rid of barely used exercise equipment, bicycles, sports equipment, paintings, antiques, furniture, unwanted presents and more.

INTRODUCTION

After you've been paid to haul it away, you can keep what you want or might need in the future, donate items to charity, sell items that have value or recycle reusable materials. Most haulers have found that only about half of what they're paid to haul away actually ends up in the dump.

Businesses, including contractors, offices, property managers and real estate agents, often need to dispose of worn-out equipment such as computers, printers, files, furniture and debris left behind when a tenant moves out. More work for your new haul-away service!

Whenever there is a recession, more and more homes slip into foreclosure and are abandoned. When people lose their homes and leave, they tend to leave a lot of unwanted stuff behind. That has created another specialty niche for haul-away services – foreclosure cleanups.

Before the bank or other lender can put the house back on the market, it has to be show-able. The real estate agent who is handling the project will hire the specialists to clean out, clean up, repair and get the house ready to sell.

In addition to cleaning up the junk left behind, many haul-away services also do other related foreclosure cleanup services to bring in even more income. Although this book is not about foreclosure cleanouts, you'll find more information in a later chapter.

According to the U.S. Bureau of Labor Statistics, over half of all businesses are home-based. Join the crowd, and start your haul-away business at home, where there is no rent to pay, or additional utility costs. In addition, you may be able to deduct part of your mortgage payment or rent, and other household expenses, like utilities, at tax time.

It's time to declare your independence and get your share of the American dream with a haul-away business. If you follow the simple steps in the chapters that follow, you can be earning a good income in no time!

How Much Can I Make?

Most haul-away services charge customers by the size or weight of the load, plus a surcharge if the junk has to be removed from difficult spots, like attics or basements. After deducting expenses for dump fees, fuel and vehicle maintenance and other overhead, the national average rate is around $58 an hour (more in large cities, less in small towns and rural areas).

INTRODUCTION

Working 8 hours a day, that's $464 a day, $2,320 a week, or $116,000 yearly working just five days a week. Re-selling some of the "treasures in the trash" can add quite a bit to that as well.

Success Factors

To succeed with your new haul-away service, there are four qualities that are essential. Without exception, all successful haul away business owners have these qualities, and you should as well.

- ✓ Willingness to work – You'll never get ahead in the haul-away business unless you are willing to work hard. If it was easy, everybody would be doing it.

- ✓ Persistence – If you get up each time you stumble, and keep moving forward, you will succeed. Don't let problems or the occasional unhappy customer slow you down or discourage you. Keep focused on your goal of a successful, profitable business.

- ✓ Marketing ability – If you think just being a hard worker is enough, think again. You need to continually let everyone know about your haul-away business and give them a reason to hire you the first time. While you can expect satisfied customers to call you back regularly, you still need to take the initiative, and sell yourself to keep busy and profitable. Fortunately, there are several free and low-cost ways to do that, which we will explore in a later chapter.

✓ Service – The haul-away business is a service business, and if you don't provide good service, your business will struggle. Service is all about the small touches, like being sure to sweep the area you just cleaned out so it looks neat and tidy, or showing up when you promised so the customer isn't kept waiting. If you provide good service, you will never have to worry about the competition.

In the chapters that follow, you'll learn about the essential start up steps of starting your haul-away business, from getting a business license to finding customers. The material you'll read is designed to provide the basic information you need to get going.

CHAPTER ONE

Business Basics

Legal structure

Before you can offer your haul-away services, you'll need to set up your business, decide on a legal structure, pick a name, get a business license and get a tax identification number from the IRS. First, let's take a look at the three most common legal structures for a haul-away service business: sole proprietorship, partnership and limited liability company (LLC).

A sole proprietorship is an unincorporated business that is owned by an individual. You are the sole owner of the business, and the liabilities and risks of the business are yours as well. The income and expenses of the business are included on your personal tax return. As a sole proprietor, you are responsible for paying income tax on your earnings.

If you plan to start a haul-away service business with a partner, you can form a partnership, a legal structure that allows the business to "pass through" profits and losses to the individual partners, who them include their share on a personal tax return.

A limited liability company, also referred to as an LLC, is a newer business structure that has become quite popular, as it gives its owners limited liability from debts and actions of the business, just like a corporation, yet allows the benefit of pass-through taxation, just like a sole proprietorship. Most states provide a downloadable form you can use to set up an LLC without using a legal advisor.

For more in-depth information on choosing the best legal structure for your personal situation, go to www.nolo.com, where you'll find lots of free information, as well as the best books on the subject.

Whatever your choice of a legal structure for your new business, you will need to obtain a federal tax identification number, or EIN. You can apply online, at: www.irs.gov by clicking first on businesses, then on employer i.d. numbers.

When working with contractors and other businesses, you will often be required, for tax purposes to supply your EIN. Most companies want you to supply that information on the standard W-9 form, also available from www.irs.gov. As it's one of the most often requested IRS forms, you'll see it listed on the home page, where you can just click, and then download a copy.

Licensing

Check with your town or county to find out the specific requirements for licensing your new business. If you plan to operate out of your home, a separate license may be required. Most states also have business licensing requirements as well. The U.S. Small Business Administration has an online list of state business licensing web sites – just click on your state to learn more: www.sba.gov/hotlist/license.html.

Solo or Employees?

Many small haul-away owners are "lone eagles" and prefer to keep their business small and simple. A few, lured by the higher income potential, hire employees to do most of the field work and focus on managing the business. While it's true a larger haul-away service business can generate a substantial income, it can be a lot of work.

You need to hire and manage employees, handle administrative tasks, and spend less time out in the field. It's up to you to decide which direction to take, and there is no hurry to decide. Start small, and after a while the right decision will be easy to make.

The majority of the local haul-away services are one or two person businesses. The main reason given by most for staying small was they started a haul-away service business for independence and flexibility, and wanted to stay small, rather than becoming a manager, with the added responsibilities and stresses that can bring.

Naming your haul-away business

Start by making a list of possible names for your haul-away business. For ideas, do an internet search for "junk hauling business" or "haul-away business." This should produce a long list of names used by other haul away services. Whittle it down to a dozen or less that you like, then ask friends and family what they think of the names on your list.

Next, ask yourself the following questions about the names on your list:

- ✓ Is the name easy to remember? For example, Junk-Away.
- ✓ Does the name connect your business to your community, as in: Lynden
- ✓ Haul-Away Service or Chino Valley Junk Removal?
- ✓ Does using your own name appeal to you, as in: Logan's Haul-Away
- ✓ Service?

The drawback to using your own name is if you ever sell the business, the name may be inappropriate for the new owners.

Your phone company can often get a special phone number for you with your local prefix and 3867 or 5865 as the last four digits. They spell DUMP or JUNK, so you can have an easy-to-remember number that can be used in marketing your business. For example, imagine 296-DUMP or 302-JUNK in big bold letters on your truck!

Here are a few names to get you started:

- Good Riddance
- Dump-It
- Clutter Trucker
- Clutter Busters
- Eco-Haulers
- Dirty Deeds
- Junk Away
- Junk Hauling Pros
- Green Junk
- Junk Be Gone
- Grunt-N-Dump
- Too Much Junk?
- Haul Away
- Junk It
- Junk Express
- Junk Hunters

- Trash Takers
- Rubbish Riddance
- Trash Raiders
- Junk Haulers
- Junk Patrol
- Get Trashed

Another option that can help "brand" your business is to use a slogan in your ads, business cards and other marketing materials. Possible slogans include:

- Consider It Done
- Mission Accomplished
- At Your Service
- Rubbish to Haul – Give Us a Call
- Don't Distress – We'll Clean Up the Mess
- We Take the U out of Junk
- You Call – We Haul

After you've chosen a name, check with your county or the Secretary of State for your state, to make sure no one else has registered a business with the same name. It's also a good idea to check with the U.S. Patent & Trademark office to make sure the name is not trademarked by another firm or individual. To do a free search, go to: www.uspto.gov.

After you've found a name that is available, you can "claim" it by registering it as a business name. The laws vary from state to state, so check with your state's secretary of state to find out the procedures in your area. Registering your new name prevents anyone else from using the same name.

Looking Good with a Logo

A well-designed logo, or symbol, is one of the best tools in building recognition for your business even if you're just getting started. A logo helps people remember your business. When they see the logo in advertising, on a sign or package, on your stationary or on your web site, they make that visual connection to you.

A well-designed logo helps establish that your business is legitimate and credible. If you have a logo, people tend to believe that your business is here to stay and trustworthy.

Today, thanks to the many internet-based sources for logos, you can get a basic logo for just a few dollars. If you're on a very lean budget, visit Fiverr.com and search the site for "logo design."

You can spend as little as $5 at Fiverr, but my suggestion is to get a basic logo from two or three designers there and pick the one you like the best. (Give each one the same instructions about the look and color you want.) You can also have them take the finished logo you pick and make it into a "banner" or "header" for the top of your website.

At Fiverr.com, just enter "logo design" in the search bar to get started. You'll find hundreds to choose from, so I recommend using a "level one" or "level two" seller/designer who has at least 100 five-star reviews. That will narrow the field down and make it easier to find the best ones.

Explain to each logo designer what you want, such as text only, text and images, and the colors you prefer. When you have the 3 finished logo designs pick your favorite and add any extras from that designer you may want, like a header for your website using the new logo. Here are a few points to remember about planning your logo:

- ✓ A logo should be timeless, so it can be used for your business for decades.

CHAPTER 1 - BUSINESS BASICS

- ✓ A logo should be simple, easy to understand, and not confuse people.
- ✓ Never, ever copy or design a logo similar to another, as it's an invitation to a lawsuit, as well as just plain lazy and unethical.
- ✓ Will the logo still make sense as your business expands and grows?
- ✓ Is the logo easy to see in all sizes, from a yard sign to a business card?

Insurance

Insurance is essential for a haul-away business. It can protect you and your assets in the event of a lawsuit or other claim.

Vehicle Insurance. Check with your insurance agent to find out what is required in your state. Most states require either a rider/endorsement or a separate insurance policy if you use your vehicle for business.

Business Liability Insurance. Make sure you work with an insurance agent who understands your haul-away business, and its unique insurance needs.

CHAPTER TWO

Setting Up Your Business Office

When you're setting up your new office, simple is best. You can always add the fancy new computer and scheduling software after you've earned a few thousand dollars. For many junk haulers, the office is a day planner or notebook on the passenger seat of their vehicle, and a box of customer index cards at home. Here are a few suggestions about the essentials you'll need to run your business.

Telephone. While you can use your home phone for business, it's best – and more professional – to have a separate business line. Most junk haulers use a cell phone for their business line, as it allows them to stay in touch with customers even when they're on the job. In addition, voice mail means you'll never miss a call.

As cell phones become more sophisticated, it's easy to check your Email or web site on the go. Check with your favorite wireless service provider to see what would work best for you.

You can also sign up for an additional phone number with one of the low-cost web-based services such as www.ringcentral.com or www.freedomvoice.com.

My favorite, Freedomvoice.com provides a new phone number to use for your business in your local area code, plus faxing capability for around $10 a month. You can forward calls to any phone, voice mail or have them emailed to your computer.

Scheduling

Organization is the key to making money as a junk hauler. Your days need to be booked, but not over- booked. Customers need to know the day and time you'll be there to pick up their junk. The secret to making it all happen is a scheduling system.

Some junk haulers love their day planners and couldn't imagine how to get through a day without it. Others have gone digital, using a computer calendar that's usually included with the software bundle in any new computer, or accessed with their cell phone or tablet. It's really your choice – if you're more comfortable with one or the other, that's the one for you.

One advantage of a paper day planner is that it can be easier to take notes when you're talking to customers about future visits, add-on work or price quotes. A tablet like the iPad could be a good choice for a paperless substitute, with the portability of a day planner, plus the ability to access calendar software to schedule jobs and take notes.

With prices starting around $300, they are worth considering as a part of your toolkit. All can be used to access the internet and Email anywhere there is Wi-fi, and all the major cell phone carriers are now offering plugins to allow you to use a tablet on their network.

Organization also applies to filing systems, as you'll need to keep track of your customer's information, such as service dates, price quotes, preferences and contact information. Although much of your junk hauling work will be one-time, you will have quite a few repeat customers, like property managers, to keep track of.

A simple and affordable system that works well uses standard 4-inch by 6-inch index cards, filed alphabetically in a card file box. You'll find a sample customer card in the resource chapter at the end of this book.

If you prefer a computer for record keeping, there are several programs that will handle your customer list and scheduling together. Google has a free contact management program at: www.google.com/contacts Two other programs worth considering are the contact and calendar programs provided with most computers and tablets using either the Apple or Microsoft operating system.

Estimates. When you give a customer an estimate for junk hauling and any other add-on work in your bid, be sure to put it in writing and have the customer sign it before you start. Blank estimate/bid forms can be purchased at any office supply store.

Business cards

Once you've picked a name for your junk hauling business, it's time to order business cards. Vistaprint has hundreds of designs to choose from. To view them, go to: www.vistaprint. com, then choose: business cards/premium business cards, and type "junk hauling" in the search box.

Magnetic signs.

You'll be amazed at how much junk hauling business you will get from customers who see the sign on your vehicle. Unlike a yellow-pages ad, there is just a one-time cost of around $50-$60. Vistaprint.com can also create a custom magnetic sign for you, as can www.magneticsigns.com. If you prefer a vinyl sign for the rear window of your vehicle, try: www.fastsigns.com

Taxes and Accounting

There are three types of taxes you'll be responsible for as a business owner, employment taxes, income tax and self-employment tax. If you do not have employees, you rarely have to pay employment taxes, but just a self-employment tax.

It's a good idea to visit a tax pro, such as an accountant, to learn just what taxes are due for the legal type of business you plan to start, such as an LLC. They can also advise you what information they will require to help you at tax time, such as a profit-and- loss statement.

To keep accounting costs low, do as much as possible yourself. Today, most accounting software for small businesses has gone online and is called "cloud" software, as it is web- hosted rather than from a program installed on your computer. This allows the software company to update programs regularly to reflect changes in tax laws and other regulations.

A small service business does not need a high-powered, expensive accounting system, but something that is simple enough to be easy to understand and use. It should also be capable of generating invoices for your customers and reports needed by your accountant or tax professional.

As I write this, there are over a dozen capable accounting software programs suitable for your small business. They all have the basic capabilities covered, so it's up to you to choose the best fit for you. Here are my current favorites:

Fresh Books. This cloud-based accounting program is considered one of the best invoicing solutions available, which is important

CHAPTER 2 - SETTING UP YOUR BUSINESS OFFICE

if you have customers to bill regularly. You can also add auto-billing and automatic payment reminders and thank-you notes!

Like most, they offer a free trial period so new users can see if they like the program before spending any money. They base their pricing on the number of clients you bill. Because it is web-based, there are no downloads or installations, and it is compatible with all operating systems as long as you have internet access.

Fresh Books is very easy to use, a big plus for a non-accountant like me (and you?) The setup is simple and quick, and the interface is easy to figure out and logical. Help is available online and by phone.

GoDaddy Bookkeeping. This software, formerly called Outright, is more user-friendly than most accounting programs. It's more of a bookkeeping program aimed at small businesses that just need to account for income, expenses and taxes. The company was started by two guys who worked at Intuit, the parent company of QuickBooks, to offer a simpler solution for small business owners who didn't know much about accounting but needed to have accurate data for their taxes.

This software is also cloud-based, so there are no downloads, and you can access your account anywhere you have an internet connection, even on your iPad or smartphone. There is a free plan if you just need to track income and expenses, and a paid version which is affordable–currently about $120 per year.

Like all the other cloud accounting programs, you can link your accounts, such as bank accounts, credit cards, Paypal and other payment processing accounts. Then it automatically downloads the information daily and it can create and send invoices to customers.

Unlike most of the other online programs, there is no extra charge for additional customers. Whether you have two or two hundred, the cost is the same. To learn more, visit: https://www.godaddy.com/ email/online-bookkeeping

QuickBooks Online. Everyone has heard of Quicken, which has been available since the mid-80s, followed by QuickBooks. It is the Big Dog of accounting software and is used by thousands of companies.

QuickBooks Online has a 3-tier pricing plan and a 30-day free trial. The basic "Simple Start" plan includes invoicing and estimates and all the normal accounting features. The "Essentials" plan adds an accounts payable function to track and pay bills. The "Plus" plan allows subscribers to track inventory and generate 1099 forms.

The software is web-hosted, so no downloads or installation is required, and is compatible with Windows and Mac OS X operating systems. Setup is easy and quick and includes several how-to videos. There are a huge number of features available to users, but the less-used ones are kept in the background for regular users.

When you send an invoice to your customers in FreshBooks, GoDaddy bookkeeping and Quicken, your customers can pay instantly by credit card, thanks to built-in payment processing. This means you'll get paid faster, and they don't have to hunt for a stamp and write a check. It's a win-win for both you and your customers.

Another advantage of using accounting/bookkeeping software is that you can set up the billing cycle so you receive a "red flag" reminder when the invoice is unpaid past a certain number of days.

The billing cycle used by most businesses is 30 days, so make it clear to your customers that there is a late fee for past due payments. Most businesses charge a percentage of the unpaid balance, such as 2% per month. If the bill is unpaid 10 days after the due date, the late fee applies.

Tax deductions. Be sure to keep track of all your business-related expenses, as they may be deductible at tax time. Top deductions include:

Startup Expenses. The costs of getting your haul-away business started are usually deductible. Check with a tax guide or tax professional to get specific deductions.

Education Expenses. If you take classes or workshops to maintain or improve your job skills, they may be deductible.

Professional Fees. Fees paid to accountants, tax professionals, lawyers or other professional consultants are deductible.

Equipment. Check with a tax pro to see if there are any special "stimulus" deductions available for the purchase of capital equipment such as vehicles and computers.

Interest. If you use credit to finance business purchases, the interest is deductible.

Advertising. Any marketing costs, such as a newspaper ad, flyers ad, a magnetic sign for your vehicle or promotional costs, such as sponsoring a little league team or buying equipment for them, is deductible.

Vehicle expenses. At the current 58 cents per mile, this is a huge deduction for most haul-away businesses. For many, the mileage deduction alone will cover the cost of a new fuel-efficient vehicle in a year or two. To keep track of those business miles to take full advantage of the IRS deduction, you need to keep accurate records.

Fortunately, there are many apps that work on your smartphone that can track your business mileage so you don't waste time or forget to record trips. Here are a few of the best free apps to do that. Just visit the Apple store or Google Play to download them.

- ✓ **Easy Logbook.** This is one of the simplest mileage tracking apps to use. All you do is hit the start button at the beginning of a trip and the stop button at the end, then label the trip. Then enter a trip description and you're done.
- ✓ **Everlance.** Has great features for tracking business travel and is also designed to reduce the battery drawdown. You can even add receipts for gas and other travel-related expenses.
- ✓ **Mileguru.** A simple yet complete app for tracking mileage and other deductible expenses. When you're ready, just send a report via PDF.
- ✓ **TrackMyDrive.** This automatic mileage tracking app runs in the background on your phone and detects all your drives, then let's you store the information in the cloud. Also

generates IRS tax reports. Like most mileage tracking apps, the first few trips are free, then you need to upgrade. But this app is currently less than $10 per year, so it's quite affordable.

An excellent book on the subject is Deduct It – Lower Your Small Business Taxes, available at www.nolo.com.

Keeping track of your new business income and expenses can be a struggle without basic accounting software. If you don't plan to have employees, Quicken Home & Business will do just fine. If you plan to have employees, Quickbooks is the best software program.

Business Supplies

Reliable vehicle. Customers will count on you to be reliable and dependable, so you need a vehicle that will do the same for you. Your existing truck or van can be used to start up, but a fuel-efficient diesel-powered truck is the best choice, as they get good mileage and last much longer than a gas engine powered truck.

Most of the larger junk hauling services use either the Isuzu NPR or Mitsubishi Fuso cab-forward diesel truck, with an open or closed box for hauling. There are lots of these available used – start looking at: http://truckpaper.com, www.commercialtrucktrader.com or http://truckertotrucker.com.

While compact diesel trucks are commonplace in Europe and other places where high fuel prices are the norm, they are becoming more popular in North America, and are more widely available now in the U.S. With fuel costs 30-40 percent lower than gas vehicles, the savings on fuel alone can cover the payments.

Dump Trailer. If you're on a budget and want to add to your hauling capacity without buying a larger truck, check out the heavy-duty dump trailers available from a variety of manufacturers. A 6' x 10' model with added wood sideboards can haul up to 10 cubic yards of junk – big enough for almost all haul-away jobs. Start your search at www.trailertrader.com

GPS Unit. A GPS unit for your truck isn't absolutely necessary when you first start out, but it will save time, fuel and money with regular use. If you're not familiar with GPS, the system uses satellites to track the location of your vehicle, and help you find your way easily to a destination, or several, even if you're in unfamiliar territory. As you drive, the GPS unit displays your route on a screen, announces streets, and tells you when to turn and which way.

This is a much safer way to drive than fumbling with a map while you're trying to drive as well. The newer units offer a feature that is perfect for haulers – route optimization. The Garmin Nuvi 760, for example has this feature, and it's called "multi-destination routing".

CHAPTER 2 - SETTING UP YOUR BUSINESS OFFICE

All you need to do is enter your starting point, your final destination and all your delivery and pickup stops in between, and then use the "optimally reorder points" command to plan the most efficient route for all the stops. If you're new to GPS, you'll find Garmin units really easy to learn and use.

In addition to never getting lost again, using this feature could cut your fuel costs by as much as ten percent, as well as reducing wear and tear on your vehicle. If you live in an area with traffic congestion, most GPS units now allow you to use the Clear Channel Total Traffic Network (TTN) to get live traffic information displayed on your GPS screen. This allows you to avoid the jams and take a less congested route.

Most of the newer GPS units will also track and record your actual mileage, so you can use the data instead of logging odometer readings if you bill customers by the mile or for a mileage log for tax purposes.

If a GPs unit is not in your startup budget, you can use the free trip planning at www.maps.google.com or www.mapquest.com. Another option to keep costs down is buying a refurbished GPS unit. For reviews and sources for refurbished GPS units, try www.refurbishedgpsguide.com or do an internet search for "refurbished gps."

Hand truck & moving blankets. A hand truck is another essential tool for picking up heavy or awkward items. Get a hand truck that is lightweight and capable of carrying at least 500 pounds. The dual- purpose models that convert to a platform truck are even more useful when you are hauling extra-large items.

You'll find a good selection of hand trucks and moving blankets at www.amazon.com. When you haul fragile items, like computers or furniture, moving blankets can protect them, and keep them from breaking, scratching or denting.

Hand tools. When you pick up a load of construction debris or yard waste, you'll need to leave it "broom clean", so be sure to carry a regular broom, a heavy-duty push broom, shovel, rake and a basic assortment of hand tools to cover unexpected situations.

If you've been asked to take remove and haul away items like a fence, deck or shed, you'll need basic demolition tools, such as a small sledgehammer, bolt cutters and a crowbar.

Other useful items in the hauler's tool kit include duct tape, scissors, pocket-knife, two crescent wrenches, large and small channelock pliers, visegrips, a 4 in 1 screwdriver, and wire cutting pliers.

Unless you have a lift gate on your truck, carry a pair of heavy-duty planks or loading ramps so you can roll appliances and other large items into your truck or van using a hand truck. A pair of metal ramp ends attached to the wood planks will make them safer. You'll find those at most auto parts stores, or online at: www.etrailer.com/c-ramp.htm.

A battery operated screwdriver/drill and reciprocating saw will come in handy on many jobs when the stuff you're hauling needs to be dismantled before you can load and haul it. If you're using an open vehicle, like a pickup truck, carry tarps and a cargo net to cover the load and rope and bungee cords to secure the load.

A supply of heavy duty (contractor grade) plastic debris bags are essential when you are hauling loose debris or yard waste. If you can afford it, a gas engine leaf blower will save cleanup time, as it's much faster than a broom for larger areas.

CHAPTER THREE

Services to Offer

Providing a list of the services you offer will help generate calls and jobs. Don't worry about being too specific with your list. Just cover the general services you plan to offer, and add a line at the end, such as: ***"Don't see what you're looking for? Call us to discuss your needs."***

CHAPTER 3 - SERVICES TO OFFER

DEPENDABLE HAUL-AWAY SERVICE

What: Anything two people can lift that's non-toxic.
When: We are ready to go when you call.
How Far: Most of our work is within 30 miles of Anytown.

SERVICE OPTIONS

- ✓ **Regular:** Same day service.
- ✓ **Rush:** Two-hour service.
- ✓ **Economy:** 2 to 3-day service.

WHAT WE HAUL AWAY

- ✓ **Appliances:** Dryers, freezers, refrigerators, stoves and washers.
- ✓ **Building materials:** Concrete, drywall, fencing, lumber, remodeling debris and roofing.
- ✓ **Electronics:** Computers, copiers, monitors, printers and other office equipment.
- ✓ **Furniture:** Beds, bookcases, chairs, dressers, sofas, tables and more.
- ✓ **Garage/Attic:** All non-toxic junk.
- ✓ **Garden/Yard:** Branches, clippings, dirt, sod and stumps.
- ✓ **Wood:** Decks, fencing, firewood, lumber and sheds.

> ## WHAT WE DON'T HAUL AWAY
>
> We are not licensed to haul or dispose of hazardous materials such as asbestos, chemicals, oil, oil drums or tanks, paint or solvents. Your county recycling department can advise you how to properly dispose of hazardous materials.
>
> *"Don't see what you're looking for? Call us to discuss your needs: 555-1212."*

To determine what services are needed in your area, visit or call potential customers, such as property managers. Tell them you plan to start a haul-away service and want to find out what services they may need.

Here is a short list of questions to ask that will help you determine the best services to offer:

- ✓ Are you using a haul-away service now?
- ✓ If yes, which service do you use, and are you happy with them?
- ✓ How frequently do you use or need a haul-away service?
- ✓ What haul-away services would you like to see available?

Don't try to sell your service. This is just an information gathering visit. It also allows you to get acquainted with potential future customers, so a future visit to sell your services will be easier. If you're visiting a larger company, ask who is the best person to contact about haul-away services.

If you're in a smaller town, where there are few or no haul-away services, you may want to do your research without revealing that you plan to start a haul-away service. Another option is to simply have a friend do the calling for you. Here's what you need to know about the competition:

- ✓ Rates
- ✓ Hours
- ✓ Services offered
- ✓ Service area
- ✓ Web site – If a competitor has a web site, visit it to see how they
- ✓ market their business.

WHO USES A HAUL-AWAY SERVICE?

- ✓ **Banks** – When a bank forecloses on a home, there is usually trash to
- ✓ be hauled away.
- ✓ **Businesses** – a regular user of haul-away services, to dispose of everything from old office furniture to surplus or damaged inventory.
- ✓ **Contractors** – a remodeling project or new construction creates lots of debris, and contractors are often too busy to haul it away.

- ✓ **Estate attorneys** – they need a haul-away service to help with the cleanup and disposal of a client's household possessions when they die.
- ✓ **Homeowners** – most homeowners don't have access to a large truck or trailer for hauling and are glad to pay someone to clean up and haul away everything from furniture to yard debris.
- ✓ **Property managers** – when a tenant moves out, they often leave a mess behind, which needs to be hauled away.
- ✓ **Professional organizers** – these "de-clutter" specialists help folks simplify their lives, which always means disposing of much of what they have accumulated.
- ✓ **Realtors** – A steady source of referrals, as homes need to be neat and clean to attract buyers.
- ✓ **Seniors** – many seniors are unable to do the heavy lifting and need help.
- ✓ **Senior move managers** – when seniors relocate to a retirement facility, someone has to haul away what won't fit in a smaller apartment. Senior move managers facilitate the move and need help with the haul away. Find your local senior move managers at: www.nasmm.com

Foreclosure Cleanouts

The number of U.S. families losing their homes to foreclosure increases with every recession, as more people lost their jobs and are unable to make their monthly mortgage payments. The

CHAPTER 3 - SERVICES TO OFFER

foreclosure crisis has affected millions of homeowners, and housing experts don't expect the crisis to end anytime soon.

According to a recent realtytrac.com report, thousands of Americans are losing their homes to foreclosure. Banks and other mortgage lenders have repossessed most of these homes and expect to take back even more in the next few years.

This mortgage meltdown has created an opportunity for those already in the haul-away business, and anyone planning to start one, to add this very profitable "niche" market to their business plan.

A word of caution though – contrary to what you might have read on the internet and elsewhere, this is not a "get-rich-quick" business. Yes, it's true you can make a lot of money doing foreclosure cleanups, but it's dirty, hard work. When folks lose their homes in a foreclosure and have to leave, they have no reason to leave the house neat and clean for the new owners!

The exact opposite often happens, as angry folks may trash the house before they leave, leaving a big mess to be cleaned up and hauled away. The good news is that, in the foreclosure cleanup business, the bigger the mess, the larger the paycheck when the cleanup is done.

Many foreclosure cleanout companies offer a full range of services, from carpet cleaning to window washing to repairing damage, in addition to simply hauling away the junk. You may want to just bid the haul- away portion of the project and leave the rest to someone else or offer to do it all.

It's important to remember that, in most states, you will need a contractor's license before doing repairs to a property. Check with your state to see what is required before you bid any projects.

Many haul-away companies choose to focus on just cleanup and haul away, as that just requires basic cleaning skills. You will get more foreclosure work if you offer cleaning as well as haul away services.

The two types of cleaning are referred to as "white glove cleaning" and "broom-swept cleaning". White glove cleaning, as the name implies, means you clean everything – inside cabinets and appliances, baseboards, doors, ceiling fans, toilets, sinks and windows. Broom- swept cleaning means you clean the surfaces, sweep the floors and pick up and haul away all the junk and debris.

If you're working as a subcontractor for one of the large REO contractors, (REO stands for "real estate owned" – just another

CHAPTER 3 - SERVICES TO OFFER

way to say "foreclosed – the bank owns it") they will have a very specific cleaning checklist you'll be expected to follow. Be sure to get a copy before your quote a price to make sure you've priced in all the items on the checklist.

One way to handle larger foreclosure cleanout projects that require more services than you offer or have time to do is to partner with other folks in the trades to wrap up the project quickly.

For example, you could have a carpet cleaner, a handyman for repairs, a house cleaner, a carpenter, a plumber, a painter and an electrician on your "team." When a big foreclosure cleanup job comes up for bid, contact the folks on your team that will be needed, go over the project with them and have them price out their portion of the project.

When you're all done, pad your bid by 15-25 percent to cover your overhead, and submit the bid. You'll get more jobs using this method, as so many property owners want "one-stop shopping" to get a home back in habitable/saleable shape quickly.

Resist the temptation to be a "jack of all trades" and do everything yourself. The foreclosure pie is big enough to share, so find others with specialized skills and spread the profits around.

Other services you may be asked to provide as a foreclosure cleanup service, in addition to cleaning, include:

- ✓ Changing the locks to secure a property.
- ✓ Lawn and yard maintenance, often until the home is sold.
- ✓ Winterizing a home to prevent weather-related damage.

- ✓ De-winterizing in the Spring – both following FHA guidelines.
- ✓ Vacancy verifications – to make sure the home is not occupied.

The best source of new business for foreclosure cleanouts is, of course, the realtors who specialize in foreclosure listings. To find out who's currently active in your area, call local real estate offices and ask to speak to the realtor who specializes in foreclosures.

If there is more than one, ask for the one with the most foreclosure listings. Then call or visit them, introduce yourself, and tell them you are interested in doing cleanup/haul-away work on new foreclosed properties.

Another source of jobs is the banks and other lenders who own foreclosed properties. When they foreclose on a property, they must "preserve" it to prevent any future loss in value. Each lender has property preservation specialists whose job is to do just that. You can contact them directly to let them know about your services.

The U.S. Department of Housing & Urban Development (HUD) works with approved regional contractors, called "management & marketing" contractors, to handle maintenance, repair and sales of all HUD-owned properties.

The M&M contractors in turn subcontract all the actual work, such as repairs, haul-aways, cleanups and maintenance, to others. By contacting the M&M resource in your area, you'll find out what truck. **Hint: don't forget to check bagged junk, as it may contain valuable items.**

- ✓ Items you keep for your own use. The hard part is learning to say no, as you will find more useful items than you have room for.
- ✓ Items you can sell, such as furniture, toys, computers or recycled material such as scrap metal. For quick sales without having to do a garage sale, post a picture and a price of each item on craigslist.com.
- ✓ Items you can donate. After a few loads, you'll be able to determine at a glance what you want to keep or sell, and items that can be taken to organizations like Goodwill.
- ✓ Junk that really does need to go to the dump.

Sideline Business – Storage Unit Auctions

If you've had a haul-away business for a while, you know there will be days when your schedule is light. Here's a perfect sideline gig to fill those vacant spots in the schedule and bring in some extra income. Best of all, you don't need any new equipment to do the work. The sideline is attending storage unit auctions and there are three ways to profit from them.

According to the self-storage industry, one in ten American households now has a storage unit. Most use a storage unit to store what won't fit in their home. But with a tight economy, more folks use a storage unit because they have lost their home, but don't want to give up their possessions.

Others are in the middle of other life transitions, like a move or divorce, and hope to retrieve their stuff when they have a place for it again. All these storage units have created an opportunity for haulers to profit by helping move people's stuff in and out of storage units.

The first profit opportunity is to attend storage unit auctions with your truck or van to help the winning bidders haul away what they've just bought at auction. It is quite common for bidders to win more bids than they had planned, and so they need help hauling it all away.

In most states, the law, and the owner of the storage facilities, require that the winning bidders empty and clean out the storage unit within 24-48 hours, so they often need help. Also, many bidders are not aware that storage facilities will not allow them to use their trash bins for the unwanted junk. Someone has to haul it all away – why not you?

It's best to arrive at least a half-hour before a storage unit auction so that you can park your truck in a visible location for the arriving bidders. This will also give you time to pass out business cards to those who may need your hauling services.

The second profit opportunity is to introduce yourself to the owner or manager of the storage facility. Let them know that you're interested in any hauling they may need, as some abandoned units are full of junk and attract no bids at all.

The manager still has to clean out the unit before it can be rented again, and that's where you come in. Often the storage facility managers you meet at auctions become a regular source of new jobs, as there is a steady turnover of units.

The third, and most exciting, profit opportunity is to actually participate in the auction as a bidder. As anyone who has watched the TV series "Storage Wars" can tell you, an auction can be an adrenaline-filled adventure. A winning bid can be a lot like a lottery ticket – either a dud or a bonanza. Here are a few tips to get you started right so you increase the odds of a bonanza and reduce the chances of a dud:

- ✓ To find storage auctions in your area, go online and search for "storage unit auctions – your state." Two other online resources are auctionzip.com and storageauctions.com
- ✓ Essential tools. Bring a powerful flashlight to check out larger units, a bottle of water or hot days, padlocks for each unit you bid and win, a notepad and pen to record information about opening and selling bids for units and cleanup supplies, such as a broom and garbage bags to finish cleaning the units you've won bids for.

- ✓ Finally, bring enough cash to pay for winning bids. Many auctions do not accept checks or credit cards. Include enough to cover the security deposit required in case you fail to clean out the unit after emptying it.

- ✓ Be sure to get on the registered bidder's list, if that's required, and sign a bidder's agreement.

- ✓ You will not be allowed to go inside the storage unit, so use your high-powered flashlight to look for treasures from a distance. If you spot high-end brands, designer labels or high-quality furniture, that's a tip-off to the overall quality of the items in the unit. Remember that most self-storage unit customers put their most valuable items at the back, so shine that flashlight deep to look for visible clues.

- ✓ Think like a detective when inspecting a unit. Usually, a tidy and well-organized unit has more potential than a junk-strewn, disorganized unit. A unit that is used regularly, with trails of dust and footprints on the floor, has less potential, as the tenant has likely been back to remove any valuable items.

- ✓ If the contents are commercial rather than household items, chances are good you'll be able to make more money when you sell the items.

CHAPTER 3 - SERVICES TO OFFER

- ✓ Set a limit so you don't get caught up in the bidding fever and spend more than you intended. It's hard to make money when you're in a bidding war with other bidders. Keep in mind when you're bidding, that about half of the items in an average unit will be junk and need to be hauled away to the dump or recycled.

- ✓ After you've attended a few auctions, your notes will give you the average opening and selling bids for various size units. For example, if you know most 10x15 units start at $60 and end at $200, you may want to pass on an auction with an opening bid of $`150, unless you've spotted something worth the price during your flashlight inspection.

- ✓ Don't limit yourself to just one venue to sell the items you've bought. In addition to a garage sale, try eBay or a free ad on craigslist.org. The more exposure you get, the faster you can turn your treasures into cash. If you must, cut the price to see if that brings a buyer. If not, think about donating the item to your favorite charity or saving it for your next garage sale.

- ✓ Be careful not to get so addicted to storage unit auctions that you forget this is a sideline, not your primary business! Also, beware of "blind" auctions where the storage unit door is closed and locked and bidders are asked to bid "blind." Just like a casino, the odds favor the house, so be extra careful if you run into this kind of auction.

Sideline Business – Ikea Hauling

This won't work for everyone, but if your nearest Ikea store is far away, this could be a good sideline revenue source for you. You are probably familiar with Ikea – they make stylish and affordable furniture and other housewares and their products are in high demand even in towns that have no easy access.

Dustin Culton lives in Omaha, Nebraska, far away from the nearest Ikea store in Minneapolis, Minnesota. He simply runs classified ads in his hometown offering to pick-up and deliver items that local folks can purchase online from Ikea.

He uses a 6' by 10' enclosed trailer, going through the checkout line once for each customer and loading an average of 150 items, big and small, into the trailer for the drive back to Omaha. Over 300 local customers have used his Ikea delivery service, usually about 20 per trip.

Dennis charges a fee of 30% to 35% of the Ikea price to purchase and deliver each customer's order. His spare-time sideline has taken in over $35,000 in the last year.

CHAPTER FOUR

How to Find Customers

Conventional marketing

For many, finding customers is the most challenging part of starting a new business. Don't worry. There are many free and low-cost ways to spread the word about your new haul away business, and we'll explore a few of the best here.

Newspaper ads. Most newspapers have a "service directory" or something similar, where you can run a regular classified or display ad for your business at a reduced rate. It's best to keep the ad small but repeat it regularly – once a week is about right. Repetition is the secret to successful advertising. After a few months, readers will remember your ad, and look for it when they need your services.

Specialized publications. Every community has specialized publications devoted just to businesses, or seniors – both good target markets for your haul away service. Try to run a small classified or display ad in these as well to let these two important groups know about your services.

Free classifieds. You can place a free classified at www.craigslist.com. It has region and city-specific sections, so you can get the word out to just those in your target area. Try a general haul away service ad, as you may attract others in need of your services, such as busy professionals or businesses.

Business cards. Business cards are an essential sales tool to pass out to everyone who is a prospect for your haul away services, and to those who may be in a position to refer customers to you.

For the best selection and pricing on business cards, try www.vistaprint.com. Vistaprint has hundreds of "stock" designs to choose from. Use both sides of the card. On the front, include your business name & slogan, address and phone, e-mail address and a web site address. On the back, list the services you offer, and if you have room, "Don't see a service – call and ask."

Online services. When you're just starting out and not well known in your community, sign up for one of the online apps that help people find everything from electricians to junk haulers. Some allow you to set your own rates and others have rates posted on their website, and they bill the customer directly.

Many junk haulers find this is a great source of "filler" jobs for filling open time between your normal hauling projects. Keep in mind they all charge you a fee or commission, which cuts your net pay a bit, but after all, these are jobs you probably would never have found on your own.

www.curb-it.com

www.lugg.com

www.thumbtack.com

www.goloadup.com

www.goshare.com

www.homeadvisor.com

Your own "billboard". Your vehicle is a free rolling billboard, visible to thousands of potential customers every day, if you take advantage of it. You may have noticed that the larger franchise firms, like 1-800 GotJunk, use a bright visible color, like yellow, green or orange to enhance the truck's visibility, and added the company name and phone number in large letters on the sides and back of the truck.

You can do the same, with a magnetic sign on both sides of the cab. When you're done, be sure to park your truck in visible, high- traffic spots where it will get seen by as many drivers as possible. Other haul-away service businesses report they get as much as 25 percent of their new customers this way! You can order custom magnetic signs from www.vistaprint.com, www.magneticsigns.com and www.buildasign.com

Rack cards. If you're not familiar with them, rack cards are a 3-1/2 x 8-inch glossy color card designed to fit standard display racks. They are widely used because they are inexpensive and effective, and the compact size means prospects are more likely to save them than a flyer. By using both sides and keeping your story "short & sweet", you can get your message across.

Leave them with prospects, such as realtors and property managers, pin them up on every local bulletin board you can find, and carry a supply in your truck to hand out while you're working. Vistaprint has the same stock designs available for rack cards as well, so you can easily match your business card design.

Custom note pads. One of the best ways to keep your name in front of customers and prospects every day is custom note pads. Other forms of marketing materials may get tossed, but people always save and use note pads or scratch pads.

Notepads give you what marketers call "top of the mind awareness." When someone thinks of a haul away service in general, they also think of your haul away service specifically. Every time they need to make a note, they are reminded of your business. Your customers and prospects will have your name in front of them daily, and when a note gets passed on to someone else, your name is in front of them as well.

In addition, instead of having to remember your contact information when they need your service, it's right there in front of them! Don't skip this powerful marketing tool – pass out two or three pads to each prospect. Here are sources for affordable notepads:

- ✓ www.vistaprint.com
- ✓ www.printpps.com
- ✓ www.marcopromotionalproducts.com .

Press release. Your local newspaper is a good source of free publicity when you are getting started or adding new services. A new business startup is newsworthy, and a simple news release, or call to the paper will often generate a story in the business section.

If you have an interesting "hook" to your story, such as a unique or special service you provide, the paper may even do a feature story about you. To learn how to put together a basic news release, do an online search for "sample press release."

Referrals. Attracting new customers through referrals is the most effective way to build your business. Traditional marketing methods, like print advertising or direct mail may or may not work. Telephone prospecting requires a thick skin to handle the rejection.

Using referrals enables you to find customers who want to hire you because a trusted friend or business associate gave you their name. As your business grows, you create relationships of trust with your customers that will create referral opportunities for you.

The first step is to provide your current customers with exceptional service. The better you meet the needs of your customers, the more likely they are to give you referrals or recommend you to friends or business associates. After all, if you don't care about your customers, why should they care about you?

As you build your business, always have a service mindset – "how can I go the extra mile to help a customer." When you exceed their expectations, they will become loyal customers, who will spread the word about you through word of mouth or referrals.

The best time for you to ask for referrals is when you've finished a job for a customer. If they are satisfied with your service, mention that most of your new customers come from referrals. Ask your customers if they have friends or business associates that could use your services. When you contact the referral prospects, tell them that (name of your customer) used your service and suggested that you contact them.

Internet Marketing

How to Set Up Your Own Haul-Away Business Website

CHAPTER 4 - HOW TO FIND CUSTOMERS

A simple website is the best way to advertise your business. A website is the 21st century version of traditional Yellow Pages advertising, because most prospects expect to find your business, or any other services and products, on the Internet.

If you think putting up a website is expensive, think again. The cost of hosting a website has dropped over the last few years, so today you can get high quality hosting for under $10 a month, with all the bells and whistles that used to be expensive add-ons now included free with hosting.

Today, a website is an essential marketing tool for any business, and even more so for a junk hauler. A basic, no-frills website can help you find new customers and stay in touch with existing customers.

If you're new to building a website, make a list of what you want to accomplish before building your site. For example, do you want to make it easy for new prospects to learn more about your business before they contact you?

You'd be surprised at how many prospects do not know what services you provide, including all the "add-on" services you provide. An "About" page can be warm and fuzzy, with a picture or two of your family, your dog, or local scenic attractions.

Most basic business websites include an FAQ page that contains all the frequently asked questions (FAQs) and answers about your services, a contact page with both phone and email contact information and testimonials from satisfied customers. It's helpful to visit other haul-away business websites to see what others are doing.

If you are like most new business startups, your advertising/marketing budget is tiny. Why not harness the power of the Internet to build your business, without spending a lot of money, by signing up for website hosting with a company that offers not only affordable hosting services but also free help to create your website?

You may have heard about hosting companies that offer free hosting, but here's why you should only consider paid hosting for your small business website:

- ✓ You can use and control your own personal or business domain name, such as "junkexpresscom". When you have registered your domain name, you own the name which can help your search engine visibility when prospects search for a junk removal service in your area.
- ✓ Paid web hosting is very affordable, and you will get better tools and resources to help you create and maintain your website.
- ✓ No ads. Free hosting companies may place ads on your website. That's how they make money, even though your website hosting is technically "free."

I'm a big fan of WordPress to build a website. Although it started as a blogging program, WordPress has now become a capable, yet user- friendly site builder that can be customized to meet the needs of almost any business.

With thousands of free themes and free help from a huge online forum of users, it may be the best way to build an affordable website. In addition, there are hundreds of "widgets" and "plugins" that can be added to your website to provide additional features like videos, shopping carts, or customer surveys.

Even if you're not a tech-savvy person, setting up, maintaining and adding to your site is easy enough for most users to do themselves, especially with the detailed free videos detailing how to do just about anything with WordPress.

I use SiteGround for my website hosting, because it's so easy to use, with a free domain name, 1-click automatic WordPress installation, free email accounts, and great customer service by phone, chat or email 24/7. I highly recommend SiteGround for your first website.

Get started by visiting the SiteGround.com website and clicking the "Get Started" button, then choose the more affordable "Start-Up" plan. Next, register your new domain name, which should match your business name as closely as possible.

Take some time with this, as you want a domain name that makes it easy for prospects and customers to find you when searching the internet. Here are a few tips to help you do it right:

- ✓ The shorter your domain name, the easier it will be to remember. Aim for two or three words where possible.
- ✓ The fewer the characters, the better. The average number of characters in the top websites is just 9. Think Amazon.com

- ✓ Pick a name that gives visitors some idea of what they will find at your website or what your business does.
- ✓ Don't use numbers in your domain name because they are easy to forget.
- ✓ Say the name of your new domain name out loud. The best names are easy to say and stick with you. For example, Google, Facebook and YouTube.
- ✓ Make a list of domain names you are considering and ask friends and family what they think.
- ✓ Having trouble coming up with good names? Search for websites that are in the same business as you. Doing this will also help you rule out names that are already taken.
- ✓ Make sure your choice of names is not in use or trademarked by someone else.
- ✓ Pick a ".com" extension for your domain name, as it is more trusted by the public than lesser-used extensions like ".biz" or ".info"

For more domain name ideas, search for "domain name generator" online. One of the free services that pops up can generate names you may never have thought of.

To build your website, you can choose WordPress or Weebly. Both website builders are provided free at SiteGround. Weebly is the best choice for first-time users, as its drag-and-drop interface is very easy to use.

Once you've chosen your domain name, you'll be asked to choose your plan. My advice is to stick to a basic plan, as it's affordable and provides everything you need to start up and claim your slice of the Internet.

On their website, and on YouTube, SiteGround.com has dozens of free videos explaining how to set up and manage your website. Just visit YouTube.com and type "SiteGround" in the search bar. If you would rather have professional help to set up your website, visit Fiverr.com or Upwork.com and search for "build a website."

Congratulations! You're almost there with your new website. Take the time to watch the videos and add the pages you need to help prospects and customers find your business online. Be sure to add your website address to your other printed materials, such as business cards, flyers, and brochures so your customers can easily find you online.

If you get stuck, or have a question, or need a new theme or plugin, help is just a click away at wordpress.org or weebly.com. Both Weebly and WordPress have a very active member forum, where you can get your questions answered at no cost. Also, SiteGround has an excellent tech support team, which you can access at their website.

Let Google Help Your Customers Find You

If your business depends on local customers, you'll enjoy a free listing in Google Places. Today, most of your customers are using internet search engines to find local services and businesses instead of the traditional Yellow Pages. That's why it makes sense to take advantage of these free listings offered by online directories for businesses.

The most popular, and currently the largest, of all is Google Places. You can start by visiting http://places.google.com and clicking on the 'get started now' button under 'Get your business found on Google.' After signing in, or signing up, at no cost, you'll be able to list your business. You can include photos or add photos or a map.

- ✓ Getting a basic listing is simple, but there are a few ways to help your business appear near the top of the listings if you have any local competitors listed.
- ✓ First, remember Google values good content, so be sure you fill out your business profile with quality information. Follow their directions for completing the listing to the letter and don't leave any blank spaces.
- ✓ Next, encourage your customers to leave feedback and positive reviews on any websites related to your business, such as local directories published by groups like the Chamber of Commerce. You can also ask customers to leave reviews or testimonials on your own website but be sure they are legitimate and genuine.
- ✓ Last, if you don't have one yet, your business needs a website, ideally with its own domain name. Having a website will give your business, however small it is, a giant boost in the Google rankings.

As more and more businesses sign up for Google Places, those who have a website will have a better shot at a listing near the top. Almost any web hosting service, such as SiteGround, mentioned earlier, can help you get a domain name and set up a Wordpress or Weebly site, which ranks well with Google.

Besides Google Places, other major online 'local' directories worth exploring are:

- ✓ http://bing.com/local
- ✓ http://listings.local.yahoo.com
- ✓ http://yelp.com
- ✓ http://linkedin.com
- ✓ http://citysearch.com
- ✓ http://listings.mapquest.com
- ✓ http://advertise.local.com
- ✓ http://angieslist.com

Local S.E.O.

Since your new business will depend on local customers, you must use location- based keywords, such as "junk hauling your town." The reason local SEO (Search Engine Optimization) is so important for your business is because almost half of all Google searches are searching for a local business. Plus, the fastest growing search term on Google is "near me" as in "Italian restaurant near me."

Since Google and other search engines can easily determine your approximate location, this enables them to deliver the results you are searching for with high accuracy.

To make it even easier for you to find what you're looking for, Google provides a "Map Pack," a set of 3 high ranking local businesses, complete with a map of their locations from Google maps. Underneath the Map Pack, you'll find the rest of the results for your search.

How to find the best keywords for local S.E.O.

Do a Google search for words and phrases that relate to your business, one at a time, and make a list of them. For example, "junk hauler near me," "junk hauler my town."

When you enter your search term, you'll see a list of additional search terms. Take a close look at those to see if any are suitable for your business. Save your list of search terms to use when setting up your "Google My Business" profile.

How to Set Up Your "Google My Business" Profile

Google My Business (www.google.com/business) is the number one factor Google uses to rank your business in local searches. When setting up your profile, be sure to include your full business name, address, and phone number (NAP). Google uses this information to ensure that your business is legitimate.

Also, the NAP on your website should be an exact match for your Google My Business listing. If it's not a match, Google may rank your business lower in local searches. Even spelling counts here - if your business address is 123 Lincoln Avenue, makes sure it's "Avenue" and not "Ave." so the Google search engine doesn't get confused.

When filling out your profile on GMB, choose a broad category that best describes your business - "junk hauling business" for example. You can then choose sub-categories, such as "foreclosure cleanouts" Also fill out the "services" tab in your profile that describes what your business does.

Google Reviews

Reviews are another major ranking factor in the Google ranking system. You may have noticed that business with many reviews, especially positive reviews, always ranks higher than those with no reviews. That's why you'll want to get as many positive reviews as you can as soon as you can.

When you get a review, good, bad or lukewarm, reply to it inside the Google My Business dashboard. That shows you care and is also a factor in Google rankings. It doesn't have to be a long reply to be effective. For example, "Thanks for the 5-star review. We really appreciate your business," "Thanks for the feedback."

How to Get More Google Reviews

Keep in mind that most customers won't bother to leave a review, even if they love your service, unless asked. It's easy to do. In fact, Google makes it easy for both you and your customers.

Go to your GMB account dashboard and locate the "get more reviews" card. There, you can get a link to your review page that you can copy and paste into an email to send to your customers.

Apply all these simple SEO tips, and soon your new business will show up on page 1 of Google search results. All without having to spend any money. Don't put this off any longer than necessary, as it's one of the best "free lunches" you'll ever receive!

Free Social Media Marketing

Facebook - Facebook is the largest social media network in the world, with over 2 billion active users. Because of its size and the large number of users, Facebook is the best social media to get your new business shared and discovered by both new prospects and your current customers. That's why it is often called "the largest word-of-mouth marketing resource on the planet."

Facebook can also be the biggest time waster if you let it be, as it's easy to linger there for hours. But you have a business to build and grow, so let's focus on doing just that, with some help from Facebook, in less than 15 minutes a day.

First rule - don't waste your money on Facebook ads. No one visits Facebook to look for services or products. They visit to see what their friends are doing. With that in mind, here's how to get started without spending a dime.

It's important to note that you must create a Facebook page, not a personal profile, also called a Personal Timeline. They do not permit personal profiles for commercial use, so if you are already a Facebook user, you must create a separate page for your business.

You can create a Facebook Page by searching "create a page" in the search bar at the top of the page, or by clicking the "create a page" button at the top of any Facebook page.

Before you create your new Facebook page, spend some time thinking about the page name you will use. Ideally, it should be short, easy to remember, promise a benefit, and describe your business.

In the "About" section of your new Facebook Page, include as much information about your business as possible, so current clients and prospects can find all your important information in one page.

You can also optimize your page by choosing one of the pre- made templates. You'll find the templates under: Settings>Edit Page. Next, create an eye-catching cover photo for your Facebook page. Look at other window cleaning businesses both on Facebook and by doing a web search for "junk hauling business" or "haul-away business" to see what others have done.

Ideally, your cover photo should communicate what your business is all about, so take the time to do it right. The easiest way to get a good cover photo designed is to hire a designer at Fiverr.com. It will cost you around $5 to $15, but it's money well spent.

Just enter "design Facebook cover" in the Fiverr.com search bar to locate dozens of capable designers. Be sure to mention that you want the image size to be 820 X 312 pixels per Facebook guidelines.

When you've uploaded your new cover photo, click it to add a text description. Describe your business in a positive way and, if possible, encourage viewers to click on the cover photo to get more "likes."

You'll also want to add a Facebook profile photo in a 180 x 180-pixel size. Remember, this profile photo appears in a follower's news feeds, in comment replies, and all over Facebook, so use a great photo. (Don't forget to smile!)

Once you've set up your Facebook page, stay active with regular posts. Most pros find 3X a week works well yet doesn't require a lot of time. Don't forget to post about special experiences you've had, such as your most difficult junk hauling job. Share the story and a picture or two of you and your customers in a post.

Is a Facebook Page Better Than a Web Site?

Yes, and no. You can set up a Facebook page in about an hour and it's free. That page allows you to stay in touch with clients and prospects and build relationships. If a Facebook page is not working for you delete it or ignore it. Keeping your Facebook page up to date with your current information, such as a list of services and prices, is quick and easy.

But - you are not in control. Facebook is in control and can change or restrict what you can do there overnight. In addition, anyone can post negative comments or complaints on your page if they wish.

If you create a website, you're in control. You own it. You get to decide what it looks like and what it contains. You can have hundreds of pages/ posts or just a simple one-pager.

Consumers today expect a business to have a website. They trust a business more when they see a "real" website. Also, having your own website allows you to post all your business information at the site, like your services, monthly specials, testimonials and more.

My choice would be to have both a Facebook page and a website. You have the best of both worlds. That way you don't have to say: "follow me on Facebook."

Twitter - Twitter can be a powerful social media tool for your small business that can help you educate customers about your plants and services, reach new prospects for your business and connect you to other Twitter users with similar interests.

Here are just four of the many ways Twitter can help your business:

- ✓ Drive traffic to your website. Unlike other social media, you can reuse content from your website or other original material repeatedly. Your tweets can include your website URL, text, images, even a video.

- ✓ Google indexes your twitter bio and tweets, which helps you get found by search engines. Make sure your bio contains the keywords you want Google to find and index, such as your business name and what your business does.

CHAPTER 4 - HOW TO FIND CUSTOMERS

- ✓ Be sure to tweet regularly so you increase the odds of ranking higher in Google Search.
- ✓ Last, use hashtags (#) to get more attention for your tweets, show your support and help people who don't know you to follow you. To learn what topics are hot or trending up right now, check Twitter Trends or hashtagify.me.

It's free and easy to open an account - just visit twitter.com, enter your name, phone and email address and create a password for your new account. After you've signed up, you can add more information for your account.

Next it's time to pick your Twitter "handle," which is the same as a username. The best handle is your business name, if it is available. You can check all the social networks for name availability at knowem.com.

If your handle/name is not available, you can add HQ to your company name, add a "get" in front of your name, or add your location, such as your town's name, to your handle.

Whatever handle you choose, make sure it is as short as possible, because you only have 280 characters to use, and they count your username in that 280 words when someone responds to your messages.

LinkedIn - LinkedIn is a place for companies and individuals to connect on a professional, not personal, level. Unlike other social media sites, folks who join LinkedIn are not joining for enjoyment and fun but to access new business opportunities and connections.

As the owner of a small business, you can use LinkedIn to connect to other local service businesses, promote your own business and build relationships with other professionals that have common interests.

Getting started is no more difficult than at other social networks. You start by creating your own personal account and profile. A LinkedIn profile is much more professional. You won't find funny cat videos or cute baby photos.

Keep that in mind when creating your profile. In your profile be sure to include your best work-related qualities so others will see the advantages of working with you.

Although you can upgrade to several higher levels of paid subscriptions, the basic account should be fine for your business. Your basic profile can include a summary of yourself, contact information, links to your blog or website or other social media pages, like Facebook, and what you're doing now professionally.

Be sure to add a high-quality photo of yourself, as people are much more at ease connecting to someone with a photo. Once you've completed your personal profile and published it, you can:

Look for connections - people you know or would like to know.

Join a group of other users who share common interests.

Have an online "business card" where potential clients can learn about and connect with you.

Boost your online reputation as a professional.

There are hundreds of other social media sites, as you may have noticed when you visited knowem.com. but most are useful only for entertainment, not helping you grow your business. These three, Facebook, Twitter and LinkedIn will help you stay connected, expand your network, and increase your profits.

CHAPTER FIVE

Pricing Haul-Away Services

After you have checked other haul-away services in your area, you will have a better idea of local rates. In general, most haul away services charge by the size of the load, usually calculated by the cubic yard, with a minimum charge for just one item, like a couch. Here are some basic capacities to help you do the math:

- ✓ Compact pickup – full bed – 1-1/2 cubic yards.
- ✓ Compact pickup – top of cab – 3 cubic yards.
- ✓ Full size pickup – full bed – 2.2 cubic yards.
- ✓ Full size pickup – top of cab – 4.5 cubic yards.

When a customer calls to ask for a price, you can give them an estimate, based on what they say needs to be hauled away and the size of the load. For example, if you estimate their scrap lumber pile will be a half load, and your full load price is $300, quote them $150, but explain that you only be able to give them a firm price after seeing the job.

CHAPTER 5 - PRICING HAUL AWAY SERVICES

If the material you're hauling away is in the basement or attic, the job will cost more than if you can simply back the truck up and load directly. If you'll need to bag or box everything, or do cleanup beyond a quick broom sweep, that will also add to the cost. After a while, you'll get a feel for how long a job will take and estimating will be a snap.

As a rule of thumb, if you have to walk more than a few feet to load up, or go up or down stairs, or rake or shovel it, you need to add an hourly charge to the basic load charge. Most haulers use the going wage rate in their area, which, as I write this, is around $25-$35 an hour nationally.

Your rates will also depend on the size of your rig, and local dump fees. If your local dump charges by the pound, as many now do, be sure to add to your rates to cover the cost of heavier materials, such as sod or construction debris.

Most folks, when starting out, use a pickup truck with side and end panels up to the top of the cab to allow double the volume of a standard pickup bed. To expand your carrying capacity, you can add a trailer, ideally with a dump bed.

One advantage of a detachable trailer is that you can leave it at a job site to provide a "self-fill" option for customers who may need to have a dumpster otherwise. This can provide you with yet another source of income that you would not get otherwise.

Rates vary by region, with cities on the East and West coast higher, and the South, Midwest and rural areas lower. Here are some sample rates:

- ✓ Rush Service: 10 % extra
- ✓ After Hours: Before 8 a.m. and 5 p.m. to 8 p.m. $25 extra
- ✓ Late Night: Between 8 p.m. and 5 a.m. $50 extra
- ✓ Weekends or Holidays: $40 extra
- ✓ 1 cubic yard (3'x3'x3') $80 to $100
- ✓ 3 cubic yards: $199
- ✓ 6 cubic yards: $349
- ✓ 9 cubic yards: $475
- ✓ Minimum charge $99.
- ✓ Large appliances: $100
- ✓ Pianos: $200 to $300 depending on size and location in the home.
- ✓ Hot tubs: $300 to $600 depending on size and time to disconnect.

According to a recent member survey by HomeAdvisor, the national contractor referral service, typical rates ranged from $134 to $361, with a national average of $234. Prices ranged from an average of $350 in New York and New Jersey, $187 in Atlanta, $225 in Chicago, $190 in Denver, $262 in Phoenix and $300 in Los Angeles.

Other factors to consider:

- ✓ Heavy loads will almost always cost you more in dump fees, so you should add the estimated dump fees to the per yard charge to cover those costs. With landfill fees ranging from $20 to $50 per ton, this is a cost you should pay attention to!

- ✓ Most haulers charge an extra mileage fee if the jobsite is out of their normal "service area." For example, if a job is 20 miles away from your town or service area, add a fee that covers the additional truck costs plus your time.

Show Me the Money - Getting Paid

Many of your customers will be regulars, such as realtors and property managers, who will use your haul-away service over and over again. If they are one-time users, it's best to get paid at the completion of each job.

Frequent customers – those who use your service often – may want the option of paying monthly. To do this, you will need to keep an accurate log of your jobs (one log for each customer), with date, job address, signature and a printed name for each completed project.

At the end of the month, an invoice showing either individual haul away jobs or a total for the month, together with the charge, is sent to the customer.

A simple receipt or invoice book and a rubber stamp with your business information will work when you're getting started. After a while, begin using computer-generated invoices, included with software such as Freshbooks or Quickbooks. Most haul away services use Net 10th payment terms, which means you expect your customer to pay you within 10 days of the invoice date.

If you want a separate payment processing option, Square, the payment processing company whose terminals seem to be at the checkout counter of every restaurant, offers a virtual terminal, so you can take remote payments from your customers. Their "card on file" feature allows you to charge repeat customers like yours on a regular basis, say weekly or monthly, at no extra cost.

SparkPay is part of CapitalOne, the well-known credit card company, and provides a solid mobile payment system. You can start with their "Go" plan, which charges 2.65% per transaction, then switch to the "Pro" plan, when your volume hits $2,000 per month. With that volume, the fee falls to 1.99% per transaction. Users also report the customer phone support is better than Square, an important consideration. www.SparkPay.com.

I've used PayPal for many years and found them to be great to work with. Big advantage - almost everyone (over 250 million and growing) has a PayPal account. Your customers don't even need a PayPal account to pay you. It's amazingly easy to set up and get started in a day or so, and the rates are very competitive. Another advantage is that the PayPal system syncs with almost all shopping carts and accounting software.

CHAPTER 5 - PRICING HAUL AWAY SERVICES

In many parts of the world, mobile payment apps on a smartphone are becoming the default payment method of choice. In China, for example, cash is becoming obsolete, as everyone has WeChat on their smartphone, and in India, the WhatsApp is the payment method of choice. Cash, checks and credit cards are on the way out.

This is happening in the U.S. as well, with dozens of payment options such as Venmo, Apple Pay, Google Pay and Zelle. Venmo, which is owned by PayPal is the leader now, with an app that makes sending and receiving cash almost effortless. If a customer asks if you use Venmo or Apple Pay and you are not set up, the app is just a free download away at the iTunes store.

CHAPTER SIX

Success Stories and Pro Tips

Gary lives in a college town, where many of the students leave at the end of the school year. Most of the students drive small cars, and don't have room to haul away several semester's worth of "stuff."

Gary puts up a flyer with tear tabs at the bottom with his phone number, on every campus and off-campus bulletin board he can find. He offers free haul away for furniture, and "student discounts" for hauling away anything else. In the month after the last day of classes, he works 12- hour days just to keep up.

Furniture is stored in his garage to be cleaned up and resold at his big garage sale, as well as other unwanted but recyclable items students have left behind. His end of the school year garage sales often earn him as much as $4500 in one Saturday.

Brian enjoys restoring antique furniture and goes to every auction and estate sale within an hour's drive of his town to bid on and buy items. He tries to always arrive early and tells the auctioneer that he and his truck are available (for a fee) to anyone who buys a large piece of furniture and needs help hauling it back home.

Auctioneers love it, as they can announce before the bidding begins, that Brian is available, if needed, to help with large items. According to Brian, there is at least one hauling job at almost every auction, so in a sense, he gets paid to attend!

Ramon began his California hauling business two years ago, and quickly noticed how much more profitable the foreclosure jobs were. He shifted to focus of his hauling business to helping banks and realtors clean up the messes left behind by those who lose a home to foreclosure.

He and his crew try to recycle as much as possible or donate usable items to local charities. A surfer in his spare time, Ramon refers to "riding the foreclosure wave", and while he knows it won't last forever, like any big wave, this one is worth getting on for a profitable ride.

Frank started his hauling business in Ohio and does roughly half foreclosure cleanups and half regular haul away work. Frank says that when people move out of a foreclosed home, they tend to leave behind anything they can do without, even if it has value, because they are moving from a larger house to a smaller rental apartment, with no storage room. He stores, sorts and repairs all the saleable items in his home garage, and has a garage sale once a month that brings in an extra $6,000 a year.

Alex started his business, Junk Removal Dudes, in 2015, and has seen it grow to pulling in gross sales of $30,000 in a busy month. His mother owns a house cleaning business and asked him to clean out the junk from a customer's basement.

Since he didn't own a pickup truck, he asked a friend to help, and they made $200 in an hour! Mom kept finding more jobs for him, so he bought a pickup, and set up a simple website and listed his business on Google.

Brian mostly cleans out basements, barns and an occasional hoarder's home. His favorite, the "pickle lady," had stored hundreds of jars of pickles in her basement. While hauling the jars out of the basement after she died, Brian found a note saying that if the world was going to end, she could always eat pickles to survive!

His steadiest source of jobs is helping seniors move out of their homes or helping their relatives clean out their homes, many with 40-50 years of accumulated junk.

Brian Scudamore is a name you might recognize. He started his junk hauling business to help pay for college, spending $700 for a beater pickup. At the time he called his new business "The

Rubbish Boys." He called a local newspaper reporter one day, and they did a story about his new business, with a photo of his beater truck with "738-JUNK" painted on the side.

Within a day, over 100 folks called to hire him to clean out their junk, and his business was on a roll. Today, his **1-800-GOT JUNK** franchises around North America take in over a million dollars a day.

His advice to new junk haulers: *"In the service industry, the market leaders are often the most expensive, or close to it. By offering the best junk removal service in any area, raising prices and keeping them high tends to attract the best customers who are willing to pay for a quality job."*

Pro Tips

✓ To gain experience and skills, consider working for an established haul away service business, either as an employee or as an independent contractor.

✓ Build customer confidence by dressing and acting like a pro. Wearing a polo shirt and cap with your company name or logo is an inexpensive way to look professional. Your customers will be more likely to have confidence in you if you are neatly dressed and friendly. Don't forget to smile!

✓ Always check containers you are hauling away to make sure they do not contain hazardous materials, such as asbestos, batteries, chemicals, medical waste, oil, paint, solvents or any other hazardous waste.

✓ Make sure the customer can meet you at the job site so you can give them an in-person bid, get detailed instructions about what is to be cleaned up and hauled away, and pay you when the job is completed.

✓ Be sure to get the customer to sign and print their name if the job will be charged to an account, so there will be no confusion about who signed for a job. You'll be amazed at how illegible some signatures can be.

✓ Use a separate job log sheet for each repeat customer so you can mail copies of the log sheet along with an invoice at the end of the month. This can prevent problems, as the customer can see exactly what they are being billed for.

✓ Check in with your regular customers once a month, and ask "How am I doing?" This regular feedback will help you address any specific issues and ensure that your customers remain happy and loyal to you.

✓ Don't forget to ask those happy customers for referrals, either in person or with a simple postcard.

✓ Build a "time cushion" into your driving schedule whenever possible. This helps when, for example, a customer isn't quite ready when you arrive to pick up a load, or you get stuck in traffic.

✓ Visit one new prospect every business day to plant the seeds for future business. Leave a printed notepad and your business card. Every time they make a note, your business name is right there!

Why You Should Love Complaints

Complaints can be a powerful marketing tool if you encourage them and handle them well. Once a month or so, check in with your regular customers to ask them how you're doing. Ask if they are happy with your service. Could it be improved? Any services they would like to see added?

In the course of this chat, you might get complaints – some mild and some not so mild. That's okay. You want customers to complain, and here's why:

- ✓ Unhappy customers tell others about you. That won't happen if you listen and correct any problems.
- ✓ If your customers don't complain, you'll never be aware of any problems, and won't be able to fix them.
- ✓ If one customer is having a problem, others could too.
- ✓ Even if customers don't complain, when they are unhappy with your service, they are likely to switch to your competition.

Here's a simple four-step method for turning complaints into happy customers:

1. Say "I'm sorry." These two powerful words can calm an angry customer and let them know you accept responsibility.
2. Find a solution. First, let them talk to be sure you understand the reason they have a complaint. After you are sure you "get it", do what is necessary to resolve the problem quickly.
3. Thank your customer. Let them know you appreciate bringing the problem to your attention and ask them to let you know the next time there is a problem.
4. Follow up. After you have solved the problem that prompted the customer's complaint, follow up in person, if possible, to let them know what you did for them, and ask if that is acceptable for them.

CHAPTER SEVEN

Setting Goals & Networking

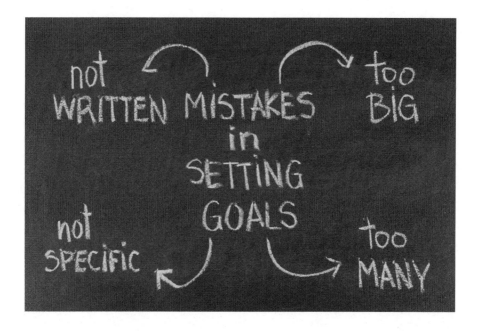

Goal setting is at the top of my "must-do" list for business success. Setting goals helps you think about your future and close the gap between where you are now and where you want to be next year or even further into the future.

The key to goal setting success is writing your goals down on paper. Just the act of writing them down makes them seem real and make them part of your new reality. Get started by writing all the goals for your new business as if you were guaranteed to succeed no matter what.

Think about what you really want, no matter how impossible it may seem to you now. Take some time to dream big! Next, list your goals in order of importance and pick your most important goal. Then ask yourself "What one small step can I take to get me closer to that goal." Then do it today, no matter how small it may seem to you. Just getting started is what counts.

> **"A goal without a plan is just a wish."**

Never forget - every goal, large or small, can be achieved by taking tiny steps every day toward that goal. Breaking your goal into smaller steps can build momentum and reduce the pressure of trying to deal with large goals.

Starting a new business is a large goal, and can seem overwhelming at first glance, but by breaking it down into small daily steps, it becomes much easier and not so overwhelming.

Action Steps:

- ✓ Write down what you really want.
- ✓ Write down how you'll get there.
- ✓ Write down your first step towards your most important goal

CHAPTER 7 - SETTING GOALS

*"Find something you love to do,
and you'll never have to work a day in your life."*

GROUCHO MARX

Setting Realistic Goals

If you don't feel you can reach a goal because it seems overwhelming or you doubt your ability to achieve the goal, it's time to break it down to more manageable "mini-goals."

For example, if your goal of making $100,000 yearly in 2 years with your new business seems too big, break that goal into smaller goals. Set monthly goals, a 6-month goal, and a 1-year goal that are smaller and easier to achieve.

Deadlines

It's important to set deadlines for your goals and the smaller steps to reaching the big goal. For example, say you'll visit two new potential wholesale customers by October 30th. As you meet your deadlines, you'll build self-confidence and strengthen your belief that your goals are within reach.

Action Step: Write down deadlines for all your goals - large and small.

"Most people overestimate what they can do in one year, and underestimate what they can do in ten years."

BILL GATES

Most of us are too optimistic when setting goals and making plans. That's why it's not uncommon for things to take longer than expected. If that happens, don't quit or give up! Stick with your goal and realize that you WILL get there, even if it takes a while longer than you thought.

The 80/20 Rule

In working toward your goal, you'll find that 20% of your efforts will bring 80% of your progress towards that goal. This rule may not seem logical, but it has proven to hold true across a wide variety of situations and businesses.

"A goal is a dream with a deadline."

That's why it's important that you find the things that will have the most impact and spend more of your time on them. Here's how to find your personal top 20%:

- ✓ Make a list of all the things you can think of that could help you achieve your goal. Aim for at least 10 things, 20 is better. Next, ask yourself, "If I could only do one thing on my list, which one will help me the most in reaching my goal?"

CHAPTER 7 - SETTING GOALS

- ✓ Now go through the list again and identify the second item that will help you the most. If your list has 10 items, the top 2 gives you your 20%.

Daily Actions: When you work on your goal every day, you'll see progress and help make your goal a reality. By taking small steps every day, you'll feel like your goal is closer and it will empower you to push on.

We all have busy lives, so it's important to set aside enough time each day to work on your goals. Just do what is comfortable at the start, and pledge to stick to it. As you become more at ease with your new daily routine, you can spend more time on it.

> *"You cannot change your destination overnight, but you can change your direction overnight."*
>
> JIM ROHN

If you think you don't have enough time in your day to start a new business, you need to identify the distractions in your life and avoid them or get them under control. Some examples: Turn off your technology alerts! When you need to focus on starting and growing your new business, turn off your email, phone, social media and chat.

Next, stop watching so much television, especially the news. The average person now spends several hours a day watching TV, and you can put that time towards growing a profitable business and a better life. Don't let these distractions control you!

Limiting Beliefs

Limiting beliefs can hold you back and create a false reality that can keep you from succeeding in your new business. The most common limiting belief when you're starting a new business is "It's too difficult" or "I'm not smart enough."

These limiting beliefs can cause you to put things off or quit at the least sign of failure or difficulty. Having these negative thoughts is normal, but never allow them to prevent you from moving forward.

When you have negative thoughts, give yourself permission to let them go. Replace these negative thoughts and limiting beliefs with more positive and empowering ones. Instead of "I can't do this," use "My new business will allow me to have a life I love."

Visualize Your Success

Imagination is one of the most powerful tools for improving your life and increasing your odds of business success. The more you visualize your goals, the more confident you'll become about your ability to reach those goals.

Take a few minutes every morning to visualize your goals and imagine how you will feel when you reach those goals. This will give you confidence and empower you to continue to take the steps necessary to reach your goals.

CHAPTER 7 - SETTING GOALS

Action Steps:

- ✓ Focus on positive visualization every day that encourages action.
- ✓ Remove negativity from your life and focus on the positive side. Your glass is half-full, not half-empty!
- ✓ Every day imagine your business is a huge success and be confident it will be.

"For things to change, YOU have to change. For things to get better, YOU have to get better. For things to improve, YOU have to improve. When YOU grow, EVERYTHING in your life grows with you."

JIM ROHN

Networking - How to Do It Right

Networking is the most effective way to build your small business. It cost almost nothing - just your time. It's about building relationships with others with the goal of mutual benefit. It's more than passing out business cards.

Networking is a two-way street, not just about trying to get something out of someone.

Networking is also about building trust. People always prefer to buy a product or service from someone they know, like and trust. Think about it. Would you rather buy from a friend or acquaintance or a total stranger?

Yet, if you're shy like me and so many others, just the thought of networking can be intimidating. When networking, remember you are building relationships, not make a sale. Here are a few proven tips to get you started:

- ✓ Be genuine. Don't try to be someone else. If you're not a natural extrovert, that's perfectly okay.
- ✓ Networking is about making friends. If you've ever made friends, you know how to network.
- ✓ No one cares about you. All they care about is themselves. That's why you need to give something to other people you meet, whether they're potential customers or existing clients, without expecting them to do something in return.
- ✓ When you give something to others, it creates an unspoken, often subconscious, need to return the favor. That's why networking works so well.
- ✓ Be visible. Networking is a contact sport and the more people you contact and become visible to, the more you will build your business through networking.

- ✓ When you're talking with someone, listen more than you speak. Give them your full attention and make them feel important by listening to them. When you do that, they will trust, like and respect you.
- ✓ In your conversations with others, practice your ABCs (Always Be Curious). Ask what they do, ask about their family, what they do for fun.
- ✓ Just do it - start a conversation with someone you haven't met yet and don't forget your ABCs.

Networking is an easy way to gain exposure for your new business in the community. Groups such as the Chamber of Commerce, Rotary and Kiwanis can provide an opportunity to meet, greet and become better known. Also spread the word among related businesses, such as carpet cleaners, house cleaners, handymen and other tradespeople.

CHAPTER EIGHT
Is a Franchise Right for You?

Starting a new business can be a challenge for most of us – after all, it's not something most of us do every day. That's why a franchise can be a life saver for those who want an experienced partner to help them start up and grow their new business.

But the cost can be high, and you may be wondering why not go it alone and start out on your own. Before you make the decision to do that, take a minute to consider the benefits of buying a franchise to start your new haul-away business.

A franchise offers you a proven, time-tested framework for starting, operating and growing your new junk hauling business. You'll learn from the pros, who have demonstrated that they can build a haul-away business over and over again and make money. What this means for you is that you will earn more and spend less time learning the tips and techniques of junk hauling success than if you "go it alone."

Most of the list of junk hauling franchises that follows offer the following benefits to new franchisees:

CHAPTER 8 - IS A FRANCHISE RIGHT FOR YOU?

- ✓ Group advertising resources that are often beyond the reach of new business owners, such as a centralized referral service to find and send local customers to you.
- ✓ Name recognition to help build credibility for your new business. For example, who hasn't heard of "1-800-Got Junk?"
- ✓ Comprehensive training from seasoned pros.
- ✓ A much lower risk of failure than if you start up on your own. This can often mean better access to business loans, as lenders are more apt to say yes if you are part of a national, proven organization with a track record to back them up.
- ✓ Operational support from company headquarters, during your start up and after, in areas that most of us are unfamiliar with, such as financing, accounting, employee training, scheduling and marketing.

According to the U.S. Small Business administration, the success rate is much higher for franchised businesses than it is for non-franchised businesses. That's why you should consider the advantages and disadvantages of franchising carefully before making a decision. Also, be sure to ask each franchisor you contact the "average gross sales" for their franchisees and compare that number to what you guess you'll make on your own.

1. College Hunks Hauling Junk

You've probably seen one of their bright orange trucks in your area. With over 120+ franchises operating in the U.S, this is one of the more popular and successful junk hauling franchises. They have also adding local moving, so franchisees have a dual opportunity.

Founders Omar Soliman and Nick Friedman started the business with one truck and $10,000 in the Washington, D.C. area, which became a million-dollar business in just two years! Franchisees pay a $40,000 franchise fee, and a 7% royalty rate on gross sales.

Capital required to start, including the franchise fee, is around $100,000. Keep in mind, because of the proven track record of this and other franchisors, most franchisees will be able to qualify for a small business loan to cover the startup costs. Contact them at www.collegehunks.com

1-800-Got-Junk

Brian Scudamore started his junk removal while in college and dropped out of school to grow his junk hauling

business. In hindsight, that was a great decision, as his company has grown to over 150 franchisees in the U.S., Canada and Australia.

Total startup investment for a franchise is around $110,000, including a $30,000 franchise fee. The royalty on gross sales is 8%. Contact them at: www.1800gotjunk.com

JunkLuggers

Josh Cohen started his junk hauling business with a strong focus on recycling as much of the junk they collect and haul as possible. In fact, his goal is to either donate or recycle 100% of everything they collect. The total startup investment is around $105,000, with a $50,000 franchise fee. www.junkluggers.com

J Dog Junk Removal

This franchise is offered only to military veterans, those on active duty and their families. By using trailer-based hauling, the overall startup cost is reduced to as

low as $42,000. As with other junk hauling franchises, SBA loans are available to qualified vets. www.jdogjunkremoval.com

Junk King

This king has king-sized trucks and territories. The trucks are 20% bigger than competitors, which means bigger loads and bigger profits. Their territories are far larger – up to 400% larger – than competitors, and their franchisees typically recycle 60% of everything they pick up and haul away. There are currently over 70 franchisees, and startup costs begin at around $90,000. www.junk-king.com

CHAPTER NINE

Forms & Safety Tips

You will find three forms that you can adapt for your own use on the following pages: a customer service request form, a haul away log form and a service agreement. Simply add your company information at the top and make as many copies as you need. (For your own use only). The forms have not been reviewed by an attorney and are meant as a guide only. We encourage you to have your attorney review the forms to ensure that they are appropriate for your business and your state laws before using them.

Haul-Away Log

- Driver:
- Customer
- Date
- Job Address
- Number of Items
- Signature
- Printed Name

Customer Service Request

Date:_____ Customer Name:_____

Contact Person:_____ Phone:_____

Company Name:_____

Service:_____

_____

Ready Now:_____ Ready Date & Time:_____

JobAddress:_____

Deadline:_____

Number of Pieces:_____ Weight:_____

Type of Service: ❏ Regular   ❏ Rush   ❏ Economy

Special Instructions:_____

_____

_____

Payment: ❏ On Customer Account   ❏ Credit Card   ❏ Cash

❏ Visa   ❏ Mastercard   ❏ Amex. Card #_____

Name on card:_____ Expiration Date:_____

Signature:_____

Comments:_____

Date completed:_____

Service Agreement

This service agreement, dated _____
is between _____(Customer)
and _____

(Company). The customer and the service provider agree as follows:

Junk Removal Services. Company agrees to collect and remove from Customer's home, office or other designated location all items listed in the Customer Service Request.

Prohibited Materials. Materials shall not include any personal property which would result in the violation of any law or regulation of any governmental authority, including all laws and regulations relating to Hazardous Materials, waste disposal and other environmental matters. For purposes of this Agreement, "Hazardous Materials" shall include but not be limited to any hazardous or toxic chemical, gas, liquid, substance, material or waste that is or becomes regulated under any applicable local, state or federal law or regulation.

Ownership and disposal of Customer materials. Customer Represents and Warrants that Customer owns all materials to be hauled away. Customer agrees Company may dispose of materials in its sole discretion.

CHAPTER 9 - FORMS & SAFETY TIPS

Access to Customer Property. Customer represents that they have an ownership interest in the property upon which the Company shall enter to haul away the materials or that Customer is an authorized agent of the owner(s) of the property.

Customer authorizes Company to drive on Customer's lawn or other non-paved area to retrieve the materials from the area(s) designated by Customer, or drive on a paved surface. In either case, Customer assumes full risk for all damage resulting from Company's entrance onto the areas designated by Customer and relieves Company from any responsibility for such damage.

Cancellation. Customer must cancel by email any scheduled work by noon on the day before the work is scheduled. If not, customer agrees to pay a Cancellation Fee of $_____

Exemption from Liability. Company will have no liability for claims or losses resulting from Customer's failure to comply with these Terms and Conditions, including but not limited to Customer's inclusion of prohibited materials among the customer materials.

Except in the case of negligence or willful misconduct, Company will have no liability for any damage to, or loss of any of Customer's property while Company is engaged in removing the Customer Materials, from any cause whatsoever.

Any Company liability resulting from instances of negligence of Company, or Company's agents or employees, shall be limited to the amount of the actual damage incurred.

Default. In the event that Customer shall fail to pay the amount due or shall fail to comply with any term, provision or covenant contained herein, Company shall have the right to pursue any remedy provided for under applicable laws under this Agreement. All expenses incurred in collecting any unpaid balances will be added to the final amount due, including reasonable attorney's fees.

Indemnification. Customer will indemnify and hold harmless the Company, and its employees, from all claims, demands, actions, or causes of action whatsoever that are brought or made by others arising out of, or connected in any way with Company's removal of the customer materials, other than claims based upon the gross negligence or willful misconduct of Company, its agents or employees. This indemnity obligation specifically extends to any actions, orders, penalties, or enforcement procedures made or brought by any governmental agency in connection with any Customer Materials.

Governing law. This agreement and the performance under this agreement to be construed in accordance with and governed by the laws of the State of _____

Force Majeure. Company shall not be held liable for any delay, interruption, or failure to perform any of its obligations under the Agreement, and shall be excused from any further performance, due to circumstances beyond its reasonable control.

Succession. All of the provisions of the Agreement shall apply to, bind and be obligatory upon the heirs, executors, administrators, representatives, successors and assigns of the parties hereto.

Entire Agreement. This agreement sets forth the entire agreement of the parties. There are no representations, warranties, or agreements by or between the parties, which are not fully set forth in the agreement, and no representations, promises, agreements or understandings, written or oral, not herein contained shall be of any force or effect.

Safety Tips

Because haul away work often involves cleaning up dusty, dirty and sometimes dangerous (boards with rusty nails, for example) materials, it's important to take simple steps to protect yourself and your helpers. Here are the minimum requirements to work safely:

- ✓ When you arrive at the job site, take a moment to evaluate it for possible safety hazards, such as broken glass, hornet's nests, slippery spots and hazardous materials.

- ✓ Heavy-duty work boots or shoes offer better protection than sneakers and can prevent toes from being hurt or rusty nails from puncturing the soles.
- ✓ Always carry a supply of disposable dust masks to protect against dust, mold and other harmful airborne particulates. Use the masks marked "N95", as they are rated to block 95 percent of particulates.
- ✓ Work gloves can help prevent cuts, scrapes and contact with possible toxic materials.
- ✓ Eye protection, whether goggles or glasses, can keep your eyes from getting damaged. They are a must when doing demolition work.
- ✓ A tetanus shot is essential protection in case you get a cut, scrape or puncture from a rusty nail or other material. The shot is good for ten years and is just about the cheapest "insurance policy" you can buy.
- ✓ A first aid kit should be kept in your truck for emergencies. Chain stores like Walgreens, RiteAid or CVS often have them on sale for just a few dollars.
- ✓ Your state may have additional safety requirements, such as ear plugs, hard hats, safety vests and so on. Be sure to check to find out what requirements are enforced – it may save you a hefty fine.

CHAPTER TEN

Growing Your Business

Hiring Employees

Whether you plan to hire new employees now or in the future, it's important to do it right. Because of the complexities of today's labor laws, federal and state regulations and record- keeping involved, you need to know of these requirements before you even place your first help wanted ad.

Hiring the best people for your new haul-away business will free you to focus on the "big picture" that will help you grow your business, give you a backup person who can take over when you are sick or on vacation and increase your profits as you add new customers.

After you have hired and trained your new employee, you will also gain precious time to keep build your network of prospects which will help your business to grow.

As your business grows, you will gain new customers, but without help, you may have to turn away those new customers because you're already over-extended and over-worked! That's not good. In addition, with good help, you will serve your existing customers better.

When is It Time to Hire Employees?

- ✓ Do you feel you just can't ever take a day off? Without employees, you can forget vacations or sick days. Just one employee can give you the personal time you need and deserve.

- ✓ Are you turning down new customers? When you have to say "no" to new customers or work longer hours just to keep up, it's time to get the help that will allow you to expand your business and become more profitable.

- ✓ Are your customers unhappy? When your customers complain about poor service, that's bad for business. It's a sign that you need to add an employee so you can spend more time keeping your customers happy.

- ✓ Do you feel overwhelmed by your workload? Do you look forward to your work every day, or do you dread it? When you're stressed or unhappy about your work, it shows, and your customers will sense it. When you love your work, it shows, and a smile on your face sends a huge positive signal to your customers.

- ✓ Do you have a life outside your work? When you neglect your personal life because you're working all the time, guess who suffers? Your family and friends. If this describes you, it may be time to add and employee and get your "real" life back!

- ✓ You want to grow your business, but you never seem to have time to pursue new opportunities or plan your business future. Hiring an employee can give you that vital time to plan for your bigger and better business.

If found yourself saying "yes" to one or more of these six reasons, read on while we cover the right way to find and hire your first new employee.

How to Find Good Employees

Start with a job description. To attract the right applicants, you need to write a simple job description. Focus on education, experience and "soft skills," such as a "people person" ability to organize and time management.

A G.E.D. or a high school diploma is a reasonable minimum requirement. Also, I've found new hires with a recent military background to be excellent employees, as the military service has trained them to be punctual, courteous and eager to succeed in the civilian world.

What to Pay Your Employees

To find good employees, you will need to pay competitive wages. If similar jobs in your area are paying $18 an hour, you need to match that, or finding the best employees will be difficult.

To get started, go to the help-wanted job boards listed earlier and note hourly wages for similar jobs in your town. Jot down 10 posted rates, then divide by 10 and you've got the magic number you need to match.

While you're checking the job boards, also study the job descriptions. This will help you write an effective ad or post at the job boards. Some job boards, like Indeed, have a template you can use by simple filling in the blanks for important items like job title, start date, pay rate and required background checks.

Pre - Hiring Setup

Before hiring your first employee, you will need to determine whether you want independent contractors or employees. The main difference between independent contractors and employees is who is in control of the work, according to the I.R.S. and most states.

If someone is responsible for their own work and scheduling, they could be considered an independent contractor. If they depend on you to supply a list of customers, scheduling, and pay, they are considered an employee. There are a lot of "gray areas" here, and laws vary from state to state, so check with your state to find out what their guidelines are.

Background Checks

A pre-employment background check is recommended for all new hires. Better to get any bad news before you hire than after. What information you can check on depends on your state regulations, but almost all states allow a criminal background check and a drug test, the two most important checks for you to consider.

To order a background check, do a web search for "criminal background check in (your state)" Compare prices from at least 3 providers before you order a check. The U.S. Equal Employment Opportunity Commission has strict rules that must be followed if you do a background check. You must notify the applicant in writing that you intend to order a background check.

In addition, the applicant must provide a signed consent to the check. If you are ordering a credit check, the same rules apply, plus you must notify the applicant if you refuse to offer the applicant a job because of information in the credit report.

Drug testing is often included in a complete background check, especially because of the nature of this work. Just imagine for a moment what could happen if a person employed by you was involved in a serious accident while driving a company truck and was found to be under the influence of illegal drugs!

Your insurance company would drop your coverage, those injured could sue you and your business could go bankrupt. So just do it! According to the current federal regulations, an applicant can refuse to take a drug test, but if they do, you probably don't want to hire them, anyway.

The U.S. Civil Rights Act makes it illegal to ask about age, race, ethnicity, color, sex, religion, national origin, disabilities, marital status or pregnancy, whether in a background check, an interview or on a written application.

Advertise Your Job

Once you're prepared, it's time to get the word out. Almost all jobs are listed on online job boards. Explore several to see which one might be the best for your employee search.

Here's a list of the larger national job boards:

>   **Indeed.com**
>
>   **Careerbuilder.com**
>
>   **Craigslist.org**
>
>   **linkedin.com**
>
>   **Monster.com**
>
>   **glassdoor.com**
>
>   **simplyhired.com**
>
>   **seek.com**

Employee Record Keeping and Taxes

First job - insure your new employees. When you hire employees, you must add worker's compensation insurance. This insurance is required in all states and covers injury or illness while on the job.

For an example, if you hired a new employee who injures their back or slips on an icy sidewalk on the job, worker's compensation insurance pays for their medical care and wages while they are unwilling to work.

In most states, worker's compensation insurance is available through private insurance companies. Only four states, Ohio, North Dakota, Washington and Wyoming, have their own state- run insurance plans. If you're in one of the other 46 states, contact your current insurance agent or insurance broker to set up this insurance. Your agent can also add a new employee to your surety bond.

Why Hire a Bookkeeper?

When you add employees, the quantity and complexity of record-keeping can be overwhelming. Don't make the mistake of trying to do everything yourself. Your focus should be on running and growing your business.

Few small business owners have the in-depth knowledge of accounts receivable, accounts payable and taxes, and the yearly changes in tax laws and regulations. It's better to hire a

professional who has the training and skills to handle this part of your business.

It's also a form of insurance, as missing a bill or a tax filing could affect your business credit rating or result in substantial fees or tax penalties from your state or the I.R.S.

Be sure to hire a bookkeeper that can handle both taxes and payroll so they can handle estimated tax payments, 1099s for independent contractors, Form 940 employment tax forms, W-2 forms and give you a schedule of what is due and when. Unless you enjoy handling these details daily, do yourself a favor and hire a pro!

Never forget ... your time is money that can be used towards running your new business and taking it to the next level. A good bookkeeper can save you money by ensuring that you don't make costly accounting mistakes, forget to file a form or a tax payment or forget to send reminders when a customer forgets to pay their bill on time.

If you are on a tight budget, you can use one of the bookkeeping software programs covered earlier to handle the more routine tasks, then transfer the data to a pro for the rest. Quicken, for example, is widely used by bookkeepers and accountants, so sharing date with your bookkeeper is almost seamless.

CHAPTER 10 - GROWING YOUR BUSINESS

First, thank you for purchasing and reading this book. I hope it has provided both the resources and the motivation for you to start your own haul-away business. Starting your own small business is the ticket to a better life and a prosperous future, and freedom from worries about job security.

If you have a moment, I'd really appreciate a review. If you enjoyed this book, please take a minute or two to post a review on Amazon. Just enter the title of this book at Amazon.com, then scroll down to the bottom of the page and click on "customer reviews," then "write a customer review".

When you leave a positive comment on Amazon, the world's largest bookseller, it makes a huge difference to help new readers find my books.

Thanks so much for your support!

Craig Wallin

Made in the USA
Columbia, SC
13 November 2020

I Dedicate This Book To My Long-suffering Husband, Richard, Without Whose Encouragement I Would Have Buckled After My First, Second And Third Rejection. "Don't Give Up," He Says. "That's When Success May Be Right Around The Corner."

A Perfect Day

Copyright © 2003 Peggy DePuydt
All rights reserved.
ISBN: 1-58898-915-1

A Perfect Day

Carrie Jacobs-Bond, The Million Dollar Woman

A NOVEL

Peggy DePuydt

2003

A Perfect Day

ACKNOWLEDGEMENTS

Carrie Jacobs-Bond Autobiography
Carrie Jacobs-Bond, *As Unpretentious As The Wild Rose*, author, Marcia Bernhardt, Curator, Iron County Museum
As Time Goes By, author Marcia Bernhardt & high school students of Iron River, Michigan
The Pasadena Tournament of Roses Association
The Third Annual Cascades Festival, Jackson, Michigan Chamber of Commerce.
Roycroft Renaissance, American Heritage Magazine
Ad Travels: *The Roycrofters' World*, East Aurora, New York
The Iron County Historical Society
Forest Lawn Museum
Monica Irvine's summary of Carrie's late years.
East Aurora, New York Chamber of Commerce
Rock County Court House, Janesville, Wisconsin
Alaska State Library Historical Collections
Thornyhold, a novel by Mary Stewart

A story of the life and times of
Carrie Jacobs-Bond, Composer of Down-Home Songs

When you come to the end of a Perfect Day,
And you sit alone with your thought
While the chimes ring out with a carole gay
For the joy that the day has brought;
Do you think what the end of a perfect day
Can mean to a tired heart
When the sun goes down with a flaming ray
And dear friends have to part?

PROLOGUE
A Perfect Day

The chronicle of Carrie Jacobs-Bond gives reason to confirm that truth is stranger than fiction; her life was a record of struggles against odds and triumphing over obstacles. No easy effort was it to introduce something new to the American public and make a success. The endeavor required years of arduous incessant work, for Carrie Jacobs-Bond's success was one of gradual growth from the time that she began her publishing in one little room to the enormous business that she and her son later controlled, a business known from Chicago to the Antipodes.

With unlimited faith in herself and her gifts, she knew that she had something to give the public, something that would make appeal to the better nature of people, a wholesome sentiment, and a belief in human nature she could exemplify in song.

As head of the music-publishing house known as *Carrie Jacobs-Bond & Son,* she earned laurels as a businesswoman.

Her concerts were not in the stilted manner of a professional; rather, they revealed the rare combination of poet, singer, and composer. Her voice was viewed not as a singing voice exactly, but more adapted to a recitative voice that in speaking was music itself. Even when she *talked* her songs, or half sung them, there was the joyousness, the note of pathos that would have made Carrie Jacob-Bond famous as an actress if she were not a composer.

It is the mission of some people to bring joy to the lives of others, but seldom is a woman gifted to bring joy to millions. Yet this is said to be the good fortune of Carrie Jacobs-Bond, whose songs deal with everyday life affairs, love, happiness, friendship, and sorrow, but not much of the last, as she had known too well the sadness of life to wish to bring it too close. Her songs are enduring wherever there is home life, and where friends gather.

No career of today reads more like a fairy tale than this of the most successful songwriter, who not alone wrote the music, but the words. Her gifts were originality and charm, and there are few of the commonplaces of life that she has not made uncommon. She had sentiment, mind, and a genius for combining the two. This talent was fortunate, for in the beginning of her career she was obliged to utilize her own judgment, her son being too young to have the knowledge demanded for the conduct of a business. The entrepreneurship, in its day, was size and scope scarcely smaller than that of the publishers who were bringing out the works of dozens of different composers.

Her entire publishing plant was one most interesting, and puts one to wonder how a single mind could have created such a comprehensive piece of machinery or to keep such a splendid organization going year after year.

Carrie Jacobs-Bond was the *works* of The Bond Shop. She was the power that built up one of the most remarkable of all businesses. An education it was to visit the home of the Bond songs and spend a day there experiencing the many details that pertain to the carrying on of Carrie's enterprise. In its seventeenth year, The Bond Shop had an output that would run into the millions each twelve months. When one remembers her many discouragements, wonder and admiration are born.

Carrie, when thrown on her own resources, began her simple narratives with only the hope that she might be able to solve the problems of existence and in the way most natural to her. The path she walked required courage and infinite faith. How well she has succeeded needs no hype.

Carrie Jacobs-Bond is an American Institution.

A PERFECT DAY

CHAPTER ONE

Through the screen door in the kitchen, seven-year-old Carrie Jacobs saw before her a wide expanse of farmland every bit as adventurous as the county fair. It was half past eight on a Monday morning, and the warm humus of spring saturated the air stirring the birds to sing, the sap to run, and a child to dream. Dressed in a pink, percale dress ending at the ankle in a ruffle and tied at the back with a sash, Carrie was ready to fly like the breeze through the yet-naked hardwoods, her blonde curls bobbing like a cork on sea foam. From a distance, the horses nickered in the barn.

It was 1869 and Carrie lived on a farm situated three miles from Janesville, Wisconsin, a village only thirty-five miles north of the Illinois state line. Life was a daily delight, and Carrie a daily adventurer. Focused on fun, she darted about the house, hitching into her pinafore. ("Don't you go anywhere without your pinafore. I can't be buying you new dresses faster than you abuse them.") Carrie had memorized the admonition from her mother's tongue.

Her patience peaked this day, mother shrieked, "Get outside; it's a beautiful day...what's wrong with you, child? How many times do I have to tell you to stop running through the house? Shoo!" Her long fingers flicked *scat*.

Carrie would rather be outside anyway. To provide peanuts for her pet chipmunk was the enchanting mission in mind when she ran headlong into the hired girl who was carrying a tub of scalding water for washday.

Carrie was sure she was dead except dead people did not hurt as much as she did. Her small body was steam burned. She suffered shock and pain for weeks, from which her nervous system never fully recovered. Words would not form; guttural moans emitted without harnessing. Around the clock, a nurse administered balm and eased Carrie's small body into new positions to disallow skin loss.

Carrie's father, a physician, assessed the use of morphine to stem her inestimable pain, but the medium was a short-lived pleasure. The mythical Morpheus seemed to hold out his taunting hand of relief when he withdrew it. Pain did not die quickly and release the weary prisoner.

"The fiercest agonies are short-lived, Carrie," Dr. Hannibal counseled, the words hoarse and broken, all too aware that pain is the deepest affliction we have in our human nature.

The grand house became a grim place for an only child, thus her early years were as unadorned and cheerless as life on a prairie could be at its worst.

"You're a lucky girl to be recovering from these burns," her father said with amazement, love flowing through every word.

Carrie nodded dutifully.

Dr. Hannibal Jacob's administrations and solicitudes were the comforts to which Carrie clung during those pain-ridden days and nights. In the deep recesses of his heart, he thanked God that the child would have no disfiguration.

"God has meant you for some yet-unrevealed intention, Carrie. Indeed, He works in strange ways; we must bear with Him."

Carrie stared, her eyes large and fixed. Although attentive, she was nothing but a marble presence, responding in monosyllables to save her strength.

Not as solicitous as her father, Carrie's mother appeared only intermittently in the sick room.

A PERFECT DAY

"How are you, child?"

"I'm *Carrie*, mama."

"Yes. Of course, you are." No gentleness remained in her eyes, just dark things.

In time, Carrie came to realize that her mother gave of herself as best she could, and that time and terrors had molded her into what she was: cold and detached. She supposed that her mother could have pursued life as a musician if she had the bent to do so. She had met, however, the intimidating Dr. Hannibal C. Jacobs, and he foreshadowed any such aspirations.

"My family is musical enough," he said. "My aunt composes waltzes, (the doer of the devil's work), and my uncle invented a guitar that he plays second to none. John Howard Payne, author of *Home, Sweet Home,* was my mother's cousin, and I play the flute. Let's have an end to this balderdash. I will not have my wife sitting at the piano all day."

***

Grandfather Davis was not musical but he owned a prosperous hotel, and he idolized Carrie's mother. To retain a niche of her own personality after marriage to Hannibal, Carrie's mother ran their home with an iron hand that rarely saw a kid glove. Struggling for dominance, her personality became cruel in her intolerance of errors or incompetence. As Carrie reached adulthood, she would realize that her mother's harsh judgments were a form of weakness, a despicable game in which she found pleasure in creating another's anxieties.

After Carrie's birth on August 11, 1862 in Janesville, she had minimal nurturing, especially as she grew into later childhood. Carrie was a fragile child with frightened, aqua-blue eyes, and never referred to as a beauty.

Her mother sighed, "Look at those chubby cheeks and

thick lips." The verbal carping shrunk Carrie to the bone, rending her round-eyed with inadequacy.

In a farmhouse belonging to her Grandfather Jacobs, Carrie lived with her mother, father, grandmother, and grandfather in her early youth. The family farm was sprawled on fifteen acres of prime farmland. Surrounded on three sides by apple orchards, grape arbors, and cultivated fields, the front of the home faced a county-maintained dirt road, dry and dusty in the summer and virtually a bog after a Midwest thunderstorm. The two-story homestead was perfectly square and built of brick, with a large cupola sitting atop the dormered attic. In front of the farm home, supporting columns ran across a wooden porch with overhang, which protected large, shuttered windows typifying the pre-civil war period. A circular drive extended to a *porte-cochere*.

Inside, great French doors extended from floor to ceiling of the large rooms boasting hardwood floors, beautiful fireplaces, and antique woodwork. Old-fashioned bleeding hearts, irises, and honeysuckles bloomed beneath the parlor windows in the spring and summer.

The house, although well built, was far too big and hard to heat. The water was laced with limestone deposits and as hard as sin. Heated by pipes running through the enormous Kalamazoo range, hot water was provided for once-a-week baths consisting of three or four inches of quickly-cooled-down, sudless water. ("If the water is covering your toes, you've used too much!") Trees from the farm's wood lot provided heat energy for the vast home. Resultantly, firewood was not considered a rationed item. Yet, in her small room at the top of the stairs lighted by a single dormer, Carrie was allowed one bundle of wood a day that had to last through bedtime. She never knew what it was to be comfortably warm all winter, and in the summer, the small attic room hissed in the heat. Discomforts and complaints by the child were dismissed as spineless, and were quickly discredited.

Carrie shuddered at the photographs of her austere Grandmother Davis: tight-back hair, condemning eyes, and lips that disappeared into the cavity of her cheeks. She had been an innkeeper's wife and had shown all the hard-bitten unscrupulousness befitting her position. Moreover, to the world outside the hotel she appeared as a mother, a teacher, and an herbal nurse, who was viewed in those rugged times as an enviable wife, even a sage.

Carrie's mother, a gentler version of her, had the same adeptness to discipline, and grousing dislike for other women, especially those tended by Dr. Hannibal. "Are you sure she's sick, or does she seek your nearness to her bed?"

Whenever misfortune struck, she was always there along with her husband, and the field hand, and as useful as either. (Jealousy would not allow her to stay away.) Well known around those parts as that her volunteerism was as much for self-adulation as goodwill. Instead of sending homemade soups and jellies to Hannibal's patients, she goaded the hired help to prepare the same commodities to sell.

"No one appreciates that which they get for nothing," she hammered home until the cliché was practiced by rote.

***

Juxtaposed was Carrie's father, Dr. Hannibal Jacobs, who traveled with his horse and carriage a wide surrounding territory, ministering to the sick. He spent all his free time in the orchards, grape arbors, and wheat fields in which he grew cash crops, and was accompanied by a single field hand, Old Pete. A backward man with a slow grin and even slower speech, he was wholly devoted to Dr. Jacobs.

("I'm a mighty strong hand, right Doc?")

Later in life, Carrie would cherish memories of her father, would keep them in a mind niche, and awaken them frequently to examine. His intelligent, aqua-blue eyes leapt with warmth whenever they fixed on Carrie. Even at four years old, she recalled sitting on his lap and tracing the circles under his eyes, feeling his full mustache, and cupping his smoothly shaved chin.

Before Carrie could catch her breath, Dr. Jacobs tickled her ribs. "You're my own crystal magic, Carrie; I love you so much."

"I'm your watchacallit, too, Daddy."

At this time, Carrie discovered she could play by ear almost anything on the piano. Dr. Hannibal Jacobs was extremely encouraging, while her mother, her own musical aspirations squelched, considered Carrie's experiments on the keyboard an amusing oddity. By age seven, however, almost anyone could recognize what she was playing.

Carrie's love of the piano was equaled by her adventures in the orchards and the arbors where she pretended she had many friends. When again she was well and able to walk the familiar paths of the homestead, she visited with non-existent friends, talked to the birds, and with the help of peanuts in the shell, Carrie tamed a chipmunk. By the devil, he was nobody's fool. Standing on his sturdy hind legs, he would chuck as many as four peanuts into his cheek pouches before scampering away. On a late summer's day, the chipmunk ran into the barn to stash his cache, and Carrie scooted behind him, interested in discovering the creature's winter quarters. There she found her father swinging by the neck from the rafters of the barn shortly after he lost his fortune in a grain panic.

"Daddy!" The word wrung hoarse and ragged.

"Nooo!" She shrieked, the sound rising like cracked

thunder and reverberating about the barn continually, the anguish deepening with each echo.

Old Pete rescued Carrie from her rigid immobility immediately, but the extraordinary agitation of Carrie's mind was so all encompassing as to stifle functionality. She spoke not a word for months afterwards, and her frightened eyes grew rounder, more solemn, and intense.

The incident grew to trauma in her memory and imagination, questioning her source for love, her idyllic father-worship, and all that lie in the human heart. In her bucolic life, cheerfulness vanished seemingly as if it had been sucked into the curves in the road. The incident raised phantoms of horror in her child's mind, terrorizing her thoughts. Would she find her mother in the same straits? Who would love her as her father had?

Her father, her champion, her hero was gone.

CHAPTER TWO

Unable to come to terms with the death of her cherished ally, Carrie whispered Dr. Jacob's name repeatedly, denying reality.

While yet faltering, Carrie was dealt additional difficulties in her young life. Because of the economic reversals experienced upon Dr. Jacob's death, the family was forced to abandon their home and move to grandfather's hotel, The Davis House. Grandfather Davis was not the epitome of a father substitute, the kind with whom a young girl could be secure and friendly. Resultantly, she invented a grandfather whom she commonly referred to as **My Old Man**. Through this medium, she could tell about people and places that she could not voice so well herself. **My Old Man** was an inventive entity possessing compassion, pride, and honor. She could resurrect him at a moment's notice and realize companionship.

Although only seven years of her life she had spent on the farm, even after multiple decades, Carrie found some memories were indelible, still distinct, and undamaged through the nebulous gauze of times past. Remaining focal was the pasture with its grazing horses, and the spires of the country church peeking from a canopy of green. The centennial trees of the woodlot defined the meadows and shaded the winding road. Cutting through her memory was that road with its deep ruts made by wagon wheels and horses' hoofs—the road over which Dr. Jacobs had taken Carrie to town, to church, always seeking what lie around the curve, while sunshine and shadow played on the buggy's occupants. The delightful squeals when the carriage lurched rang in her mind's ear.

"Yee, we're going to tip over, Daddy."

"Don't worry, Carrie Bug, I'll just slow down. See?"

The busy village had a general store holding a potpourri of smells and merchandise: cinnamon sticks, horehound drops, root beer barrels and a plethora of paint, leather goods, yard goods and groceries. Sugar, coffee, flour, peanut butter, pickles, cookies, and lard were sold in the bulk, the customers ordering pounds, half pounds, and dozens. The come-alive smell of freshly ground coffee beans permeated the mercantile.

The village smithy clanged his hammer, and the fierier shod local horses as they snorted in protest. Farther down the street, Carrie breathed deeply of tantalizing bakery smells. Leaning her nose against the display case, she pointed to the exact cinnamon bun she desired. The public pleasures of the village, Carrie never found counterfeit. She found there many diversions, which she caught with delight, never questioning or analyzing; her enjoyments were boundless.

In the spring, clouds of fragrant lilacs and pungent snowballs grew in profusion within enclosures of white, picket fences. A vivid picture was her Grandfather Davis's first-rate hotel where wild roses grew along a maze of paths leading to a gazebo and tennis courts. These wild roses were to become part of the Bond logo in later years.

At age nine, Carrie played Liszt's Second Hungarian Rhapsody by ear. Resultantly, at age ten, Grandfather Davis consented to piano lessons for Carrie. Upon learning to read music, she lost some of her ability to play by ear, but she practiced faithfully for eight years with **My Old Man** sitting warm and snuggly next to her on the piano bench. Never did he abandon her. Never.

A PERFECT DAY

Bemused, Grandfather Davis thought the *Old Man* crutch quite harmless to offset this young phenomenon. Regardless of whoever was within earshot, he proclaimed, *"Thou shalt become astonishing, and a byword among all nations."* Whether the quote was keen perception or wishful thinking, Grandfather Davis was one of Carrie's greatest sources of encouragement and promise.

In addition to the friendship of *My Old Man,* Carrie inherited a real friend, a golden cocker spaniel named Schneider. He was her friend and confidante for six years. As she played the piano, Schneider lay on his belly near her, his nose on his front paws, his ears oblivious to sour notes. She reached down and scratched his head. A raised eyebrow, an alert ear, and a wag of the tail were applause from an audience of one.

Carrie cherished the golden memories, but there were no friend remembrances—except one. No cloudiness hovered in the picture of the day she met Frank Bond. He was the son of Dr. Bond, the Janesville General Practitioner. Surely, she had chanced upon him at school or downtown, but the first time she recalled talking to him was on a warm summer's day on the grounds of The Davis House when she was fourteen years old.

The day was forever dear so it could not have been a special day like her birthday, a day she looked forward to all year, but when it came around, it was just like any other day, nothing. This meant that she spent that once-a-year event all alone because her Grandfather Davis was too busy running his hotel, and her mother was too busy keeping them both alive to bother with such ballyhoo as birthdays.

"And, above all things, you're not allowed to play with the village children," mother said.

Carrie remembered every moment of that afternoon, though it began as only a haze, a surfeit of mutations like a watercolor painting. Sitting in the gazebo, Carrie allowed the mid-afternoon's cacophony of sounds to lull her: bird choruses from the gardens surrounding The Davis House, the sigh of lazy breezes around the whitewashed, octagon ramada, and a dog barking at nothing in the distance. The openwork trellis through which purple clematis wove its seeking vines was constructed over a wooden platform. The day was August hot, and the smell of freshly cut grass and warm earth drifted around her drugging an already sleepy day. She sat dreaming, eyes wide in vacant restfulness.

Something happened. Did the gazebo move? Carrie's vision had been interrupted by various light flows. The dreamy spell was enveloped suddenly by shadow. The clematis bowed and cocked as if wafted by a sudden breeze. In the slipstream, the air quieted again, heavy with fragrance. Birds ceased their concert, and katydids stopped their burring. Carrie froze in time, hushed as a quail at twilight, in the center of a real and alive world, and sensed herself to be part of it, vital and energized.

She blinked her eyes to the sudden reality, and Frank Lewis Bond was standing with one foot on the platform of the gazebo as if hesitant to approach without invitation. Frank was eighteen years old, but to Carrie he seemed older, as her mother, in her thirties, seemed old. Frank had the proud look and stature of one self-confident in one's role, his family wealthy and of excellent lineage. Even then, Carrie remembered, he had a black mustache that drooped just a little at the corners of his mouth. His dark hair was combed straight back; gentle brown eyes browsed Carrie with amusement and quick approval. She could not remember in later years what he wore, but his attire was dapper and cool white.

With a look of pure innocence, her eyes widened. She smiled.

Frank sank down beside Carrie on the bench. He seemed to manage the transition without appearing forward.

"Look," he said, pointing. "It's a Monarch butterfly. In the Southwest, they are known as Queen butterflies, but are much smaller than the Monarchs are. Do you know who I am, Carrie?"

"You're Frank Bond. I've seen you with your parents at church, or, long ago, in school?"

"Yes, so you would have, and I, you. What are you doing out here on such a warm day?"

Carrie was apprehensive to answer. Quite apart from the dallying in the garden, (*A great waste of time,* mother accused,) she was not supposed to be talking to a young man, unchaperoned. Hypnotized by Frank's direct query, she blurted the truth. "Just day dreaming."

"About what?" Amazingly, he seemed not put off, but interested. Carrie removed her gaze from Frank and looked round about her. Experiencing the mesmerized velvet of the trance she had been in, her eyes widened again, and the green lawn and border flowers morphed into a watercolor.

"I don't know. Things and nothings."

It was the kind of response that usually produced disapproval; however, Frank Bond, nodded as if he had understood every word of Carrie's undetailed explanation.

"Whether measles ever come around twice, for instance?"

"Well, yes. Do they?"

"No, they never come around again; once you've had them, you develop immunity."

"That is the truth, isn't it?" Carrie found herself speaking barely above a whisper.

"Yes. Measles are a highly contagious viral disease spread by droplet spray from the mouth, nose, and throat during the infectious stage. Once bitten by the measles bug, never again you entertain the malady. It's one of God's miracles."

"Do doctors make that happen?"

"No. It is truly God's work. Some things doctors can make happen, but not that. Some day, if I'm allowed, I'll try to assist God in his miracles. Do you understand?"

"No. You will just be able to make things happen? Are you going to become a doctor then, Frank?"

"Yes, I'm off to Milton College, Wisconsin State University in Madison, and then to Rush Medical College in Chicago."

Carrie's eyes grew wide sucking in the information. He may as well have said he was going to Mars to study monsters.

Laughing, he rose, pulling Carrie up after him. "I hope that becoming a doctor isn't undesirable to you. Well, never mind. That is neither here nor now. We'll get back to the hotel where it's cooler, shall we?" He offered his hand. "Come."

The magic afternoon was not over yet. They moved slowly back through the garden where they encountered more Monarch butterflies.

"Monarchs *are* Queens," Carrie breathed.

Frank laughed from deep within his chest and did not press to correct her. He picked one flower and herb after another and told Carrie about their functional uses, ("Dandelions are used to make salads and also wine. An extract from the sap of unripe, poppy seed pods is used in medicine, and sprigs of rosemary are used for cooking.") Therefore, by the time they found the shade of the hotel porch, Carrie knew the usefulness of some half-dozen plants. By the grace of God, though she waited to be punished for being in the garden alone with a grown man, Carrie's mother said nothing, and all was well.

"I'd like to take Carrie to Myers Opera House to hear a concert pianist," Frank entreated Mrs. Jacobs.

"Why, yes, of course. That would be an experience suited to her interests, Frank," Mrs. Jacobs replied wearing a wide smile, (as hard to find as black orchids at midnight).

A PERFECT DAY

This was the first time Carrie had ever been allowed out without a chaperone. Frank stopped by often for the next few weeks before leaving for school, spending time with Carrie. She thought her young heart would never slow its frantic pace. Evermore her smile increased in his presence.

Placid weather prevailed as always in those memorable summers, and Carrie and Frank were seen often at the soda shop and on picnic walks. Carrie realized in reflection that the cornerstone of the rest of her life was laid that summer. When Frank left, the life went out of the fields and woods, but what he had kindled in Carrie remained.

CHAPTER THREE

In the cool days of autumn, there were no Monarch butterflies, no flower and herb studies, no cozy walks, or band concerts. Carrie, having lost Schneider to a digestive disorder, begged for a pet to fill the void of Frank's absence. ("Excuse me! No, I don't think he was poisoned.")

"Any kind," she pleaded, the need being ignored.

As with all hotels of that era, the hostelry boasted a stable and hay bales a plenty to make a home for a pet, but all suggestions were disallowed. Encouraged by her early successes with a chipmunk, she attempted to tame a new one, but the city chippies were much more cautious than the country chippies, and she had no success.

The chickens in the hen house, situated a stretch from the hotel, always welcomed her. Stretching their necks through the wire pen, they picked corn out of her hand. How she delighted in creating need in a creature for what she had to offer. It became a daily ritual for Carrie to feed the busy chickens. One, Suki, ate out of Carrie's hand and lingered her long neck in the warmth of Carrie's palm. Oh, to have a friend…to be needed by a creature that returned your love!

Within weeks, Carrie's mother insisted she stop the practice. "You're going to catch fleas or some dread disease from those filthy creatures."

Many disappointments Carrie found in the mean spirit of her mother, who had turned even sourer after her father's death. Like a small bird in a thunderstorm, Carrie tucked within herself and sought the shelter of her room much of the time. The storms outside were storms inside, fearsome and wild.

In the shortened days of fall, Carrie tread lightly back to the chicken coop where she heard a racket indescribable. There she saw Old Pete chopping off the heads of chickens. Throwing them into the air, he laughed heartily as they ran in circles, their heads missing, and their feathers flying.

Carrie flew back to the hotel where she became sick all over the flagstone garden walk. Her Grandfather Davis, surprisingly considerate, cleaned up behind her. Old Pete stayed scarce for some time as well as chicken on the table.

***

It is said that the psyche produces its own defenses. In the hazy mist of years gone, Carrie remembered amazingly little about the next four years. There were trickling treats: business trips to Madison, trips to the Rock County Fair, and evening concerts in the park with Grandfather Davis. She warmly recalled the kindly solicitations of hotel visitors, who called her **Carrie Chord** for all the sweet music she pulled out of the piano.

Many hours were spent alone in her small bedroom, reading, or standing and staring out the window overlooking the hotel gardens. There she watched the red sun disappear for yet another day. It was the yearning time of evening, yet she yearned for what? She did not know. Whatever her soul wanted was out of reach. Hopes that could cheer deserted her. Yet she sought strength that could sustain through indelible memories of her father, and through the God he had taught her to know.

***

One day when Carrie was seventeen, he came again: Frank Bond, paying what he called a farewell visit before entering Rush Medical School in Chicago.

"I'll be gone for some time," he said.

Carrie knew he spoke of the truth; a year was the measurable time before he would return home.

"There are so many places I want to see: Fort Wayne, St. Louis, and Detroit," his voice drifted on.

She nodded slowly and miserably. The names passed over Carrie's head like so many pigeons. Now she added even more time to his absence, years instead of a year.

"I'll return when I've seen them all. Meanwhile," a smile broke his face.

He drew a buff, cocker spaniel out of a tote bag.

"Meet Miss Schneider," he said, a grin spreading across his face. The small bundle was warm, and nuzzly, and loving. "You need to think of me when you go for walks with her. She'll be your companion while I'm gone."

"Schneider?" Carrie faltered. Then sinking to her knees, and cuddling the puppy, Carrie giggled while Schneider licked Carrie's nose, her mouth, and her cheeks. She dared not look at her grandfather sitting on the porch glider swing.

"Schneider it is. She's yours."

"I shall call her Schneider Two," she said, holding the dog above her.

Frank exhaled long and slow. Carrie was so young, so vulnerable. He smiled.

Carrie had hoped Frank would kiss her before he left, but he did not. He never had kissed her. ***Perhaps it is because I am so plain,*** Carrie thought. Frank descended the porch steps, and a moment later disappeared down the street. The hollowness of his absence was felt sorely, as if she was being torn from herself.

Carrie's mother, wiping her hands on a dishtowel, came onto the porch smiling; however, the smile was short-lived upon spying the dog. "Whaaat," her voice dragged out. "That young man needn't think he's going to saddle me with the care of a dog."

"I'll take care of him; he'll be no bother at—"

"You're not going to be here."

Carrie's mouth gaped. She waited. No one questioned her mother, who snapped the dishtowel and crossed her arms looking incredibly like grandmother's portrait in the hall; her lips skinned back.

"You're going to go away to school. You need social exposure to other young women of fine breeding. You must be rousted out of your day dreams."

"What?" Carrie exhaled, mouth gaping. "When was this decided?"

"When I agreed to pay for your higher education is when the decision was made." Grandfather Davis cut in, his voice straining for tact.

"It's the chance of a lifetime for you to maintain musical studies. Surely, even someone as thick as you must see the value of the plan," her mother said razor-like.

Grandfather Davis look flattened. "You need this chance, you do see, don't you, Carrie Chord?"

Schneider Two squeezed close to Carrie's legs; she stooped and picked him up, putting her arms around him. At once, the dreamy vacancy of the last few years were preciously coveted—the hotel gardens, the gazebo, the walks to the general store, to the bakery, and to the post office. All took on new importance as heartfelt places.

"No, please," Carrie said. "Oh no, please, is this necessary, Mama?"

Mama had already turned away, back to her previous preoccupations, undoubtedly making mental notes of travel needs for a young woman. She chose not to reply.

A PERFECT DAY

Carrie knew even then that her mother found the prospect of her daughter being at boarding school for nine months of the year delectable.

"Grandpa, do I have to?"

"It's best..." He dismissed whatever else he was going to say or could have said.

Schneider Two licked Carrie's face again; the tears made no difference.

CHAPTER FOUR

Her mother, for Carrie's extended studies, chose Milwaukee's Notre Dame Convent.

"My granddaughter is going to be cloistered with nuns?" Grandfather Davis was appalled; he had no previous knowledge of these arrangements.

"From the prospectus, the school sounds promising. Maybe she *will* choose to become a nun, but, if not, she'll graduate as a musician of note, and with excellent scholarship credentials."

Autumn of 1880 saw the *Chicago and Northwestern* hiss out of the Janesville station. Carrie and her trunks were on board. The last thing she heard was her mother's pressured goodwill laughter. The last thing she saw was her grandfather's unabashed weeping.

Their visions grew fainter as Carrie turned from the window. In resignation, she leaned back, the train soothing in its lulling concert. Snatches of conversations returned to her.

"It is bad enough that Carrie attended the primary and secondary local schools. She is not going to end up with all the wrong friends. Never!"

"But, a convent for a young lady in the spring of life..."

"Yes, when the blood is dancing, it's time for the discipline of nuns." Carrie's mother crossed her arms over her chest punctuating the end of the conversation.

It was the conviction of an unfulfilled woman subjected to a fate she had not chosen, Carrie realized. The attitude was common enough, nourished in her mother's case by a rural upbringing in which a woman's place was in the home. In addition, Carrie recognized even then that it was shades of repressed ambition. Her mother wanted Carrie to have more in life than she had had. She needed to have the independence and freedom that only an education could give her.

So it goes, mulled Carrie, her chin cupped in her hand.

She surmised it all, even her grandfather's repetitious tune that a girl should get married, and find in that way the greatest happiness. Carrie knew her limitations; she was not a pretty woman, although socially correct and amiable. Supposing she never married, never found fulfillment in that status? Supposing she never received a proposal. Yes, surely the university education was quite necessary.

"She must have qualifications to earn her own living, and get out of this little town. Who in the world, proper for her to marry, will she ever meet in this godforsaken place?" Her mother's words rang hollowly in Carrie's mind.

Into her eighth decade, Carrie would look back and see beyond her own unhappiness to what must have been her mother's burning ambition for her. As a young woman marrying a country doctor, she had been enthusiastic. The layers of enthusiasm had been slowly peeled away by hard work and the loneliness resultant of her husband's attentiveness to his patients. In addition, the vast difference between the obscurity of the farm, and village living in The Davis House was disillusionment. A social life, at which her mother would have been adept, was a situation to which Carrie's father never subscribed.

"At the snap of a finger, it could have all been his. Doesn't he realize how coveted a doctorate is?" Her mother verbalized her revulsion to anyone who would listen.

Carrie, at the time, gave no heavy importance to the

situation. She simply knew that some unhappiness, unspoken, lie between her parents. Her mother became mute and unresponsive to fun or funerals, her father melancholy and far away, so far away, he ended it all. Carrie acknowledged that it *was* best that she get away; it was time to get on with her life.

※※※

The red brick fortress was formidable, and occupied a full city block deep in the heart of sooty Milwaukee. Carrie looked up, up, up to the fourth floor of the Notre Dame Convent. Parapets encircled the perimeter like a Moorish citadel. The late afternoon sun reflected dully on windows coated with years of pollution. A sudden cold chill gripped her. Would she be relegated to the fourth floor? As if perception were reality, she was indeed packed off to the fourth floor where there lived an attic-like dormitory. After spending her childhood in attic rooms, her stomach burned with the realization that her next four years were condemned to a barren booth, where the only privacy provided was by a sliding curtain around her bedchamber.

A uniform of navy blue, worsted blazer and skirt, and a white blouse was the dress order of the day. "There will be no discrimination in this convent between the haves and have-nots," Mother Superior snapped during orientation. Therefore, Carrie wore the same garments day after day, her brain cursed with acquiescing to conformity in lieu of individualism.

The uniqueness mattered not to the nuns for they had long ago accepted the oneness of identity. Their habits were full length, full-sleeved, black tunics. Wimples and headdress linings were stark white.

Always pulling something out of their sleeves, (missals, handkerchiefs, test papers), Carrie maintained that the teaching sisters could produce half of Janesville from their sheathing. In chapel after receiving communion, the nuns slipped an opaque, black veil over their faces to concentrate on words of worship instead of worldly distractions.

Carrie's designated Dormitory Nun, Sister Claudia, (commonly referred to as Countess Claudia by the students), was a ghostly pale woman with the square-jaw set of a lion, and deeply-set, dark eyes, eyes that probed seemingly by remote control. Robotically, she rang a hand bell for everything. The clanging announced the Angelus, a devotional prayer at morning, noon, and night to commemorate the Annunciation. Bathroom time was scheduled by bell. ("Twenty minutes only; please observe".) A tinny, bell indicated breakfast.("March in line, now,") The harsh ringing continued for mass, class, and exercise in the courtyard, which mandated marching to martial music. The hand bell for dinner was sharp. ("No talking, please.") Napkins folded into a ring were the order of the day. ("Please be reminded there is only one napkin issued per week.") By the end of the day, the peal for evening prayers had become second nature. The lineup at the foot of the bed for nightly inspection was regimentation to exercise control. Lights were snuffed, and Countess Claudia exited, hands folded within her sleeves where surely she kept voodoo sticks. Only dull streetlights permeated the murky windows, giving small comfort.

Carrie, accustomed to a dictatorial mother and filled with fear of the directive nuns, drifted through the terms of that first year. Her assigned piano resided in a room so small, it must have been, at one time, a closet. The only flicker of light and warmth was the thought of holidays. It wasn't her attic room at The Davis House, or even her grandfather's gentle ways, but the consuming love of her dog, Schneider Two, that kept her sustained and filled with sweet quietude.

Two was faithful to a fault and followed Carrie like a shadow. Begrudgingly, her mother put up with the small dog because Grandfather cared for it, but eventually, the dog had to be tied up when Carrie was not home. At the end of the second term, Carrie came home to find Schneider Two was missing.

"She ran away. That is the end of it. Gone."

Carrie dared not ask; her mother would consider it interrogation and smart-lipped. Her mother predictably squint-eyed her, if she cried. "Do you want something to cry about?" Privately, Carrie cried with pain of loss, and Schneider Two was not there to lick her face. The chipmunk, ailing birds, chickens, and the dearest Schneiders all removed from her life. Should she ever try again? She gasped for air, sighed, and closed her eyes resignedly.

***

The new term came when the earth was blanketed with snow, the wind moaning like some tormented soul. What a ray of light it was when she observed a visiting white pigeon roosting on her window ledge. With fierce determination, she managed to work the window ajar amply to slip breadcrumbs to the faithful bird. Having the affection of this small creature warmed her heart. In time, the warm, fragile bird binged bread from her outstretched hand. Thus, Carrie stayed content within herself secreting the knowledge that she would see her feathered friend at the end of each day. Despite of all her caution, one evening she returned to find the window nailed shut, the bird pacing, cooing, and stretching its neck to the bottom of the window, searching for the kindly hand that fed it. With her heart broken, she vowed to own never again a pet until she had complete control of her life. For months afterward, Carrie heard the visiting pigeon summoning her friendship in the midst of swirling snow and threatening winds.

Aid came via a diversion. Carrie found a new best friend, Gina Smith, an animated, dark-eyed, dark-haired girl, whose family lived nearby and made Carrie welcome on weekends away from the convent. It must be admitted that the sheltered life she lived at home was duplicated by the cloistered life in the convent, forming a conspiracy to push Carrie into the joy she found in a warm and loving family.

"Smith," she tossed over her tongue repeatedly…"Gina Smith, Edward Smith, Edward E. Smith," Gina's older brother.

In stunned surprise, Carrie could not remember how it started, or how much she loved, or if she even knew what love was, but she floated through every day with happy thoughts of Edward Smith. She harbored secret desires to know him better, to vie for his attention in the circle of a warm Italian family, (mama's maiden name was Caccani), their strong values, traditions, and table foods.

Soon, the petite Gina was bringing notes. "For you, from Edward," she breathed in shared confidence. Carrie secreted the private missives out to the courtyard to read, and respond, always drawing a wreath of wild roses in the upper center of the paper. Every gust of wind played with her tortured nerves fearing she may be found out, quizzed, and denied visitation to the Smith home.

Carrie walked taller resultant of the first physical attentions paid her by a man. Frank Bond was wonderful, but always left Carrie wondering if he really reciprocated her strong attraction to him. A direct opposite, Edward was aggressive and passionate. His letters metamorphosed from, "Dear Carrie Jacobs," to "Dear Carrie," to "My Dearest Carrie, the Wild Rose." Carrie saw Edward as a chance to be her own person and start a new life.

In June 1881, Carrie Jacobs married Edward E. Smith.

CHAPTER FIVE

Clever and resourceful, Carrie remained content to be Edward's wife. Asking for something better was the farthest thing from her mind. Her musical talent was superior and admired by the family. (She quickly learned that she had married The Family.) The years went by smoothly enough living in the same home as The Family. Nevertheless, she missed the solitude of her younger years, and at every opportunity, she got away to an old storage shed, dilapidated and dingy. One could collect one's thoughts there, she found, as the birds and squirrels ran in and out, and swallows nested under the eaves.

Edward, sensing her melancholy, interpreted it as loneliness for her family in Janesville. Deep into August, he encouraged, "Go home for two weeks, visit, and relax." Carrie, concerned about entering Milwaukee Normal College in September, thought it a timely idea.

There, in Grandfather's gazebo, it happened again like *deja vu*. It was summertime quiet, and, contentedly, she sat alone, humming a song; she would find words later. She had snipped snapdragons and zinnias from along the garden path, and these were lying limply on the railing encircling the summer place. A light footstep on the flagstones, and there he was.

Frank Bond said with gusto, "I knew I'd find you here. Are you ready for some lemonade?"

"Why, Frank! Yes, I am."

Carrie never asked where he had come from, or how long he had been in Janesville. He seemed to sense that Carrie would not go to the ice cream parlor for lemonade, so he produced from a bag a thermos of cool refreshment. "That song you were humming was quite catchy. Have you been writing music?"

"Yes. It seems to be my fortress against restlessness."

"You've always been adept at arpeggios and grace notes, and now words?"

"The words come more slowly."

"And at the university...teach maybe?"

"It's difficult to know. I'd really like to be a concert pianist."

Having only recently reached the age of nineteen, Carrie believed that being a concert pianist meant a kind of glamorous life laced with bright lights and surrounded by musician admirers. She longed to go to an exclusive music school, but there was no way Edward would approve because of the expense. He had come to resent her time at the piano as it was, interrupting and complaining about the *noise*.

Since Grandfather was still paying for her education, even after marrying the unapproved Edward, there was no appropriate way she could mention private school to him.

"I'll stick with the teaching certificate, and then, maybe, some day..." her voice drifted off.

"That's a waste of talent. You are underestimating your capabilities. Allow me to give you a word to the wise. The only breaks you have in life are the ones you give yourself and the God-given gifts with which you are born. After that, it's up to you."

"You're right, of course, but there are—" she bit her bottom lip and stopped, lowering her head to look at her hands resting on her lap.

Frank's eyes became empathetic. "Sunday sermon finished. Enjoy your lemonade."

Carrie held the tall glass; droplets of condensation touched her fingers like a soothing balm after a hard day's labor.

Frank told her about the far away places he had visited during his breaks from medical school. His descriptions were painted so clearly that Carrie, upon seeing them in later life, recognized what Frank had seen: the mammoth width of the Missouri River, the towering timber of the far north, and the awesome curve of the Atlantic Ocean.

The tower clock at city hall struck five; the sound floated over the still, warm air. It was time to get back to the hotel—back, in fact, to reality.

"This is like that other time when you visited and invited me to the concert, isn't it?" Carrie said. "You simply appeared from out of nowhere on a quiet afternoon. You said that sometimes doctors could make things happen, like magic. Remember that?" She flushed.

Frank chuckled softly. "I do. Indeed I do. What about it?"

"Well, is it true?"

Frank withdrew from his vest pocket a black, leather-bound, manual about the size of an address book. *Physician's Handy Reference*, it read. "I can sometimes make things happen with the help of this book," he said, tapping it with his finger. "I can also forecast what *will* happen by the indicators posted."

Carrie stood, enthralled at the possibilities of the small book. "If I gave you symptoms right now, could you tell me what may be wrong with me, or what will happen to me later?"

"Yes, sometimes that is possible, but not with a 100 percent guarantee. That's why it's called, *practicing* medicine," he laughed.

Carrie took a long breath, and released it with a sigh. "How wonderful it is to be able to do that."

Frank looked down at her, the afternoon light casting a

halo around her golden hair, pink cheeks in fair skin, plump mouth in a determined chin. He thrilled, but quickly turned away.

"I've found a home in medicine now," he said with determination and self-control. "It was made for me; I'm certain to see it through. Some day you'll see that."

Carrie processed that it was not, "*Maybe* you'll see it," but, "***You will.***"

They were walking back through the garden now, Carrie carrying her faltering flowers in her arm as if cradling them from further harm. "Where will you practice?"

"It will be in the north, far north, perhaps Michigan's Upper Peninsula. I want to have a home where woodland is ample, where there is room for a garden, and where a river flows nearby. I'll grow my own herbs in the summer and listen to the silence in the winter. It'll be remote and restful."

Carrie thought he was describing heaven, but it lacked an essential. "Will you have animals?"

Frank gave her a sideward glance. "I'll have a dog named Schneider, for sure, and a grand piano for visiting dignitaries such as yourself, Mrs. Smith, my dear."

They had reached the steps of the grand entrance to The Davis House. With her foot on the first step, Carrie said, "Fulfillment such as your dream almost never happens, you know."

"Not completely, perhaps," Frank said gently. "Sometimes not even for a short time, but one's happiness requirements change as one gains in years. Happiness is in you, Carrie." He took a step to move on. "You make sure you grab all the happiness you can in the coming years. I won't be around anymore. I leave for Chicago tomorrow on the early train, so I'll say goodbye."

A PERFECT DAY

"Oh," she murmured, suddenly wide-eyed and sober. "Goodbye Frank. You take care of yourself and your little black book," she said softly.

A curtain of finality dropped between them.

CHAPTER SIX

Carrie did not gain her teaching certificate.

She did not gain much of anything but abuse and hard times. Edward's criticisms were always a word away, and with them, he controlled. Five acquiescing years into the marriage, Carrie bore a son, Fred. Two years later the marriage ended in divorce after much unhappiness marred her life: Edward the violent, Edward the womanizer, Edward the spendthrift, Edward the non-presence at the birth of Fred, where Carrie lay exhausted and spent, her face lined with trauma. At the age of twenty-five, she was on her own with a small child to rear. She was awash in fear, not knowing where to go. The wind would not cease nor the great oaks in the yard stop shaking...Like her, she thought.

Grandfather Davis, without hesitation, offered her sanctuary at The Davis House. Clinging only to the hope that The Davis House had succored her once before and might well do so again, she traveled again the long journey from Milwaukee to Janesville, Fred nestled at her side.

Carrie's mother never knew that Carrie did not get to be a teacher, and that she had a grandson named Fred. Three years ago, her mother died as she had lived —pursuing society, crowding days into hours. With her horse and carriage raising a long curl of dust while attempting to outrun a train at the Main Street crossing in Janesville, the train won.

In the months and years following the funeral, Grandfather Davis was listless and had difficulty getting out of bed in the morning. In spite of her infuriating ways, Carrie's mother had been the torque that kept him going. His keen mind often drifted into the vast reaches of nothingness.

Indecisions were non-existent that onto Carrie's shoulders would fall the responsibility of caring for him, and, in addition, managing the hotel upon her arrival in Janesville. Forever grateful for her grandfather's largesse in folding her and Fred under his wings, Carrie reciprocated nobly. The strength and success of the hotel rested upon her intelligence and virtue.

"It's all yours, Carrie Chord." Grandfather winked conspiratorially. His unexpected flash of deep bonding brought sparkle back to Carrie's eyes.

"It'll be my pleasure."

The tender years of her life had come and gone it seemed in a blur, and sometimes, in worn-out futility. The far away places with exotic names would never be hers to see. After the thrill of being independent, the disillusionment of a better life, and the evaporated promise of love ever after, she found she had come full circle back to where she had started.

If she were sunk in despair, it was short-lived. The tenacity of youth clung on she loved two-year-old Fred dearly, as well as her grandfather. In truth, the hotel took on a completely new light without her mother, less of a prison, more of a new door opening. It amazed Carrie how fulfilling the management of the hotel was without her mother's derogatory remarks.

The golden-haired, blue-eyed Fred in his exactness of Carrie captured Grandfather's heart. The two were inseparable. A new fire ignited in his soul, a radiating glow from his gentle eyes, an inner pride bursting forth.

Sometimes Carrie surveyed Grandfather Davis with love and often with sadness. Ever watchful, she waxed empathetic for the dear man. The passing years had stooped his once sinewy shoulders, had drawn together his hectic brows in an acquiescing frown. His quick business acumen wobbled undermining his bold confidence. Sciatica terrorized his left hip and leg without letup reducing him to rely on a cane. Having pressing thoughts of his own demise, he arranged for Carrie to realize whatever profit was available from the sale of the hotel, but that would be of slightly more than a dowry. The expenses inherent to raising a small child would quickly drain the gift. Then, and what were her chances in Janesville of marrying again?

There had been friends made in her year at the Notre Dame Convent, and the following year at Milwaukee Normal, but the male associates had quickly melted away upon her marriage to Edward and the subsequent birth of Fred. At times, Carrie found herself in the clutches of wary tension that strung her senses taut. Nonetheless, every sunset found her a stronger person.

In the same manner, life went for another two years. In the mornings, she awoke with her senses renewed. Alive were her motivations, glossed with what she would accomplish that day. Carrie found both privations and privileges as manager of The Davis House, but fear of the future became less daunting.

She fell into bed exhausted at night sometimes missing the mark of her morning enthusiasms. Fred growing and needing many attentions, consumed her time, and took her on many tangents. His third birthday came and went and his fourth. The child grew delightfully, his senses quenched in search of the mysteries of his environment: a flower of blue, a clover of violet, or a grasshopper of green. All things he viewed like the dawn of a new day. What Fred did not discover on his own, Grandfather Davis pointed out with his cane, the tow-headed tot alert to all teachings.

"Whazzat, Grandpa? Whazzat?"

Carrie, out of necessity, had lost contact with Frank Bond, or, with gentlemanly courtesy, he had lost touch with Carrie. She had not seen him since his visit at the gazebo the day before he had left for Chicago to further his medical studies. Carrie wondered if he had ever realized his dream of a doctorate, or if he had decided to travel extensively. "Maybe he also married," she surprised herself speaking aloud. She had no way of knowing, and he slowly faded into the vapors of her green years. Carrie had no quality time to waste in idle dalliance of what might have been. Wherever he was, she was sure that he was making other people's lives enjoyable.

When Fred was four years old, Grandfather Davis died. Fred in his loneliness followed Carrie like a shadow, his arms raised to her. A big boy for his age, nevertheless, he sought the comfort of being close. Carrie's heart went out to him. All too vividly, she remembered her father's death, and her mother's subsequent indifference. How *she* could have used a soul mate.

Serene and concerned, grandfather's last thoughts were for the welfare of Carrie and Fred. Every holding of his mortal lifetime was Carrie's. The funeral was large and, with great respect, was attended by a myriad of townspeople. After the aplomb and eulogies, Carrie found she was alone, and revisited the gravesite. It was late September. The paths between graves were strewn with fallen leaves, fading blossoms, and pungent with the smell of rich, damp earth. The trees yet clung to anemic-colored dressings in the still air.

She never knew she could miss someone so much. ***Don't it always go that you don't know what you got 'til it's gone;*** she recalled the old saying. Grandfather had literally come to life when she and Fred again entered his world. His zeal was a fire of love and returned him to his youth. Dazzling smiles broke into his deeply lined face as if he had come upon a powerful potion of restoration.

A PERFECT DAY

At his graveside, she lingered until dusk was fast approaching. His trackless past had ended here. Had he fulfilled his dreams? Gathered in his fruit? Why had she not asked more questions? Tears came unwanted.

※※※

The hotel, although bustling with guests, was empty, no longer the stunning castle of her youth. Carrie sat down in the room that had been her mother's, the rocking chair inviting company. Old Pete, (never quite comfortable after the chicken episode), had set aglow the fireplace, and then disappeared. Settled near the fire, she raised her arms, cupped the back of her head, and contemplating, stared at the ceiling. Flames licked around the log energy until there were only embers that alternately flushed and faded.

You need an education so you can support yourself, Carrie. Indeed, don't wait for a knight in shining armor to sweep you onto his white steed. Her mother's words flew at her like a condemnation from the high court. Only twenty-five, and having the responsibility of a small son, she recognized her boundaries; managing a hotel for the rest of her life was out of the question. Proceeds from the sale of The Davis House would sustain for a while. However, afterwards, what would happen? She would have to seek employment and make the best of a bad bargain, but, admittedly, she was scared to her bone marrow.

Carrie was licensed to do nothing, and, it occurred to her, that her mother would have reminded her briskly that was what she was: nothing. She flexed her shoulders and sat up straight with the thought, the rocking chair halted to stillness.

Things always look better in the morning, Carrie, grandfather had told her repeatedly. Maybe she *would* see things more clearly upon awakening. Chunky ashes fell through the grate with a flicker of never-say-die. The cushy sound was like an avalanche in the silent room.

She arose and gathered the mail from her desk near the door. Carrie sifted through the letters that Old Pete delivered daily to her room now, as if saying the myth and meaning of the cocoon you've been living in have been rent. You are the boss now, the decision maker, the planner, the bill payer, and the check writer.

She took a quick breath at the return address on a long envelope: **Dr. Frank Bond, 32 Adams Street, Iron River, Michigan.** Carrie's feet glided back to the cooling fireside, not ever remembering in later years how she ever got there; her legs had turned to jelly. She slapped the envelope gently against her palm, the paper feeling rich and textured.

She opened it, read it.

Slowly she sank into the rocking chair. Her heart hammering in her throat, she read it again.

Carrie's fingers held the letter as if it were about to disintegrate. Handwritten, the letter spoke to Carrie as if Frank were standing in the twilight of the room, his arm outstretched over the fireplace mantle.

Dear Carrie,

    I have not kept in touch with you because of the inappropriateness of the situation. News has reached me of your grandfather's demise, about which I extend my deepest sympathies; he was a Janesville hero, if not a national one.

    I have established my medical practice in this far north, iron ore mining village, whose population is escalating daily because of new assays of iron ore. The scenery is as unspoiled as the fearless settlers are. I have found a home.

I would like to make this home yours as well as mine when and if you should decide to accept a marriage proposal. You will find, as I did, that everything is here that you ever wanted: peace, contentment, nature's playground, hearty neighbors, and, above all my devoted love.

Take it, Carrie. I have been caring for a dog named Schneider all this while in the hopes that someday you could still be mine…Schneider's and mine.

Your long-suffering devotee, Frank.

When the gasping ashes fell to the last one with a soft poof, Carrie sat hypnotized by Frank's letter. It had been written months earlier but postmarked only days ago.

A PERFECT DAY

CHAPTER SEVEN

Dr. Frank Bond, at age thirty, married his hometown sweetheart, Carrie Jacob, age twenty-five, on June 10, 1888 in Janesville, Wisconsin. Within days, Fred snuggled between them, they journeyed by railroad to Iron River, Michigan. Carrie, in later life, would remember how she imagined the village. The mental fantasies she had drawn for herself were polarized from reality. She had mind-captured a small town with church steeples, picket fences, lilac bushes, towering pines, and, tucked away unobtrusively in mythical never-never land, mine shafts. The name itself, Iron River, should have been Carrie's first clue that the village ran red with iron ore dust.

She saw the settlement for the first time on a windblown day in June, ten months after her grandfather's death. All legalities had been settled, and The Davis House sold. A few pieces of furniture she saved and had in storage until she settled into her new home. A small number of her possessions, she had packed into two suitcases for the trip, and bid Old Pete a tearful goodbye.

***

Stepping down from the train at the station, great gusts of steam belched from the engine *a-shush, a-shah, a-shush, a-shah*, as if in conspired cadence in honor of the musical guest. Carrie saw cows ambling along graveled Selden Road, dogs trotting along behind them—the tinkle of the cowbells and an occasional bark to disturb the stillness. Carrie reminded herself that it was too early to make a prognosis. ***Say nothing***, she thought prudently.

The station attendant lifted Carrie's bags onto the buggy back. "So, you're Dr. Frank's missus, ay?" A short, pleasant man with a push-broom mustache, he winked at Dr. Bond.

"Yes," she said, nodding her head in acknowledgement.

He patted the suitcases securely into the rack. "I hear your grandfather died last fall; sorry 'bout that, yeah, sure sorry 'bout that." His dark head bobbed in deference and respect for the village doctor and his new wife.

Carrie was helped into the buggy's passenger seat beside Dr. Bond. "Yur gonna be comf'table here, missus. Anyways, that's how I see it, yur husband a doctor an' all."

"I'm glad to know that," Carrie said, trying to put the right touch on the words so as not to sound lofty.

The attendant touched his hat in acknowledgement of Carrie's response, and shuffled off to the waiting freight.

Carrie mulled the word, *comf'table.* She had realized a modest balance after probate of Grandfather Davis's estate, and in all likelihood, Frank would provide ample needs for the foreseeable future. Carrie hoped that would be forever. It is all she wanted. Good together, they and would stand the test of time. Their mental links had been soldered since childhood.

She saw house after house, some wood frame, some log, until Selden Road intersected with the busy corner of Genesee Street. Carrie craned and looked twice to study the wooden street signs carved to the likeness of Indians!

"Those were crafted by hand by Tony Krajewski," Frank advised, the name rolling off his tongue with respect. "Most are ten to twelve feet tall bearing likenesses of feathered head pieces, and tomahawks. Some are women in buckskin dresses, papooses on their backs."

"How unique," Carrie whispered. Although her voice held an element of surprise, her eyes showed appreciation.

A PERFECT DAY

There were businesses such as there were in Janesville: two banks, a bakery, a general store, a post office, a livery, and various independent merchants. After that, there was forest.

Carrie knew, of course, that *forest* did not mean a small plot of ground dedicated to the growth of deciduous trees, but what she saw was magnified farther than her imagination had ever stretched. The village was simply a small space carved out of thousands of acres of virgin timber.

Cattle grazed in back yards, in vacant lots, and in small meadows, for every family had their own cow and oftentimes, two. Towering white pines, wearing their signature brown bark and long needles stood proudly in the yards of homes, the owners reluctant to bring down such giants. On the horizon not a half-mile away, was the edge of the village where there was not a house in sight, and the forest encroached to within thirty yards of the road. Harnessing her dreamer image of the village, she sanded it down to bare wood and started over again.

From the north, she heard the rushing sound of water.

"That's the *Ir'n* River," Frank said, tongue in cheek.

"The *Ir'n*?" Must she learn a new language?

"No," Frank laughed shortly at his own joke. "You'll hear it referred to as such, nonetheless. It is the *Iron* River. The Iron River flows west to east and feeds into the Brule River, which angles southeast and empties into the Menominee River, and that, in turn, runs south into Lake Michigan."

"It's my geography lesson for the day?" Hmm, it **was not** language but topography.

"It is." He clucked at the horses for the left turn at Adams Street.

Frank slowed the carriage after three blocks. "Home sweet home," he said as the horses stopped. They had reached the corner of Sixth and Adams Street where Carrie stared in awe at a new home built on lands granted to the village by co-founders Selden and MacKinnon in June 1878. It was a white, two-story frame home featuring a wrap-around porch supported by six great pillars. The width of the home faced Adams Street, and the length of the home bordered Sixth Street. As was the architecture of the day, the porch had no railings.

Their carriage stopped at the Sixth Street entrance to the home where there were three steps leading up to the porch. The windows were plentiful and extravagantly large for a time in which there was no central heating. Two tall chimneys well above the roofline silhouetted the sugar maples that stood smartly beyond. For Carrie the chimneys held promise of no more chill blains from freezing, damp rooms. Attached to each first-floor window was a planter alive with geraniums, petunias, and trailing ivies. Nothing, not even a pouring-down rainstorm could have hidden the fact that the home was built with the same care Frank was now showing her, and showed to everyone he met, equally. A fair wind is a fair wind, is a fair wind, lifting all spirits as it passes, she reminded herself.

Before she could turn the doorknob, Frank reached around her, snuggling a kiss into her neck and pushing open the door. "Your castle, milady."

A bright, airy kitchen greeted her. When in the sitting room she saw a four-section bow window into which a melodeon piano was placed, tears sprung to her eyes. She was so full of emotion, she could hardly speak, so she turned quickly to the adjacent bright, cheery room; it was the living room highlighted by large windows facing the front porch.

Immediately off a long hall, leading from the front door was a stairway guiding to the upstairs. The hall contained Frank's desk upon which was situated a Smith Corona typewriter. Carrie had seen few of them, the contrivance only having been

A PERFECT DAY

marketed four years ago. The hall continued giving onto the living room and sitting room on the right, and farther on to the left, the dining room, and the kitchen. Carrie, opening a door at the back of the kitchen, found a large room embracing a pantry, a storage room, and a housekeeper's stairway to the upstairs.

Fred ran through the home as if he had a bee in his britches. "Mama, come see my bedroom," his voice rang through the house.

Carrie found him upstairs flitting from room to room.

"This one's mine. This one's mine," he shouted happily.

Carrie had only a glance before Fred pulled her into a large master bedroom, a nursery, and two guest rooms. Glistening hardwood floors were laid throughout the home.

Reeling with the speedy tour, she found herself again downstairs via the back staircase, where she found Frank grinning as if he had just spooled in a prize brook trout.

"I arranged for Hilda Benson to stock the ice box, and have dinner prepared."

"How thoughtful," Carrie breathed her face radiant as she inspected the kitchen now flooded with late-afternoon sunshine.

"The ice man will deliver fifty pounds of ice and set it in this chamber of the ice box," Dr. Bond indicated, pulling open that particular compartment of the device with multiple doors. "He'll remove a coupon from an ice coupon book, that is when new, purchased for the delivery of five hundred pounds. When the coupon book is depleted, I'll go to the icehouse and buy another book for five hundred pounds of ice, delivered." Frank's eyes devoured Carrie, the girl of his youth, the maid of his dreams, all soft and blonde, but with hurting blue eyes. He vowed silently to change that.

There was a brief silence as Carrie's gaze swept the modern

kitchen where four clothes irons rested upon tripods clustered on top the range. When one iron grew cold, she simply need notch another onto a wooden handle. She knew from experience at The Davis House that each iron weighed about twenty-five to thirty pounds. The porcelain kitchen sink was long and possessed a drain board and an indoor pump. Mrs. Benson had left a clump of lilacs in a vase on the kitchen table; a breeze pirouetted from the window and swirled the heady fragrance throughout the downstairs.

Carrie clutched at a small purse made of netting and beading; the sterling chain dangled. "Oh, Frank, how wonderful," she cried, her eyes brimming over. "I wasn't sure I should come to Iron River. I was not sure of anything anymore. Now this lovely home appears. It's much more than I dreamed, too much for you to have done." Shook out of her composition, Carrie rambled, embarrassed. She knew she was talking too much, too rapidly. As if, she thought, she was never to measure up to such grandeur. She felt guilty to have so much, and Fred, patting her long skirt, shared her joy.

After being removed years ago from her disciplined nest in Janesville and settled in a strictly controlled convent, she seemed to feel guilty about everything. The feeling wrapped her in its familiarity and reflected in her voice, the voice of trying to please, aspiring to be satisfactory.

"Frank," she said looking up into his dark brown eyes filled with compassion, "How can I ever describe how I feel right now? How wonderful you are. How pleased Fred and I are." The plains of her face reflected earnestness and concern.

"Well, well. There are many ways in which you can thank me, Carrie…ahem," he cleared his throat dramatically and grinned with pleasure. "There's no need to do so madam, the pleasure is all mine, and has been mine. It's been lonely bumping around in this big house until I could capture you." He chucked her under the chin. "These walls have been waiting for laughter and music, so I'll just move you and Fred in and start living and loving and putting a day in."

A PERFECT DAY

CHAPTER EIGHT

While Carrie was yet trying to comprehend her good fortune, the kettle on the stove began whistling. Pouring the steaming water into a porcelain teapot to steep with the green tea, her thoughts were no longer consumed with burdensome responsibilities. On the contrary, she was uncannily lifted to the present wonder of what was new and good in her life.

Through the rolling hills of Wisconsin, and north to Upper Michigan, Carrie had traveled in a state of osmosis, mentally absorbing all she beheld as she moved toward the Cinderella ending of which she had always dreamed. A house and a garden of her own where she and Frank could sit in a gazebo, watch butterflies, and listen to crickets was all she dared hope. She had not lingered on the reality being better than the anticipated. Thankfulness rested gently on her mind that Frank had brought in food and supplies for their homecoming.

"It'll soon be tea," she said, smiling. "Will you look at these cream puffs from, from…?"

"Nolingberg's Bakery," Frank cut in. "It's situated on Adams Street; you'll use that homey business often." With a napkin, he swiped pilfered cream from his mustache.

"How old, or maybe I should ask, how new is this village?" Carrie poured the tea, one ear attuned to Fred making his rounds of the house again.

"Iron ore was discovered in Iron River in 1851, but option to explore wasn't granted until 1880. Ore began shipping via railroad in 1882, and that's when Dad and I came to Iron River.

Our practice has been good. We work hand in hand with the Ammerman Pharmacy, which is next door to our office. Since the inception of the mines, we have a Presbyterian Church, a Catholic Church, and many spin-off businesses."

"Tell me about these mines." Carrie's thin eyebrows pulled together in a scowl line. "How is this iron ore removed?" She trusted she was not delving too deeply into mining lore and lexicon, because, after all, Frank was a doctor, not a miner.

Unscathed, Frank jumped right in. "Here, in Iron River, it is mined by the deep, underground method, requiring vertical shafts to be sunk into the earth penetrating the ore body. In the next step, tunnels or drifts are driven horizontally into the vertical shafts or ore body at different depths. Drifts are extended into and through the ore by drilling holes and blasting the ore loose. Blasting is an important part of stope, or drift, mining. Small hand drills, dynamite carriers, boxes, and fuses are all part the miners' life. It's a dangerous occupation, and mining injuries are, with too much frequency, brought to my office."

"Damaged bodies are taxing. I'm sorry that is part of your life. I hear of lung ailments. What is the air quality down there?" Carrie's curiosity was getting the best of her, and the fount of knowledge Frank possessed in regard the mines was remarkable for a nonprofessional miner. In fact, it was so like him to take an interest in his patients' lives.

"In the early days, bad air was identified by canaries carried underground in wooden cages. If the canary fell off its perch, it was a warning there was no oxygen."

"Good lord, Frank, you can't be serious!" Carrie's aqua-blue eyes became enormous.

Her response drew a shrug and a faintly amused grin. "A contemporary tester shows the air change now days."

"What do they use for lighting?" Carrie freshened the

teacups, the steam curling its way to nothingness in the warm kitchen.

"Mining hats show the different means of lighting. Here," he said, sliding a newspaper graphic toward her. "Shown in these exhibits are the early candle, the sunshine lamp, the carbide and battery packs."

"Let there be light," Carrie replied, hoping she did not sound trite or flippant.

"By means of the modern lighting, power shovels, loaders, or scrapers break the ore that is hauled by railway cars or conveyor belts to the vertical shaft where it is crushed, and hauled to the surface in buckets, called skips. The ore is stock piled until trains remove it from the area. In some cases, sand and gravel are used to fill the underground cavities after the ore has been removed. Air is pumped down another shaft and circulated throughout the underground workings. Mines may be as deep as a mile containing underground drifts extending horizontally for thousands of feet."

"Mercy," Carrie, put her hand over her heart. "A mine sounds like a rabbit warren."

Frank laughed at the comparison, but was pleased to have piqued Carrie's curiosity.

"How and when is the ore shipped?" Carrie's eyebrows, already showing signs of becoming permanent character lines on her face, melded in askance.

"The removal of the winter stockpile of ore starts with shipping in the spring. The steam shovel is brought in and ore cars appear from the Chicago and Northwestern Railroad, and the cycle is complete."

"Interesting…the iron ore business and all it entails. I know we're going to be very happy in this growing village. Thank you dearly for the perfect arrangements, Frank."

"You wouldn't have thought so a few months ago, but I couldn't let you come here until I had everything up to snuff. Nothing but the best is fit for my bride." He reached across the kitchen table to squeeze her hand. "I've arranged for a housekeeper: Hilda Benson from Bates Township. She comes highly recommended."

"Your kindnesses have no end, Frank." Carrie hesitated. Although reluctant to say it, she neither wanted (or could they afford?) daily assistance with the house. "It's so thoughtful of you to do that, but you really needn't bother with a housekeeper. I, well, I can look after things myself. I've had much experience at The Davis House, and if the truth be known, I prefer it." She smiled. "I'm grateful for your thoughtfulness, but help from time to time will be sufficient."

"I won't hear of it, Carrie. You're not to lift a hand at anything. You must spend all the time in the world at the piano."

Carrie flushed deeply. Was it not just like him? Her great blue eyes watered over, her voice too choked to differ.

"Dad and I have made arrangements to sell our interests in the drugstore to Emil Ammerman. That way, we can devote more time to our patients. The medical practice is growing by leaps and bounds, like the village." His face radiated such confidence and strength, as if that Tony Krajewski fellow had sculpted it, himself.

"It seems so appropriate for a doctor to own a drug store," her voice trailed off.

"Not any more, Carrie. What is appropriate for me is to have time to devote to you and Fred."

Carrie was in a semi-catatonic state of pleasure when

Fred's small footsteps came down the backstairs and Frank arose, picked him up under the arms, and danced him around in a circle. Frank's honest affection spreading through their hearts, Fred and Carrie's laughter rang through the house. Had Carrie reached the apex of contentment? She would contemplate nothing *but* contentment.

As she lay secure in bed beside Frank that night, she never felt more radiant. A plain woman, Carrie had to remind herself not to regress into the cowering, suppressed child she had once been. Admittedly, child was the right word. Underwritten by Frank, it was only now that she felt a fulfilled woman.

She had overseen the entire comings and goings of The Davis House after her mother's death, surely, she did not need a housekeeper, but to refuse would disappoint Frank and erode his societal position in the village. There was rawness in Carrie's dichotomy toward a housekeeper that surely she could ripen and mellow.

Still in all, Carrie had never shed her need for privacy, to be alone, to meditate. Would this Hilda Benson come and go as she pleased? Carrie's eyes flew wide, and no locked doors? Now that she had her own home, would she indeed not have it to herself? Well, whatever the situation, she was achingly tired and problems, real or perceived, could be sifted out tomorrow. ***Things always look better in the morning, Carrie Chord,*** she recalled Grandfather Davis saying.

A peaceful, easy feeling flooded her. In the distance, a train whistled short blasts, punctuating the darkness of the night. The future was a clouded entity as she hazed into the deep sleep of a distance traveler.

A PERFECT DAY

CHAPTER NINE

"I want you to plan a trip to Chicago for some serious shopping," Frank encouraged the next morning at breakfast. "You'll want to choose your china, silverware, and stemware."

"What?" Carrie exclaimed, her glance ricocheting from her fruit compote to Frank, to Fred.

"It doesn't have to be this week or the next, but sometime soon after you've finished exploring and acclimating here," he insisted. "In addition, you'll want to purchase new clothing. The villagers are sticklers on gowns of white being worn for communion, weddings, and summer. Black gowns are worn for mourning and for winter wear. In between time, you'll want to have some happy gowns for entertaining."

"Entertaining, Frank?" She lost her breath; the tension was almost palpable.

"I wish to show off my award wife, who is gorgeous, talented, sings, and plays the piano like a concert artist." His eyes sparkled with mischief.

You can do it, Carrie Chord she tossed from her tongue to her mind. She smiled, calming her perceived short falls: hostess, entertainer, wife, and mother. What kind of a balancing act could she manage?

It was a peculiar experience for Carrie. At Frank's request, she had moved only personal items from The Davis House, so nothing in the house was familiar or seemed as if it were a part of her life. Was this a dream? Carrie's heart had eyes that could never be explained to her brain. Everything she saw, she liked, as if she had always been at home in this household. Consequently, she found herself treading lightly as if she were experiencing some kind of déjà vu. Unreal it was, unreal.

That Hilda Benson had done an excellent job at cleaning the house was a given. Dust was not to be found and the heavy, unglazed cretonnes of the window draperies and sofa arm covers were as warm as a day in spring.

The piano had been polished to mirror quality; the keyboard beckoned to Carrie. In the early morning light of a brand new June day, music spilled forth, filling the room with magic. It seemed that an angel's touch was in her fingers, and a heavenly chorus in her ears. For how long she sat in such a mode was a lost dimension, lost in the depths of complete absorption. Had her perfection at the keyboard been attained by slow increments, or had it simply required the hand of time and contentment? How her music soared, the melodies floating out the open windows as if they had an embodiment and will power of their own. The notes told a story as if they were an unfolding, divine opera.

"Come see, Mama. Come see all the things in my room!" Fred was pulling at her skirt. He led her up the front stairs to his room where the morning light had revealed a myriad of childhood delights, delights that Carrie scarcely had time to notice the night before. A rocking horse stood in the corner, and a bookcase containing colorfully illustrated stories was standing against the far wall. A picture of Ben Franklin flying a kite attracting electricity hung over Fred's bureau. A red wagon carrying blocks and puzzles sat with the handle up, inviting Fred to pull the small vehicle to any adventurous destination he desired.

"Glory be!"

"Are they for me?" Fred asked, spreading his arms as wide as he could.

"All of it for you, my child." Carrie's heart swelled so; she thought it would jump out of her chest. "Now come see the rest of this fine home," she said, taking Fred's small hand in hers.

The dining room, situated at the left of the foyer hall, had been seldom used. The room spoke of show and no go. Frank had collected, nevertheless, some handsome pieces of china. She would paint wild roses on them to make them more distinguishably her own.

Across the hall was Frank's den featuring an oak, roll-top desk, a second Smith-Corona typewriter, and two, leather chairs. Medical journals lined the shelves. With file folders ajar and papers askew, a filing cabinet stooped with overload. Abandoned on the desktop was a coffee cup. A door leading from the hall, and one directly opposite could close off this sanctuary. This second door opened onto her music room. Carrie walked across the room, her foot nudging the edge of something: a leather house slipper, its heel squashed down, its plaid lining worn. *Frank's favorites*, she smiled, and toed the footwear under the chair allowing just a shadow to protrude.

Fred shook his head in dismay, glancing up at Carrie for validation.

She squeezed the child's chubby hand.

Utility cupboards, pantry, storage, broom racks, and cleaning supplies were all found in the spacious room off the back of the kitchen. She had made the circuit. The sun was already high; Frank would soon be home for lunch. As if by some magic thought transference, she heard the front door open.

"Carrie, I'm home," swelled Frank's beautiful voice, comfortable and homey.

Manna in the wilderness had fallen into Carrie's life.

※※※

Returning from Chicago on the *Chicago and Northwestern Railroad*, Carrie was a reservoir of happiness. She had chosen her china in white in the company of a narrow gold rim, and a narrower wheat-colored rim around the perimeter of each piece. Fostoria crystal gleamed in the china cabinet.

A favorite gown she had purchased was of lightly layered, shell pink chiffon ending in a handkerchief bottom. A slim sash of taupe lace wove its way down the bodice and tied at the midriff.

With an adoring eye, Frank conceded that the gown's style gave the impression of height to Carrie's slight build, and discreetly flattered the mature curves of her slender figure.

"That's the one you'll wear Saturday night when we have a dinner party."

"I don't think I'm..."

"Everything is arranged," he said, holding up his hand to halt Carrie's objection. "Hilda Benson will cater the whole affair: crispy fried chicken, creamy mashed potatoes, fresh garden beans, in-season fruit salad, Hilda's specialty, mile-high, baking powder biscuits, and apple crisp. All you have to do is look stunning and play the piano." Frank lifted and kissed Carrie's hand, his eyes rising to meet hers.

Carrie would prefer for that not to happen, her recluse nature bubbling to the surface like air from a sunken bottle. Nonetheless, she could see that Frank was deliriously happy, and she would bend to the ways of his world.

Play the piano Carrie did, and never stopped. The gossamer dress enhanced Carrie's complexion lending a clean-scrubbed glow of summer vitality, and radiating warmth that Frank felt in his blood. Carrie's delicate hands turned her into the empress of the piano kingdom, holding Frank's guests enthralled. He picked up his brandy snifter and swirled its contents while studying her; pride of possession spoke from every pore in his body.

She was invited to play the organ at the Presbyterian Church on Sunday, and she obliged. In addition to fulfilling her duties as wife and mother, Carrie found time for poetry and music. She had never known such complacency. If, because of her heightened social status, she felt superior it was an amiable superiority rendering her new neighbors agreeable, and if not agreeable, then acceptable.

Her personality, in a constant state of felicity, made everyone she met pleased with himself or herself. At peace, she produced in others good nature and benevolence. She encouraged the shy and soothed the confused.

Carrie hugged private moments as precious. Sometimes she would go into the quiet woods near the village, and under the canopy of vast pines, think out the verses of a song. Often melodies would come to her to fit the words. She explained that the way she composed was to listen for melodies with her inner ear and, when she heard them, write them down as rapidly as possible.

Six years of silver linings followed without a cloud to dampen Carrie's spirits.

CHAPTER TEN

In 1889, after selling their interest in the drug store to Emil Ammerman, Frank and his father gave their full attention to their profession now in full bloom. It was at this, the busiest of times, that President Cleveland appointed Dr. Frank Bond to the challenging position of postmaster.

"Frank, you must snuff something out of your life. You're burning a two-wick candle." Carrie shook her head in mock scolding.

"Don't you worry about my candlepower. It's a torch, and you, my dear, keep it burning," he added kindly.

On three occasions, he was president of the village and held other responsible positions of trust, in all of which he was faithful and earnest in carrying out the wishes of his constituents. Frank had the rare ability to suppress his vast knowledge in an attempt to put others at ease.

It was a breathtaking autumn day that same year when the hardwoods were aflame in proud garb that Dr. Bond, Sr. died after suffering a stroke marked by accompanying paralysis. All was done that medical skill could devise and kind hands perform. He was interred in Milton, Wisconsin. Dr. Frank was both forlorn and devastated. He had lost a father, a confidante, and a friend.

Carrie knew the sense of great loss, the sense of being betrayed, the anger, the hopelessness, and then the acceptance. Blindly she gave of herself, her time, her patience, trying to supply what Frank seemed to be desperately seeking...a nebulous island of peace.

Encouraged by Carrie, who recognized Frank's need for diversion, he became a prominent stockholder in the Calidonia Iron Mining Company. Calidonia was instrumental in opening up a fine property, afterwards leased to the Mansfield Mining Company, the endeavor subsequently suffering a hard streak of misfortune. The mines closed. People lost work and were unable to pay Dr. Bond, and he kept no accounts.

"I'll give piano lessons, Frank, to supplement our income." Carrie, knowing what it was to compromise, found the principle a contribution rather than a demeaning factor.

"I won't hear of it." Frank, although proud of his talented wife, did not want Carrie to go outside the home as a means of beefing up the income. The secrecy of his reversals was not going to be aired on the streets.

"You know, Frank, you're granddaddy-old-fashioned in some ways."

Firming his chin, Frank nodded in agreement.

Carrie threw a quick glance at him, and then turned away. Evidently, she had struck a masculine nerve.

Still, it was not long before Carrie was giving lessons in *her* home. Over coffee one day, Frank had decided. "All right, my dear, we can't wait forever to see which way the cat jumps, but this piano lesson thing is only for a limited time...until the mines re-open."

Determined to salvage his investments, Bond, in company with the other stockholders in the Calidonia Company, became interested in some promising gold and silver claims out West; these, too, met with unsatisfactory proceeds.

Sitting in the kitchen, Frank found himself gripped with fear, his hands clasped and resting on the table. "This can't be happening to me. These investments were ironclad."

A PERFECT DAY

His disappointments he could not weave into words, could not inject some logic into his financial reversals. A successful captain of his own ship, Frank was nudged aside by a vessel of vicissitudes over which he had no control.

Carrie, her eyes soft, had an uncanny read on Frank. "I love you, Frank, with or without your mines."

Frank melted like warm wax; he wept, his shoulders shaking as if all the disappointments of his lifetime had found a crack in the damn. He cried for what he had lost and for what would never be.

***

Early in 1895, his financial reversals continuing, Frank allowed Carrie, at age thirty-three, to go to Chicago with a half dozen songs that she thought would be saleable. In her innocence, she went to the *Chicago Herald* to seek help and then referred to a citified woman staff writer known as Amber Holden. Cascades of mahogany hair swung freely around her head, and giant silver hoops jiggled from her ears.

"She had the most striking brown eyes, the shade of Amber," she later told Frank. "Her name was a *nom de plume* and fit her so well."

Carrie's first break was promoted by Amber at the Bohemian Club in Chicago.

"The club is a place where many performers come early in their careers, and they feel honored to appear there," Amber directed.

"Indeed *I* do," Carrie responded in typical self-effacement.

The work she submitted was not immediately accepted by one of the largest publishing firms in Chicago, but she was tasked to writing a children's song, so she returned to her hotel room and wrote *Is My Dolly Dead?* Two days later, it was accepted and she entered into an agreement for royalties. She introduced *The Captain of the Broom Stick Cavalry*, a children's song, written for her son, Fred. It was to become a favorite in her repertoire in later years. She quickly found, however, that the road to publication was a long and arduous one. The first lines of concern began appearing on Carrie's brow.

***

During this year of setbacks, Carrie and Fred worked on a garden of serenity in the backyard. Already there stood in the yard showy, sugar maples. "They're just far enough apart, Fred, so we can lay flagstones between them, and add half-moon benches at the foot."

"And remember, Mama, you said Dr. Bond wanted home-grown herbs in his garden?" Fred tugged at Carrie's skirt.

"Why, yes he did—a long time ago, before you were born. Thank you for reminding me." My God, Carrie thought, the child has a memory like an elephant's elephant. A small plot was cleared into which Carrie and Fred carefully sprinkled seeds for basil, rosemary, parsley, thyme, and dill.

Wild roses were dug from the nearby woods and planted along the paths where they thrived as if always there. Hedgerows of perennials grew along the picket fence that separated the Bond home on the east from the Konwinski home, a bedlam boiling over with children. Tiger lilies, day lilies, pristine daisies, purple phlox, and brilliant zinnias all fought to outshine each other. The blowing dandelion fluff was troublesome, but part of Mother Nature's regimen, thus accepted. By Autumn, the sun fell warmly on the array of gold, mauves, coral, and yellow, and sent up a maze of scent as the damp earth readied for winter.

Carrie spent her mid-afternoons in the garden reading or etching plates and serving-pieces with her unique, wild rose patterns, while Fred pulled his red wagon around the yard, picking up dead leaves or wind blows to place in the trash.

"See, Mama, how clean?" His wide blue eyes studied hers for the hint of a smile.

For Carrie, it was akin to looking into a mirror, into her own eyes.

"Fred," Carrie's voice choked as she wrapped her arms around the child. "Whatever is with you is so right."

In full sunshine, a Monarch butterfly flitted nearby landing delicately on a spike of pampas grass, sun enhanced, as if a giant stage light lighted it. It was like a flash of insight, an out-of-body experience. For a moment, she sat immobile encompassed by a violent gravity, her mind seeing Frank in the Gazebo at the Davis House in Janesville. He was smiling, bringing a precious memory.

The moment Frank had invited her to the concert lay as if in relief against the backlight of the vision. *"Do you know there are other butterflies that look just like the Monarch? There's a world of knowledge out there, Carrie, to share with someone."*

Carrie thought she understood the all-encompassing frieze. She and Frank were meant to be together. After all, a part of her had been in love with this man since she was fourteen. Thus, at the tempered age of thirty years old, her love was stamped with approval. She was still drawn to the quiet confidence and the inherent pride and integrity she sensed in him.

She watched Fred playing in the yard while Schneider lolled on his back, eyes closed.

How thankful she was for the tall, sturdy chimneys of the house that blessed them with winter heat, as opposed to memories of her childhood hours spent in the arctic attic room in Janesville. Now she lived in the perfection of Frank's love and caring. She found here excellence not consisting of doing extraordinary things, but in doing ordinary things extraordinarily well. The most trivial of actions brought delight: sweeping the sidewalk, nipping dead blossoms from the window boxes, reading to Fred in the garden, and catching in Frank's eyes the appreciation for her musical talents. She walked up the flagstone path toward the house carrying an ecstatic feeling of the sudden glimpse of insight.

The sun showing up the newness of the home, Carrie found clean lines. There were no paint chips. Deteriorating framework was non-existent. Nothing detracted from the scene of her happiness. From the Sixth Street entrance, the window box alyssum wafted silky fragrance in the late afternoon sun.

"Carrie?" said a familiar voice from down the hall, in a strong, worried tone. "Where is everybody?"

She spun quickly through the kitchen to view Frank in the hall. My, how handsome he was, wearing his dark brown suit, vest, white shirt, watch fob, and polished leather shoes. Her heart melted shyly. He was as robust as a wrestler was and as much a gentleman as Carrie had ever known. Perhaps his rearing in a fine home contributed, and, yes, education polished the boy into a man, but groomed character and instilled love for his fellow man created the final product. He relished what was decent, just, and polite.

Suddenly, she was flooded with an overwhelming sense of peace, love, and joy.

Fred and Schneider came tearing in the back door. "Daddy, I cleaned the yard," shouted Fred. Schneider, sensing the excitement, ran circles around Dr. Bond's legs nearly knocking him over.

"Good boy." Frank smiled while scratching the heads of both the boy and the dog.

"You're looking lovely, Carrie, in that heavenly blue color. Lovely. I'm the luckiest man in town...in the world!"

Carrie glowed with pleasure.

"Daddy, if Schneider got sick, could you give him mes... medicine?" Fred gazed up the long length of Frank.

"You bet, buddy. I'm not a vet but I could conjure up some magic for him."

"A vet?" In his question was wonderment.

"Yes. A veterinarian is an animal doctor."

"Wow. That's what I want to be when I grow up!"

"Then you shall. Until then, however," Frank said, lifting Fred into his arms, "We have a lot of living to do."

However, Dr. Bond was never to experience the living he hinted.

A PERFECT DAY

CHAPTER ELEVEN

Carrie's happy years in Iron River ended without warning on a day when Dr. Bond was brought home helpless after falling on an icy village street.

On December 2, 1895, Frank was leaving on a professional call. "It's harder every time I say goodbye to you, Carrie. That's the way it should be, I guess, and always will be. We know love is the greatest thing in the world." The words murmured into her hair.

There was such sweet pain at his words that Carrie could have hung forever in his arms and spent the rest of her life looking into his eyes. "Yes," she breathed quietly. "*Your* love is the greatest thing that ever happened to me. It makes life a celebration."

Unbeknownst to Carrie, the life of the active young physician was to be cut short. He was walking down a wooden sidewalk on Adam's Street, when a group of small children ran into the back of his legs, knocking him to the roadway where he was hit by a carriage, bursting his spleen. He was in agony for days. Carrie held fast to the hope that he would recover, but he had no illusions.

"My darling, this is death," he told her. "I don't want to die; oh, how I want to live." Every morning that wore into evening saw Carrie's heart break repeatedly in numb disbelief. In his last hours, he would often exclaim, "Come Carrie, my darling; let us go home. I'm tired and cold." His voice was thin.

"We *are* home, Frank, together," she responded to his

delirium. She pulled back the coverlet and crawled into bed with Frank seeking to warm him. His breathing was shallow, his pulse weak. Carrie laid two fingers on his throat to feel the surge of whatever life remained.

"He's gone, Mrs. Bond," whispered nurse, Nora Nash, encouraging Carrie to cease clutching at hope that had evaporated. Nash, her hair as dark as death sprinkled with a goodly share of silver, pleaded with her eyes.

"No, no, he's not gone. I can feel a pulse," Carrie protested. As she spoke, the rhythm of Frank's heartbeat dimmed to nothingness.

"Come, Mrs. Bond, we'll go downstairs and I'll prepare a refreshing cup of tea for both of us.

"No. I'll stay right here with Frank. Carrie was adamant, her voice squeezed.

If love had borne Carrie to heaven, then death must be its twin. Love would be the conveyance by which Frank would enter paradise. As Frank deteriorated daily, she prayed for his nightmare to be over, and he awaken from his bad dream surrounded by God's own angels.

In the same year Babe Ruth was born, and Swan Lake was performed for the first time, and X-rays were discovered, at age thirty-three, on Tuesday, December 5, 1895, at a few minutes before five a.m., Carrie's beloved husband, Frank Bond, died with Carrie at his side. His last breath was quiet, and, after such a valiant struggle, Carrie knew that the slight intake of air was his final, valued possession.

After days of home nursing and unflagging hope for Frank, Carrie collapsed as if she were a wax effigy left too long in the sun. Her strength had never wholly been regained after she was scalded with the wash water as a child. Her nerves never fully recovered.

A PERFECT DAY

Nora Nash kept watch at Carrie's bedside for days. She read from biblical passages.

> 'For he has passed from death unto life'...*John, v, 24.* '..The valley of the shadow of death...' *Psalms, XXIII, 4.* 'O death where is thy sting? Oh grave where is thy victory?' *1 Corinthians, XV, 55.* Nash read from Socrates. 'Be of good cheer about death, and know this of a truth, that no evil can happen to a good man, either in life or after death.'

However, Carrie found no comfort from any corner. She wished she could knock some sense into herself. Everywhere she looked, Frank was there, even in the cold wind that howled outside.

***

The obituary in the December 7, 1895 Iron County Reporter made sentimental observations about the Bond marriage.

> His married life was one of happiness and contentment, and his home ties were strong and enduring. In his every day life, he was all that husband and son should be, kind and affectionate to wife and his father. His every thought seemed to be for the happiness and comfort for those near and dear to him.

The death of Dr. Bond shocked the community. Two-thirds of the front page of the local newspaper was devoted to his life story and to eulogies. Long, and what today would be considered flowery, tributes were paid him by local organizations, among them the Iron River Tent, No. 336, Knights of the Maccabees; Camp No. 3273, Modern Woodman of America; The Iron River Lodge No. 162; Knights of Pythias; and the Village council.

The love story was to end the six happiest years of life for Carrie Jacobs-Bond. The Village of Iron River, Carrie called, "My idyllic life in the great pine forests." The young widow's situation was grave. Those middle years of the 1890's were a time of general business depression, and Dr. Bond had grown almost as poor as the people he served. There was little money left after bills had been paid. Was she, after finding exquisite happiness, to be destitute? Was she to be a poor widow with a small child again?

This time, there was no relief in sight, no Grandfather Davis, no Davis House, no parents, and no siblings. The status of being alone weaved an ever-thickening shroud around her existence. She was faced with the necessity of supporting herself and her son. She had been trained to nothing that offered much prospect of adequate remuneration. She was haunted by testy questions. Where could she go? What could she do? All were monumental challenges.

Before she could grasp what was happening, Carrie's life was radically changed. Although she had refined taste in clothes and demeanor, her table manners and social graces faultless, it qualified her for exactly nothing that would return sustenance.

In January 1896, widowed with fewer than three thousand dollars and no means of support, she was faced with making major decisions. She had no means of a livelihood in either Iron River or her hometown, Janesville, so she decided to move to Chicago. Her health was not good. She suffered from intermittent periods of deep depression and frayed nerves.

"My God in heaven," she repeated with a taut edge to her voice.

A PERFECT DAY

The situation seemed hopeless after Dr. Bond's demise, until Fred said, "Mother, I could do something for you. I could be as kind as doctor always was, and I always will be."

Sobbing, Carrie found solace in the small child, hugging him to herself, as if afraid he, too, would be taken from her.

She was being tested. She would not be labeled *the poor widow*. She felt Frank's energy staying with her. Thus, she stood tall and met her unknown future with a determined set to her jaw. With hat adjusted and gloves in hand, Carrie took one last look around her handsome home, and out the windows at her garden in fallow. Everything was in its place. Schneider had been cozily housed with the Konwinski's big family next door. Hilda Benson had scrubbed everything white, and not a thing of Frank's was left in view. The closed, roll-top desk looked like a decoration for a model home, no papers awry, no slippers under the chairs, no coffee cups left to mourn the loss. All was tidied away as if it were the end of Carrie's life, too. As a last gesture, a basket of dried, wild rose petals and pods she moved from the pantry to set on top of Frank's lonely desk in lieu of the coffee cup.

She straightened when Fred, forgotten in the absorption of her last minutes in heaven, tugged at her skirt. He silently pointed to the pot-pourri. "I'll help you make some more, Mama." He looked uncertain, waiting for support.

"Goodness. Yes, of course you shall," she conceded with affectionate reassurance.

"And so from his ninth year, Fred and I walked hand in hand," Carrie said of her life.

For the next forty years, she was to use her talents to make a new life and become nationally known, earning more money selling her music than any other woman in the United States, a position that she held unchallenged for the full forty years.

CHAPTER TWELVE

Carrie arrived in Chicago to find work. It was heartbreakingly hard.

At this time, she was thirty-four. She was not young and she was not lovely. Sorrow was written all over her face, her face that had always been plain. She had to earn a place with the hardest of efforts. She had nothing of particular interest to offer, except her work, the acknowledgement sinking to the bone.

"If I was just a trifle more attractive, maybe I would gain attention sooner," she confided in Fred.

Nine-year-old Fred looked troubled. He paused in the midst of home selection, and held his small hand to his chest. "Mama, you're as pretty as a million dollars, and so was Doctor Frank and so was Schneider. You'll feel better when we get our new home," he said, suddenly cheerful.

The bolstering was straight from heaven, as if Frank had put the words in the child's mouth.

"You're dessert for a skinny dinner, Fred."

The child beamed with confirmation.

Carrie and Fred took a house near the College of Physicians and Surgeons and rented out rooms to help support themselves, even if it was a pitiful income.

After a time, Carrie became disillusioned. "Some of my borders are snobs," she said under her breath.

"Snobs?" Fred puzzled.

"Oh dear, Fred, snobs are high-hats, snooty people… pretentious in all they do."

"Most are nice, though, Mama." It was more of a question than a statement.

"Yes, Fred. Most people are inclined to kindness, but some forget their own friends to grovel after those of higher degree." She hugged her arms in agitation.

"That's mean, Mama."

Carrie nodded, her assent silent, knowing the separation of social cast was anything but unifying or kindly.

Spending the better part of two years at the rental home, Fred was now eleven and took up many of the responsibilities of the household, while Carrie found herself riding the Cottage Grove Avenue streetcar for transportation attempting to get her songs published. She hoped her gift for verse and melody was not, after all, the only thing that held even slight promise of relieving herself and her son from their grinding poverty.

The songs that she had composed in happier times, she now tried to exchange for bread. Publishers were indifferent. One of them, more generous or more reckless than the rest, offered her $35 for 11 songs. She quickly learned that publishing and being in demand were worlds apart. She promoted her work by going to stores and persuading them to listen to her play and sing until her heart hammered in her head with the steady trial and rejection.

Her savings steadily dwindling, she next offered to sew in exchange for some free advertising in music magazines. The orders scarcely amounted to more than six or eight dollars a month. These she delivered herself. She wrote her own words, her own music and painted the covers. On title pages, she painted a wreath of wild roses and put a line underneath in the center: *Songs As Unpretentious As The Wild Rose.*

"Only one way there is to know people, and that is to be poor," she told Fred upon arriving home cold and weary late one afternoon. "Nobody is nice to you when you're poor unless they like you," she remarked. She crossed the small kitchen of their quarters to wash her hands as she always did after using public transportation. Carrie turned as she was toweling her fingers to see Fred regarding her with numb awakening.

"Poor? We are poor, Mama?" Fred frowned in puzzlement.

A cold chill crawled along Carrie's skin in a moment of epiphany. The child had known no sacrifices so far. He was well clothed, warm, and well fed, (while Carrie practiced fasting.) What did he know of her shrinking three thousand dollars? She had not understood how much she insulated him. While poverty was no disgrace, it was inconvenient and, unless she could look it in the face, she would deprive herself and Fred of the accomplishments for which they were fitted. She would not want Fred stifled by the hopelessness resultant of being poor.

"Look, Fred. Do you see any of the grandeur we had while living with Dr. Frank?" Her hands were thrust into the pockets of her recently donned bib apron.

"No, Mama." A faint disillusion underlay his expression.

"People with independent dollars don't bring borders into their home, but we'll manage, son. Just you see. Having little doesn't mean we're poor in spirit." A bright smile lit her face as she embraced the child and danced him around and around, singing, **Captain of the Broomstick Brigade.**

Therefore, it followed, that due to Carrie's persistence, all kinds of interesting people came to her home for her various offerings of hand-painted plates, greeting cards, sewing, or music. Some were rich and some were poor.

In later years, Carrie reflected. "I don't remember of ever being envious of any of them for a robe or luxurious woolen. What's more, my own fur coat was worn out and moth eaten. I had used the last of it for collar and cuffs on a coat I had made out of a blanket."

At the turn of the century, Carrie found that the boarding house venture was unprofitable. She and Fred moved into a smaller apartment of five rooms, taking the furniture they had used in the rooming house, and storing the extra items in the basement. When winter came, the wind from Lake Michigan blew its icy blast seemingly right through the rental. For warmth, Carrie closed off the biggest front rooms, and kept a tiny fire—all they could afford—burning in the one room that served as both living room and studio.

The rent in the smaller house was less expensive. To stay alive, she sold some of her hand-painted china bearing her trademark, the wild rose. She continued making greeting cards and worked diligently on the colored design for the title covers of her music. The logo was to be used on many of her songs and consisted of a wreath, with the inscription *Words and Music by Carrie Jacobs-Bond.*

The money, nonetheless, was still going out faster than it was coming in, and saving themselves was the first law of survival. She studied herself daily to keep her mood less bitter than the coffee. The suspense of not knowing which would expire first, she or her minutia savings, was a miserable thing. It was the life of a frightened rabbit.

"I'm going to lodge a family, Fred. They're homeless." She hoped that the idea did not scare him.

"Well," said Fred, his voice growing in confidence all at once and sounding as if he *were* Dr. Frank, himself, "Let's say they can be of assistance to us, while we can offer them shelter, and warmth, and food. That's a deal, isn't it?"

"It's more than a deal, Fred, more than. In fact, we're lucky people." Carrie knew she was lucky to have Fred, who stoked her personal furnace daily with his enthusiasms. The more adversities they encountered, the greater his enthusiasm flourished as if kindled in the hour of need and ever awakened him to deeds of courage. She closed her eyes and sighed, knowing that without Fred she would have unquestionably buckled long ago. The fabric of her hope was frayed to a thin thread.

Luck prevailed, for at that time Carrie had a severe attack of inflammatory rheumatism. For four months, the needy family she brought in cared for her. Poverty continued to change Carrie's outlook. How grateful she was to those she thought she was befriending.

When the father got a job, the family moved out. The house seemed empty without them, so Carrie and Fred visited at the family's new home and found that the father was wearing one of Frank's old suits and on the floor were two rugs that Carrie had stored in the back room.

Carrie was stunned. "That suit and the rugs were made for use and not for storage, Fred," she said on the streetcar on the way home. "I feel badly that I didn't offer them to the people."

A bright glance stared up at her. "Was that really Dr. Frank's suit?"

"It was, and it was quite a surprise to me."

Later when she looked in the trunk, she found the moths had eaten practically all of her wonderfully stored items of clothing. "No one has a right to horde things, Fred, we need to remember that," she said with terrible softness.

"You bet we do," he said brightly, sounding again like Frank. "It's a lesson in sharing, Mama." His blue eyes grew intense with conviction. Not ready to ascribe to the cruel vagaries of fate, surely Fred could have been a slayer of dragons at that moment.

A PERFECT DAY

CHAPTER THIRTEEN

In less than a year, the new quarters were to prove too expensive. As autumn leaves rustled in the street, Carrie located new accommodations for fifteen dollars a month, (three rooms), above a restaurant at 42 East 31st Street and was to spend four years there.

"Here it was that I went to the University of Great Experience," she said. "Here it was that the inspiration for The Bond Shop was born. Here it was that my son and I first became business partners. Here it was that I realized that if I lost my home, Fred and I would be adrift."

She recognized that if she had only one room to live in and could afford it, life was more livable. "The thought that if you do not pay the rent, someone can put you out on the street is a terrible feeling," she told Fred with frightening helplessness.

Circumstances were pushing Carrie closer to the poor house. The sufficiency of her efforts, although holding immense merit, only served to remind her everyday of her insufficiency. The daunting last words of Frank returned to haunt her reveries—*Come Carrie, let us go home, my darling.* Maybe that would be the route she would choose in the end...death. Nevertheless, what kind of morally bankrupt dunce would she be to leave Fred to shift for himself? Oh, how difficult it was to pull herself up by the bootstraps when in the darkness of despair, but she would live until tomorrow, and another tomorrow, until all the tomorrows have passed away into infinity, and she shall have survived them all. Just when she thought she had reached the midnight hour of bleak hopelessness, Fred came to her rescue.

"I'll leave school, Mama. I'm thirteen now and out of eighth grade. "I'll work during the day and attend school at night!" His enthusiastic glance traveled over Carrie's face.

Carrie would not dream of dampening Fred's enthusiasm, but her heart broke at the overwhelming reality that Fred's childhood dreams would disintegrate into a soft poof of dust, even if he did not think so. What would his judgment of her be in later life? Why could his mother not have provided better? Why could she not have allowed him time and money for the Cubs games, basketball on the neighborhood courts, and picnics along the shores of Lake Michigan? Nevertheless, what was, was, and her small bankroll was long past spent. How long were they going to stand back shivering in the cold blast of being victimized by circumstances? She and Fred would jump in, and scramble through this new odyssey as well as they could.

Filtering her thoughts brought her back to Fred's inquiry. "Of course you may look for work, as long as you can manage both night school and a job. Let's play it by ear," she said with a grin at the play on words and no song in her heart. Memory stirred of that day long ago in the gazebo of the Davis House, and Frank's stern sentiment: *All the success you'll have in life is the talent you were born with. After that, it's up to you to capitalize on it.* Well, she and Fred knew about luck and about hard work and ambition. Luck had evaded her since Frank's premature death, leaving only hard work and aching ambition. She reminded herself of a gerbil on an incessant wheel, the furry ball with ambition enough for a creature of even greater size; although the critter climbs, he gets nowhere.

The balances stood poised for Fred's attempt to contribute to their welfare. Carrie never doubted his enterprising capacity, or his audacious vigor in executing his plan. Fred would tackle yet another challenge. He did make a success of both school and a job, and gave every dollar he earned to Carrie, dispelling any concerns she may have entertained.

He promptly found a place with the U.S. Postal Service where he earned twenty-five dollars a month. The job consisted of long, hard hours for a little fellow, but he stuck to it courageously, looking forward to the day each month when he could move with exaggerated tiptoeing into Carrie's room. Later, she would find under her pillow a bag of candy—her favorite, gumdrops—purchased with a dime of the precious money; and under these, wrapped carefully, was the remaining twenty-four dollars and ninety cents. Carrie smiled, half in disbelief and half in wonderment. Maybe they had won round one.

The environment of Fred's success and gumdrops, and in which she had the three rooms was called the Dunlap & Smith Co. The staircase to the upper apartment was accessed from the street and consisted of a flight of wooden stairs leading steeply up between boarded walls. There were no banisters and the treads were bare.

Mr. George W. Cobb, a short, dapper man with a long testosterone beard was the person on the board of management with whom Carrie had contact. Over a cup of coffee, Cobb consoled her. "Even though you're in arrears for six months, don't worry about it, because you're a worker."

Carrie smiled tremulously. "Thank you,"

She warmed with real satisfaction afforded by the positive appraisal. The statement expressed aloud, did indeed agree with the whispers of her own conscience, but there were few in her life that showed her the encouragement of recognizing her endeavors, thus reassuring her that her efforts were not in vain. Any kind word, a friendly gesture was absorbed into her psyche as if pulled in through her every pore. She was encompassed by a vast sense of relief.

During that time of pressure from poverty, she sold every piece of china one at a time, but after a while, it was all gone. She thought she would even have to sell the irreplaceable piano Dr. Bond had given her as a wedding present. The struggle between a proud mind and an empty purse left an indescribable hollowness in Carrie's heart.

Soon, she would have to admit defeat, and life as she and Fred knew it would end. Yet, she determined herself to maintain. They were healthy and happy, though hardscrabble poor. Being rich was not a synonym for health and happiness. She would not allow the devil to find her spirit idle and morose, leading her into the dredges of depression and ruin.

***

One freezing, stormy night when it seemed almost too cold for any human being to be out, the bell rang. Carrie went to the door, and there, at the bottom of the staircase stood a shivering colored man. He wore threadbare trousers and a ragged coat.

"Can I come in and just get warm," he pleaded. "I'm nearly frozen."

She looked at him and believed, believed that the city was rife with the poor and the indigent. "Take care on those steps and come right up here," she said without preliminaries.

She rapped on the floor. That was her signal to her kindly downstairs neighbor, Miss McGraw, (a big-bosomed, motherly woman, belying the title, *Miss*), that someone was coming down for a cup of coffee. Carrie took her guest through her small back room and sent him downstairs through the back door to Miss McGraw's back door. She and Carrie understood each other perfectly, and the color of humanity did not make much difference to them. Ignoring the small needs in the lives of others sent Carrie spiraling downwards. She was altogether too aware of *her* overt small needs that masked a multitude of great needs.

"You come back, er, ah,"

"Joe. Name's Joe—Joe Bidwell."

"You come back up here when you finish your coffee, Joe."

He did. There was something about his speech and mannerisms, something about the lightning smile that suggested intelligence, what Iron River people called moxie, with a touch of down-on-his-luck.

"You can sleep in the back bedroom," she advised, and bade him goodnight.

After being there for five days, he declared, "I've been given a new lease on life, thank you so much. Your hearty beef stew, and the apple pie renewed me. It's been far too decent of you." Smiling with genuine gratitude, he then slipped off into the cold night and went away.

Carrie admired Joe's sense of manly independence as much as she admired his manly dependence while under roof. He never once surrendered his unity with dignity and virtue. Beneath his poverty, there was a goodly amount of acid and steel.

Five years elapsed. It was the day before Christmas, the weather snappy and crisp, when Carrie's doorbell rang. Answering it, she found there stood at the bottom of the stairs a colored man all dressed up looking radiantly happy, and successful. Heat shimmers rushed outside from the hall and encircled the man like Carrie's wreaths.

"Why Missy," he shouted. "Don't you know me? I'm the man who slept in your back room. You sure were kind to me, and I haven't forgotten. I've been flourishing since I left you... got a nice job at a dry cleaners. I just came this morning to see if we could have a cup of coffee together. I brought doughnuts," he gestured the box uneasily, and quietly waited for permission to come up.

Carrie drew her hand to her heart, her eyes widening in astonishment. "Joe! You just march right up here. "My, he looked so elegant, clear-eyed, and silently strong.

Looking to the sofa where Fred lay, Joe inquired, "What's the matter with the youngun?" With warmth, his eyes swept the room as he spoke.

"He's been down sick." Carrie knew the child was sicker than sick; he probably was on the verge of pneumonia from being out in adverse weather, running deliveries for the post office. In addition, Fred was depressed. Carrie recognized the signs from her own inclinations to the malady. Her father had gone through these deep pits of hell, and Carrie had fought bouts with all the strength she could muster. Depression may sink people down and out, but so do funerals. The times, she realized were not as bad as they seemed. They could not be. She stared up at Bidwell in helpless frustration.

"He needs the hospital," the suddenly take-charge man said.

Scooping the fragile Fred in his arms, blankets and all, he carefully took every worn step down to the street and hailed a cab. There seemed to be no civil way to stop him. Carrie's soul pulsed with gratitude for this unusual man who had fallen into her life. Fred, at age fourteen, was in the Cook County Hospital for almost three months.

Carrie, herself, was in the hospital several times during these early years on her own. She painted china until her trembling hands became too cold; then she would stop, and in her spare time, work at the copying of music manuscripts. Desolation fought to hang like a cloud over her bent body, but she would not allow despair to overcome her as long as there was another human being for whom she was entrusted to care. A deep wrinkle stamped her brow. What if Fred faded from her life leaving her alone on earth? No, no, that is not to happen. Death had touched her too many times: her pets, her father, her mother, her Grandfather Davis, and her saintly Dr. Bond. God would not allow her another loss. Fred was dearer to her than she was to herself. She wanted to cradle his face between her palms, his dear, earnest face.

Heavenly warmth as of electricity suddenly infused her. Her desolation began to melt in its light. Surely, she was in the care of an angel. (. . . *to light, to guard, to rule, and guide…*), she remembered from her childhood prayers.)

A PERFECT DAY

CHAPTER FOURTEEN

Her courage sustaining her every effort, Carrie trudged through the bleak, gray winter. Although poor, her humanities to humanity never halted.

On another day when the wind was snarling snow off Lake Michigan as if Old Man Winter were an all-consuming monster, an incessant ringing of the doorbell brought Carrie to the door. She found a man, young in years, who asked to be allowed to sweep the snow from the doorway and bottom steps—the last resort of the work-seeker!

"I have no money to pay you, but you might come in and get warm."

He hovered over Carrie's small fire, while she went on copying manuscripts.

Finally, he said, "Madam, I could copy that for you."

"What?" Carrie raised her eyes in askance.

"Yes," he continued, for he saw Carrie's involuntary astonishment. "I used to sing in the glee club at college. I can copy music." Taking the manuscript from her hand, he set to work. The poor derelict remained with her, so she took some of the stored furniture and fixed a place for him.

One evening he came to Carrie in genuine distress. A poor family had been dispossessed—turned out into the snow. "Mrs. Bond," he said, "they're worse off than I am, because there's a woman, and children, too. So, if you'll allow me, I'll give them my place." Carrie recognized the altruism. In the poor wreck that he was, he found it in his heart to help them. With Carrie's permission, he brought them to occupy the place where he had found a haven.

It was just a day or so after that Carrie had an attack of rheumatism again that confined her to bed for three months, and the woman nursed her faithfully during those weary days. "Desolation you say? It is non-existent." Carrie confided in the woman. "Some heart from out of nowhere responds to the hearts of others."

***

Carrie never cast off her love for creatures. In those years, she had a gentle dove that came regularly to her window seeking crumbs. Consequently, memories of the days at the convent were freshened, and the denial of the pigeon that came to her window. Now, however, she could feed the hapless bird for she ruled the roost.

"Those were real days of poverty when I couldn't go to the market as often as I wanted, and even then, there were no frivolous purchases. Bare necessities were the order of the day. Nevertheless, I took into my small home a lonesome soul, who said she wanted to learn to sing. How anyone with such a drop of cruelty as was hidden in her heart could ever become a singer, I do not know. I'm sure she never became a singer."

One day Carrie came home shivering and discouraged. Opening the door, this woman greeted her with, "Mrs. Bond, I have a surprise for you!" She placed before Carrie a 'pigeon pie.' She had killed Carrie's little dove! The smell of the warm pie and the woman's coldness created nausea such as Carrie had never witnessed. She had bright flashes in retrospect of the runaway chipmunk in the barn at Janesville, her father hanging from the rafters, Schneider Two unaccountably disappearing, and her pet chicken heartlessly slaughtered.

"Do you think that woman lost her home with me? Alas, she had never learned to love the simple things." Carrie was not made wholly of the lamb; a tooth of the lion laid buried deep within her soul when it came to retaliation for creature cruelty.

***

"My hopes and my dreams made me different from other unfortunate people whom I met daily, folks having the same struggle with circumstances that I was having. I was always expecting something to turn up—and invariably it did. It is that faith that keeps one buoyant.

"I recall one occasion when there came an appeal for five dollars, and I answered it—for it was urgent—with the last five dollars I had. Even my usually hopeful son looked thoughtful; it did not appear we could earn the next five dollars in time. Nonetheless, my faith was unshaken. In the next mail came a letter from which a five-dollar bill fluttered down!

"It was from a church for whose entertainment I had sung some weeks previously, with the understanding that we should share in the proceeds. They had paid me, but a later accounting had convinced them that I had not received my full share, and this was the extra five dollars to pay for it. Do you wonder that I was full of hope?"

Full of hope was what she was through the long years of denial. Yet, to Carrie, it seemed she would never rise above her poverty. She supposed that she would not so much estimate her poverty as a misfortune, were it not for the world treating it so. She must consider her dearth as advantage, for only then would she know the delight of seeing again fresh clusters of daisies, snapdragons, and zinnias in her garden. Only then could she aspire to know again the comfort of adequate food and clothing, and, in time, the splendor of a table set with china and crystal such as she had had with Dr. Bond. The memories were disconcerting.

***

In these poor days, if she invited someone for dinner, she would say, "Excuse me. I'll go get dinner." Then she would step on the piano stool and pull up a one-burner gas stove by its left leg to which she had tied a strong string. The piano had to be set cross-wise to give the stove a chance for connection, because the only connection for gas was in the baseboard behind the piano.

Before the surprised visitor could guess what was happening, Carrie would go to the lower part of the washbasin where she stored the cooking oven and pans. From under the laundry, she would pull a folding card table and begin preparing the food.

The coffee was made first and kept hot on top the oven while the food was cooking. It was uncannily easy to cook three things at once, providing she had them, but the coffee was always a question until she discovered it was all right to keep it hot on top and then warm it as soon as the oven was taken off the burner.

"Everyone enjoyed those meals, the impoverished, the well to do, and the entirety of humanity that passed through my life at that time. Sometimes all I had was a ring of bologna and a bowl of German potato salad that I had set myself, or well-watered-down chicken and dumplings."

Were the accouterments of style necessary? She thought not. She had friends. Her cramped apartment was warm. She could run a deep, hot bath, pull on slippers and robe, and feel richly blessed. Weather permitting; she could stand on the porch of her back-landing fire escape. The nights became warm again smelling of humidity, earth, and concrete. She could lift her eyes to a sky full of stars and wispy clumps of clouds in a lazy state of comatose.

"Surely I *am* blessed," she said in a stilled voice.

CHAPTER FIFTEEN

The June Chicago sky was lucent, and a soft lake breeze billowed out the kitchen curtains; the birds were twittering and Carrie was humming. But wait. Was that Victor Sincere she heard in the outer hall? She bustled to peek, a dishtowel draped over her shoulder.

"So, you're the dream maker," Carrie said, stepping into the hall. She addressed the man by the name of Victor Sincere, a lawyer, whose hobby was music, and who visited a friend who lived across the hall from Carrie. A giant of a man, standing well over six feet tall, he had heavily lidded, brown eyes conveying deep sorrow to Carrie.

Sincere straightened his shoulders and nodded, silently analyzing the woman who came effervescing into the hall out of nowhere.

"You'll need a cup of hot tea, then, surely, before you hear my music, if you will?"

Sincere, amused, stared at her, his eyes widening, increasing his wrinkle count. "I can do that."

Carrie played some of her favorite pieces for him, little dewdrops of celestial song.

"Are you a composer, too?" Sincere asked, setting his teacup down, his eyebrows askance.

"Yes, these songs are all my own work." Carrie hoped she did not come off sounding offended. She must not let her setbacks leak through her worldly facade, revealing bitterness or dejection. These characteristics were not entertained in her house.

Meeting Sincere was the beginning of one of the most valuable friendships of Carrie's life.

"I can arrange for you to play recitals in the homes of friends for ten dollars an evening," he said blithely, impressed with Carrie's unique presentations.

"It's a beginning for me," she breathed, genuinely astounded. "Thank you."

"Don't mention it. The pleasure is about to be all mine, I'm sure." His words were couched in polite terms, yet with warmth seeping through.

Arriving home late from her first home recital, Carrie beheld the night sky from below stretching tree branches bearing new finery, the stars pulsing and the moon flirting with scuttling Great Lakes clouds. Could a rich man observe the heavens with any more joy? She thought not, but the ten dollars in her pocket was riches to her. Besides, true to her nature, she enjoyed her moments alone, if only for a few minutes or hours on her way to and from recitals. She was reminded of her yearning hours of childhood, in which she could get in touch with her God, reminded of the hours spent alone in the dilapidated shack on the Smith property in Milwaukee.

Carrie found the evening concerts, although a Godsend, were a snail's pace manner of advertising. "I must meet public singers and performers," she confided in Fred.

"You will, Mama." His gaze softened. "You play the piano so well." Fred's adulation so profound kept Carrie from sinking. His words, so simple and direct, moved her, cutting to the heart of her life.

***

A PERFECT DAY

Her steady plodding served her properly when, on January 26, 1902, she was invited to give a recital ***Afternoon of Song*** at the Hearst Chicago American with Jan Kubelik, an Ichabod Crane-looking violin virtuoso.

This appearance beefing up her résumé, Carrie was asked to perform in one of the first, Vaudeville shows in Chicago. A firm by the name of Cole and Middleton ran the show. Carrie had never been on stage in her life. She was going to adapt, in her funny way, some of her songs to a player piano. The up-scale thought of an on-stage performance was a heady experience. A surge of powerful confidence possessed her body and mind, positive, soothing, and sweet. Her angel infused her, surely.

"I'll have to wear this black, silk dress that I made myself," she mused aloud. "To make it quite dressed up, I'll put in a white lace front and carry a bouquet of white lilies."

Fred smiled in restrained amusement. His mama was going uptown. Maybe this heralded a well-deserved new direction in her life.

For seven years, she had dressed in mourning, and the white vest seemed to her to be almost too gay. On the other hand, she rationalized that she must dress it up somewhat, and she did, hoping the addition of the white vest would not be too showy.

When she went to the theatre to perform, one of the back-stage assistants approached her. "Are you going to go on stage like that?" The glint in the assistant's eyes spoke fathoms of rejection, her appraising stance a confirmation of what she thought.

"Yesss," Carrie said half under her breath, her heartbeat picking up.

"Well, I'll fix you up a mite," the woman said, struggling to control her impatience.

When Carrie looked in the mirror, she did not know herself, with rouge, white paint, eyelashes, and eyebrows.

"All this red on my face," she gasped. "Won't I look terrible? And these awful red lips will never do." She felt her spirits sinking.

"It will scarcely be noticeable on stage," the woman replied reassuringly. "That's the way you have to go."

Carrie sang on stage and pumped the piano for her own accompaniment. She had to match her words to the rhythm of the ghost-like keys, a condition far removed from *her* performances in which she played her own tunes with a strong and steady beat coinciding with her musical story telling. Watching the crazy keys move on their own volition, set her heart to beating so, she thought it was going to jump right out of her chest. Looking down at the live audience was as if observing from a height Lake Michigan rolling and bursting on the beach. The illumination of the dazzling footlights burned her eyes and cloyed at her mind so as she had to concentrate to not come under their spell.

The next thing she knew, heavy applause met her ears, but she flew from the stage and then ran down Michigan Avenue with pink tears dripping on her white vest, flying back to her friend and refuge: Madame Marione's Rooms. After her, as fast as his legs could go, came Fred. Throwing his arms around her, tears running down his cheeks, he told her, "Mother, it was just wonderful!"

Madame Marione, a large, big-shouldered woman with masses of curly brown hair that knew no boundaries, rented rooms with board, but only to friends and relatives, and to those who needed partial assistance in living. Carrie had taken refuge at Marione's during the awful winter that Fred was in the hospital for three months, her own health flawed and fragile.

A PERFECT DAY

In a few minutes, all Carrie's friends came in, including Mr. Middleton, himself, a promoter highly esteemed, with a keen eye and ear for new acts, new entertainers, and new promise. God bless him, she thought, hanging onto whatever dignity she could assemble.

"It was splendid," he said, his bulgy black eyes rolling with masculine expectation from this new gold mine he'd found. "You'd never know it was your first time. Now you come back tonight," he added.

The makeup, the pretensive player piano, the charade of everything she was not had her frazzled in the attempt to breathe life back into what she was. To undertake that for which she was not made was extremely vexing to Carrie.

"I vow that I'll never appear on stage again. It's just not right for me." She did not go back that night. She did get, nevertheless, a check for twenty-five dollars for her appearance at that matinee.

"The right and the wrong of something," advised Madame Marione, "is in the mind of the person making the judgment."

The simplicity of the statement was earthy and supportive. Carrie nodded in appreciation.

***

It tugged at Carrie's soul that she had to leave Fred evening after evening to give recitals, and he worked hard all day himself, studying after he came home.

"I never found him in bed upon my return. He would always have a dainty sandwich of bread and butter ready and hot coffee. He learned to cook so he could help me, and he often laughingly said, "By being a chef, I have more than once been released from a hard job by promising to stay in camp and make baking powder biscuits for the crowd."

Fred's humor was a bulwark for the daily outrages visited upon the poor. He tried to learn to iron. He tried doing his own laundry and hanging it over the furniture, but the next morning he found dampness had taken the varnish off the chairs costing him $25.00 for refinishing.

"He then gave up the laundry business," Carrie said with eyes dancing at the pre-destined futility in the undertaking.

During her regimen of evening recitals, she caught the attention of the Pullman and Wrigley families of Chicago. They thought she was *the cat's pajamas*. It was the turn of the century, time of hearts and flowers and noble sentiment.

She caught on.

She gave concerts.

With the income hike, and at the age of forty-one, Carrie afforded to move to 5535 Drexel Avenue. There the idea of The Bond Shop came into full bloom, and she and Fred eventually became partners. They soon outgrew the dining room table at Drexel for their publication work. They were making about $150 a month so afforded a sign painted **The Bond Shop**. The entire apartment of five rooms was given over to The Bond Shop, so they moved upstairs in the same building to seven rooms where the rent was twenty dollars a month, and in a closet, Carrie had twelve shelves put in. The closet was the width of a sheet of music. That was her first stockroom—the future Bond Shop. Carrie found the move stimulating and vastly incredulous, given her years of cold indifferences.

The most amazing thing about the move was the discovery that she enjoyed the stretch between poverty and privilege: the ceaseless struggles, the constant improvisations, the minutia successes, and the shortfalls. All were daunting challenges. The affluence of her grandparent's farm in Janesville, The Davis House, and her home in Iron River were not the same as the gains painstakingly achieved on her own. She had been the lady of the house in Iron River, but not the mistress of the house. Neither did she know the satisfaction that accompanied being in charge. Hilda Benson had made all the decisions, leaving Carrie to live a refined life.

For the total of her lifetime, nothing was ever physically Carrie's. A child's accouterments of trinkets and books, butterflies and pressed flowers were among the treasures in her bedroom. All had quietly disappeared when she was away from home: Schneider, the chickens, the chipmunks, and the ailing birds she had, were have-nots. Carrie found that the frou frou of today did not ensure funds for tomorrow.

All the benchmarks of her life had dissipated into memories. She had come to Chicago with Fred and almost nothing else, the most depleted of newcomers. Thus, she developed a strong sense of ownership, the two-way street of possessions, and the intense desire to hang onto them. Personal property became dear because it was fortification for her and Fred against misery and physical distress. She would seek no false glories or grandeurs, but neither would she allow herself to become vulnerable again.

For a year, progress intensified until at last spring rolled around. Scrawny arms of hardwoods not yet in possession of their May array, sought the last light of day when Carrie vowed aloud to the sun draining in the west, "Never again will I fall into the pit of poverty." She rubbed two quarters together idly in her hand, ingesting the sound of their meshing.

A PERFECT DAY

CHAPTER SIXTEEN

Duly impressed with Carrie's talent, Victor Sincere lit a fire under her to contact Jessie Bartlett Davis, the prima donna of the old Boston Opera Company. He spoke warmly of her. "She is a lovely and gentle lady, who made *Oh Promise Me*, famous all over the world."

Carrie did go to Jessie Davis, and indeed found her to be lovely with black-as-night hair, intelligent turquoise eyes, and a vision in gunmetal gray silk. She radiated the vitality and exuberance of a spring morning. However, Carrie was ill, sucked down into one of her fits of depression. She looked homemade, knew it, but was helpless in her morass to rise above it. Everything she had on, she had made herself, out of necessity and innovation: her hat, her coat, and her dress. She had never been trained in the art of dressmaking or millinery with the exception of the time she tried to work at a millinery shop, and that, she remembered, was a waste of time. Her skin burned with the thoughts of the hopelessness of being caught in that niche. At times such as these, she found it difficult to cling to the flying hours of her life and remember that sunshine follows rain.

Jessie gave no hint that she noticed Carrie's clothing, but, instead, listened closely while Carrie played her book of *Seven Little Songs*. There was ecstasy and powerful emotion in the music as well as in Carrie's voice. Whatever was required to further this woman in street clothes, it would be worth it. Everyone should have the pleasure of sharing these songs.

"You must have that book published at once," Davis advised, her head nodding repeatedly with affirmative excitement.

"I have only half the money needed for that," Carrie confessed, thinking the suggestion a macabre jest.

"Don't worry about the money. I'll underwrite the publishing of your *Book of Seven Songs*."

If there had been a gale-force wind blowing, Carrie would have been oblivious. Her mind's chemistry flowed volatile between anxiety and immeasurable exuberance. In her depressed state, it was as if an old, worn-out engine had been kick-started. Yet on the piano bench, Carrie stirred half way around, her lips parted to drink in the reality of the suggestion, and the promise in Jesse Davis's voice. After an acre of performance, was Jesse finding a forty of potential in her little songs? She gripped the edges of the piano stool so tightly that her knuckles turned white with the effort.

Mrs. Davis went to her desk and drafted a check for two hundred fifty dollars, a fortune; an impossible fortune it was. The formidable hill Carrie had been climbing gave forth with an aura of light around it, drawing her out of herself, circling her with relief born of what must be, at the least, a miracle. Her angel! The dark shadows that lived in the recesses of her soul lifted and took flight as gently as gulls riding the thermals. She took a deep breath to calm herself.

Two songs made the book flyaway popular: *I Love You Truly* and *Just a Wearyin' For You*. *The Little Book of Seven Songs* was launched using Nelson's Printing Office. Nelson, a raw-boned Norwegian, was all business. "I'll print it," Mr. Nelson said, "but your *Little Book* will never sell, especially from an unknown composer." Yet, she had it published, and it sold for one dollar. It contained: *Parting, Just a Wearyin' For You, I Love You Truly, De Las Long Res', Shadows, Still Unexpressed, and Des Hold My Han'*. The two flyaway songs were eventually taken out of that book and sold as singles. This time, Carrie published them.

She was conscious of the groundswell for her music, a cohesive communication that reverberated throughout busy city gathering places. She stood taller than the woman she used to see in the mirror. A memory from the past: *"You'll only be as lucky as the breaks you make for yourself,"* swept around her like an all-embracing cloak.

The cold turf of defeat was getting warmer. The **Little Book of Seven Songs** was to be the seed of all her future business. Of such small successes, happiness was made. Carrie desperately longed for Frank's presence, and his constant encouragements. How happy he would be for her. If it was true, that mighty grief humanizes the soul, Carrie determined that her soul was as humanized as a hank of hair and a piece of bone.

Optimistic, Carrie wrote and published her **Old Man** series of poems, a succession of anecdotes about a down-home country dweller. The string of anecdotes captured the imagination of city society, and leaped to syndication in a short time.

***

MY OLD MAN'S HEAVEN
I've tried to live an honest life,
Have helped a friend or two.
An' never shirked my duties,
If the jobs were small or few.
An' I guess I've been a-walkin'
In the narrow path all right,
'Cause I've seen a heap more daytime
Than I ever seen o'night.
Now, some folks call the narrow path
A hard one here on earth,

But me an' Mary allus found
The path was filled with mirth.
Fer ain't we had the children
A cheerin' all the time?
An' ain't they kept us hustlin'
A-keepin' them in line?
An' why should I be sighin'
Fer a different kind o' life,
When I've got my thirteen children
An' my Mary Ann fer wife?
I guess, by jingo, if I do
The very best I can,
I'll find some heaven here on earth
Along with Mary Ann.
If Mary Ann was singing
On th' everlastin' shore,
S'pose I'd give up lookin' pleasant
An' I wouldn't sing no more.
But as long as Mary's livin'
An' the children all are here,
I'll keep my old face smilin',
So's to scare away the tear.

**

It was 1907, and Fred, at age twenty-one, graduated as an engineer, passing with honors. He was a most splendid sight in Carrie's eyes: straight-up tall, curly blonde hair, bright blue eyes, (that matched her own), and values without pause. He took a position with the Burlington Railroad for three years; this being arranged by a friend of Carrie is whose husband was the president. It was as if, suddenly, gentle hands were caring for her, for Fred. Carrie was overjoyed. She likened the experience to sunlight glinting off ripened fruit that she thought would never see maturity.

"It is precept and principle that make great men, Fred," Carrie had preached.

Now, here stood the man molded and prepared for the world, programmed with unquestioned precepts and principles.

Yet, that same year, at age forty-four, one of her darkest days was when she discovered she was $1,500.00 in debt to her printer, Mr. Nelson. Located on Dearborn Street, his printing plant was the best in Chicago, so she never explored further. In all the years he dealt with her, he never sent her a bill or asked her for a cent.

A good-natured man, but, like his true Viking ancestors, Nelson was unemotional. Every time she took work into him and she was excited about it, he would simply tell her, "I hope so,"...that it was going to be a success. Carrie's eyes closed fast as she gathered patience.

She quickly grew tired of the indifferent riposte. One day when she went to see him, she told him, "Mr. Nelson, don't you dare tell me, 'I hope so,' again. The next time I bring a song in and say it is going to be a success, you must say to me, 'Of course it is, Mrs. Bond.'"

Blinking, Nelson's pencil-slim mustache wiggled as if it had a life of its own; his big shoulders did a fast weave.

"Of course, he thought the winds of fate had blown me off course, but he adopted the new formula, all right. Nevertheless, the changed words did not change the luck so as far as I was concerned," Carrie recalled. From then on, Carrie could not wait for new composition so she could terrify Mr. Nelson with her newly found unpredictability.

Her deviltry was short-lived, however, upon learning of her $1500.00 deficit.

CHAPTER SEVENTEEN

It was strange how Carrie's confrontation with Mr. Nelson propped up her spine. She found grit; she found sand even though she suffered from neuritis, a lingering malady resultant of her terrible scalding as a child. It was difficult for her to write, but it never interfered in any way with her piano work. She hired a man by the name of Henry Sawyer, a quiet, competent composer, who wore heavily rimmed glasses, and who took music from dictation. If Carrie would play him a song, he would nod as if he had confirmed something, and write it. He had an ear for music such as she had. If she played a composition for him once, nearly always he would have it. At times, she heard him utter a soft, "Hmm," and give her a speculative look.

Carrie was not educated in composition, counterpoint, or any of the technical things that would have helped her so vastly, and yet her renderings were terribly vivid. For the next twelve years, Carrie worked with the keenly perceptive Sawyer in Chicago.

Together they wrote Carrie's *Little Book of Four Songs*. She used a publisher recommended by Sawyer, but he held the book promising he would sell it back to her at any point in time for what he had invested in the four songs. Eventually, she did go back to buy them.

"That'll run you *three hundred dollars* down and the balance in a month," he said coldly.

Carrie grimaced as if he had stuck her.

Hurriedly she went to three friends and borrowed the

whopping amount. It took a long time to shake the effects of the dark incident. Clinging mists of frustration wrapped her. She would never again allow someone else to hold her property at bay. It was as if she had pawned her *Little Book of Four Songs*. Carrie then stuck with Mr. Nelson, who had helped her with her accounts during the first seven years she was in Chicago, during which time there were no successes to speak of. After she did have some accomplishments, she queried Mr. Nelson in regard her indebtedness.

"How much do I have on the books, dear sir?"

Carrie had been so isolated in her poverty that she had not allowed herself to think about the money owed; it was too dreary. Besides, not knowing was a cheering armor. However, she was now of the mindset that 'out of debt' was 'out of danger'.

He went to his desk, took out a small book. His voice sounding half-strangled he said, "Slightly more than fifteen hundred dollars." For a long pause, he leaned over his desk with his back to Carrie. His shoulders twitched.

"Fifteen…Hundred…!" she exclaimed, her voice shrill like that of a sea gull in a dive.

Carrie drew herself up with a quick intake of breath. Her heart stopped. She had no idea she was so deeply in debt, and she knew that Mr. Nelson, himself, was poor. The situation was a nightmare of staggering proportions. Was Nelson aware of what a sum that was to one barely getting by? Should he not have advised her of the creeping balance from time to time? The elements of yesterday's wild imaginings and high falutin' aspirations had crumbled. Her state of debt was an embarrassment and positive misery.

Common sense deserted Carrie, losing a battle to the twisted neuroses that had plagued her from childhood.

For perhaps the only time in her life, Carrie decided to give up the tortuous fight. Her years of fierce struggle had brought her nothing but debt and ruin. These anxieties led to a breakdown, landing her in the sanitarium of a friend, Christine Forsythe, a registered nurse with a heart that held the woes of her patients. Christine's tall, lean body was as brown as a nut in the sun, and her smile as welcome as July in December. Carrie had never asked, but rationalized that Christine was perhaps Nationalist Indian. In this peaceful sanitarium, Carrie had already spent many weeks recuperating from depression spawned from insecurity and fears. From her convent days, she remembered a passage from Timothy 1:1-2: *Even in the night, my heart exhorts me.* In Carrie's mental state, the urgent appeal fell slowly into a wallowing pit. Life, she determined in her despondency, was warfare.

When she went to Christine, Carrie explained, "I've come to die. I have no money. Put me in the cheapest room you have. I don't care where it is." For the first time in her life, she was willing to admit defeat. "I tell you frankly, I have come to you to die. I can no longer feel the sun on my face, and there exists no saving wind at my back." The words came through clenched teeth, her jaw set and immobile...a talking automaton.

Christine was stunned, having never seen Carrie this morose, her battle plans reduced to yesterday's shredded newspaper. She laced her fingers together in her lap, leaning to Carrie as she would a small child. "Perhaps," she said slowly, "perhaps to understand this setback you'll have to find genuine love, for your son, for your work, a mutual respect and willingness to be tolerant and patient."

Willingness to be tolerant...willingness to be patient... Carrie shook her head in disbelief. She thought the words condemnation not inspiration. Who had been more plodding more understanding than she had during these tedious years of sacrifice? Who? She stood up, stretched her arms to encompass the air, threw her head back, and screamed, "Eeeeyeah."

Death was infinitely more appealing than life. She found herself in the throes of violent shaking, yet wearing a weary smile, unable to maintain control. She tasted blood. She was chewing on her bottom lip, and that is all she remembered.

Carrie was in a dear quiet room when next she opened her eyes. She hitched herself up against the pillows and extended her hand to take one of Christine's, gathering energy transference. Forsythe sat with her for hours coaxing normality by bringing concoctions of homemade remedies: mustard plasters for her chest, chamomile tea for restfulness, tempting ice cream dishes to thwart anorexia, chocolate recipes to hype Carrie's malaise. Carrie wondered if Christine had a small, black book such as Dr. Bond had considered his bible, one that told of inclinations, remedies, and results. But, did she care? She had fought the hard fight in this conflict and lost. She could no longer tell herself to rise again and go on. Her mouth drew in and her brows rose in resignation.

Forsythe had counted on Carrie and believed in her unwavering determination for seven years. Many times, she had urged Carrie to come and stay. When the edge of the crevasse was reached, Carrie's dreams engendered by her *healthy* mind faded into an unidentifiable oblivion. Nothing mattered. Nothing.

Nevertheless, a torturing question queued in Carrie's mind to deprive her even of the small satisfaction and peace that despair might have brought. What of her son? After all her striving was she to die now and leave him nothing, that would spare him the poverty they had both witnessed? If she felt she could do *a thing* that was successful, would not the a-symmetrical factors of doubt and despondency be sure steps to direct, indescribable heartache...to failure?

A PERFECT DAY

"Don't you have some old friend, someone who has more knowledge of business than we do, and could possibly help Fred carry on?" Forsythe took a plethora of pleasure in finding ways and means to cheer Carrie, treating every suggestion as if it were a gift. She let it hang there for Carrie to mull, and then added meaningfully. "I never knew you to be short of friends."

The implanted thought aroused the sick woman to a raw rebellion against the cruelty of life. Admittedly, cause and consequence were inseparable: fire will burn, water will drown, air will consume, earth will devour, and people will know defeat. She herself was defeated, she conceded, but she resolved inflexibly that her son would not be. Empty bags cannot stand alone, and she was not an unfilled sack to be blown away in the wind. She would build on her defeat as the first step to something better. That old tyrant, the devil, would not pull her down.

By the time Carrie had her morning bath, she had thought of an old friend whom she used to play with when she was only three years old. She made a soft sound in her throat with the revived memory.

"Cora was her name; she married and came here to Chicago to live. She and her husband know nothing of my adversities," Carrie sighed resignedly.

Forsythe tucked a robe around Carrie's lap and gentled her into a rocking chair near the window.

Cora's husband, Walter Gale, a friend whom Carrie had not seen since Dr. Bond's death, appeared at her door, seemingly out of nowhere. Christine had contacted Gale, and he had come to the sanitarium at once. He partnered in the Gale and Blocki Drug Company, and was a man of means and position. Dressed in a gray, pin stripe suit with white shirt and bow tie, he looked every bit the tall savior. An incorrigible clump of black hair strayed down over his forehead; his left hand smoothing it away was a gesture familiar to Carrie. The sound of his laughter was pleasant and easy.

"I'm in dreadful straits financially, and lucky I'm not hungry in addition. I've had a bad fright." Carrie told him the story, and that she needed fifteen hundred dollars. "I'm leaving some songs that somebody some time may want to buy. What do you think of those and my shoestring publishing business as a legacy?" She had trained Fred to be useful and spunky, and had fed him with yeas and not nays. This was no time to let him down and prove her training flawed.

"I think you've done devilishly well to start a business with no money; fifteen hundred dollars isn't that much. I really figure your business is worth nine thousand dollars," he stated, his voice strong.

In an awful mental state, Carrie was injected suddenly with hope, her load lightened. She straightened slowly and exclaimed. "What! You really believe that my small business is worth that much? Do you believe it enough to buy a tenth interest in it?" Her face was rapt with anticipation.

"I surely would do that," Gale responded without hesitation.

Who would do this for her? Her childhood, although adequate with common comforts, had never known the genuineness of caring, no matter the cost. Her grandfather had neither the time nor the inclination to understand the loneliness in which she existed; her mother starved Carrie of the basic needs of an emotionally growing little person in lieu of social successes. Her father, cut out of her life while yet a child, left her bereaved and without understanding of such an unspeakable death, a tragedy with implications beyond measure.

Gale quietly went to Carrie's desk and drafted a check for fifteen hundred dollars. Handing it to her, he asked, "When can Cora and I come to see you?"

A PERFECT DAY

It was crazy; her black nightmare was lifted. She had an angel. She must have an angel. Yes, sure, she had an angel. Thinking anything else would be absurd. Heaven itself had entered her world. It was like Dr. Bond carrying her away again. How had she remembered the Gales? Was this happening a fantasy? She turned her head slowly from side to side as if to absorb more of the aura surrounding her. Yes, she thought. Yes, yes, yes. A thought from the force surrounding her transcended into her mind. Would she not have done the same thing for a friend if she had unlimited resources? Enough of sadness; people grow lean on it. Joy is more than a happy accident; it is an ornament in one's life, and a duty.

The incident reuniting their relationship after so many years was charismatic for Carrie, for they began again where they had left off in childhood. From that day on, they were like brothers and sisters. The next day, although wobbly, she left the sanitarium in absolute command. Walter was her silent partner, and Cora, tiny and shy, was one of her most precious companions, a gleam of laughter always touching her eyes.

In a few days, Carrie was able to pay off Mr. Nelson, both resigned that he, as well as she, had been in violation of each other. Immediately afterwards, she went home and officially opened *The Bond Shop*. Carrie was rewarded when, at age twenty-four, Fred joined her in the business. His experiences in the railroad office were considerably helpful. Through his fine business ability, the shop outgrew the apartment dining room shop.

Walter Gale decided they should have a storeroom. They rented a bathroom of a pharmacy on North Michigan Blvd., and the business picked up so much that they had to have a delivery wagon. Fred tied into a bundle a package of 100 or 500 copies of music and started downtown to deliver them on his motorcycle. Soon they had to buy a sidecar for the motorcycle, and where it had been 1000 copies, it now was 5000.

Fred hunted down Joe Bidwell, the kindly border who had saved his life, and immediately hired him for the stockroom. Carrie took great delight in repayment of Joe's past kindnesses.

"Thank you, Mrs. Bond," Joe said, his voice a great rope of resonance.

"My pleasure, Joe," she murmured lightly, completely surprised that Joe reflected her own sentiments, thankfulness.

The Bond Shop became a reality, *Carrie Jacobs-Bond & Son, Inc.* In that first year after Gale loaned Carrie fifteen hundred dollars, his return on his investment was an unexpected ninety percent. After Carrie wrote *A Perfect Day*, he came in for a lion's share.

The hurricane of success baffled Carrie. After years of poverty, concentration, and perseverance, the sun shined on her doorstep. Her biggest success, she weighed, was acknowledging how long it took her to succeed. She had been subdued but not extinguished.

A PERFECT DAY

CHAPTER EIGHTEEN

Carrie and Fred moved to downtown Chicago in 1908, their enthusiasm soaring to new heights. In addition, they rented a room in the Chicago Musical College Building where they had their name imprinted on the door, and contained in the building's directory.

Carrie's second concert in Chicago was held on a bitterly cold night in February at Steinway Hall, where she successfully overwhelmed her audience. A man by the name of Carl Bronson, a cigar-smoking promoter, who owned the Cable Piano Company, became interested in her work and offered to give her a testimonial concert if she would provide the artists. Bronson furnished Steinway Hall, a Mason and Hamlin piano, and all the printing of window cards, programs, announcements, and invitations.

Carrie sailed from store to store. "Would you place my program announcements in your windows?" From where she drew her confidence she did not know, but her sails were billowed by the icy Lake Michigan shoreline gusts. Everyone was kind. She was never embarrassed for a moment in those days to travel up and down the business streets of Chicago.

She went to her old friend, Jessie Bartlett Davis. "Would you be so kind as to sing at my testimonial concert? I would be so pleased." The humility in Carrie's heart was not an abject, groveling spirit; it was a right estimate of her, as she perceived God saw her.

Only for a moment was Jessie silent. "Yes," she agreed with

genuine commitment. "I'll also help find others who will sing at the concert. Among those I'll ask is Charles W. Clark, who is Chicago's greatest baritone, and I'm sure Paul Schloessing, a cellist from the Thomas Orchestra, will also agree to entertain." Her turquoise eyes flashed as if fired by an inner light.

Carrie released a long breath, relieved at not being laughed at.

Jessie was far from laughing, indeed. Cognizant that Carrie was a rising star, Jessie was of the conviction that one had to be on compatible terms with one's peers; besides, she had taken a deep liking for this unusual woman.

"It's going to be a raving success. Wait and see." Jesse's eyes held warmth and excitement for Carrie.

"It will be now. It will be now." Carrie paused in the doorway upon leaving, a full smile dressing her face. "It will be now."

And it was.

Her income from that one evening was greater than all her previous endeavors put together.

***

Finances improving, Carrie had in her kitchen a dear old colored woman, Nancy, who was, in her younger days, the original Aunt Jemima Pancake maker.

"How old do you think she is?" Fred asked suddenly one day. "She must be nudging near one hundred years old."

Was Fred thinking Nancy was too old to be employed, to be dedicated to a family? Something in his tone caught at Carrie. Throwbacks to her repressive upbringing lead her to find Fred's questions about the elderly inappropriate. She studied him for a moment and determined he meant no subterfuge, only solicitousness.

A PERFECT DAY

Carrie took a breath and said hesitantly, "I don't know really know how old she is. Anyway, she is well into her last years, and she loves and cares for us."

Fred nodded. "Yes." A smile broke his serious face then, liberated, Carrie thought, at not being considered a prude.

Carrie in giving received in greater proportion. A comfortable old age was the reward of Nancy's well-spent youth. Healthy and cheerful, Nancy was forever young, and, when she died, Carrie was sure Nancy would die in youth, even when years would count her old. Aunt Jemima stayed dedicated to Carrie and Fred until they later moved to California.

While in The Bond Shop, she wrote *A Four-Song Book, A Seven-Song Book, A Ten-Song Book, An Eleven-Song Book, and A Twelve-Song Book.*

Accolades were plentiful and received well on her *Seven-Song Book.*

> We will do all we can to assist in the sale of Seven Songs.
> **Lyon & Healy, Chicago**

> Dear Mrs. Bond:
> The Seven Songs, which we had the pleasure of hearing you interpret, gave us great pleasure, and we shall do all we can to make them known.
> Very Truly yours, **Edward Schuberth & Co.,** New York

> Dear Mrs. Carrie Jacobs-Bond:
> I am very fond of violets and of fresh, clean, morning fields—this is the reason why I like your little songs. You have the insight of the seer and the poet—you see

deep. Simple things are difficult.
There is work in the world for you. Thousands are awaiting your message.
By Yours Truly,

David Ffrangon-davies, Berlin

I take pleasure in recommending the songs by Carrie Jacobs-Bond, which show genuine talent and individuality, and which appeal directly to the heart.
Amy Fay, New York

From phoenix in the ashes, Carrie had risen to numerous allies.

A PERFECT DAY

CHAPTER NINETEEN

In the same year, 1908, Mrs. Henry Howe, a graceful and ingratiating woman, of Marshaltown, Iowa and President of the Twentieth Century Club, wired Carrie. "We would consider it a tremendous favor if you were to give a recital here to kick off a concert tour. Please advise."

Carrie danced around and around the office upon getting the dispatch, the goldenrod communication waving in the air. "Fred!" She said in amazement. "What an opportunity."

"Grab it, Mama. It's a grand break and will give you needed exposure." Fred smiled indulgently from behind a stack of orders.

Joe Bidwell shook out of the mailroom, his expression soft. "It sounds like a good bargain to me, an exposure to the Midwest."

It was more than a good bargain and excellent opportunity for exposure; the tour enabled her to meet Elbert Hubbard, Editor of *The Philistine*, who gave her important publicity. He was also the founder of a turn-of-the-century arts and crafts village, *The Roycrofters*, flourishing in East Aurora, New York from 1895 to 1915. A man of medium height, he wore an aura of authority, his dark eyes scrutinizing deeply, yet not unkindly. A rakish grin pulled at the corner of his lips, almost a trademark.

Carrie later established that the village was eighteen miles southeast of Buffalo, and, upon her first visit, she found everything she looked for in a small town: a wide main street, and Victorian houses growing out of well-tended lawns. The home of U. S. President, Millard Fillmore, was situated there, where Carrie discovered the precious jewel of peace, a peace that could not be denied to such a peaceful people. *The Roycrofters*, a community within a community, consisted of mostly local people Hubbard had trained in printing, bookbinding, metalworking, and other crafts.

A one-time soap sales representative, Hubbard was disturbingly charismatic.

Carrie fell under his spell.

He told Carrie, "The love you liberate in your work is the love you keep."

No one could deny that Carrie flourished in an avalanche of love in her music, and Hubbard returned it triple fold. After a life of sorrow, grief, and tragic losses, Carrie drifted easily into the indefinable magnetism of Hubbard's charms. Her work ethic of total application never made her happier. She bloomed in the headiness of his presence as a May flower ascending from last fall's crush of leaves.

Maybe she had too much imagination, but she entertained thoughts of love at first sight. Maybe she was too impressionable even though her years on earth numbered in the forties. The sensations that washed over her in his presence knew no resolution. *Be sensible, Carrie. It is just his mesmerizing personality.* It is simply the sexuality he exudes, the masculinity of his posture, the power and confidence he radiates that you find attractive. Alternatively, was it a rare cocktail of all those things? Maybe her senses had left her, and her mind put on 'hold'. Upon second look, she discerned, as by instinct Hubbard's inner feelings. What could be more sharp-sighted or sensitive than that, than that of true love?

After the Iowa concert tour, she gave for Hubbard many impromptu concerts, first in his Roycroft Shop and later in a fine-looking music room. Her performances had never demonstrated more gentleness or love. She knew that with the slightest invitation she would fall into his arms, his life, and his bed. Did not Lord Byron say *Man's love is of man's life a part; it is woman's whole existence.* Carrie knew this to be a truth, for her soul had lived and flourished on love.

Hubbard, who wore his hair long, favored Byronic black ties, loved to ride, and settled in East Aurora in 1895 because this was horse country. He had sold his shares in a soap business to become a writer. When editors in New York City rejected his work, calling it, as Hubbard told the story, "too plain, too blunt, sometimes indelicate, it would give offense, subscribers would cancel, et cetera, et cetera," he started his own magazine *The Philistine.* Following its success, he launched a larger format publication he called *The Fra,* short for Fra Elbertus, suggesting his tongue-in-cheek view of himself as a preacher giving a monthly sermon to his flock.

This talent of Hubbard's varied ministries grabbed insidiously at Carrie's heart that had 'Open Season' carved upon it. Knowing he was married and had a son as old as Fred, cast him as out of reach, placed him in the never-never land of her Victorian upbringing. Besides, whoever told her that she measured up to what Elbert wanted in a woman? *You are plain and can count but few glorious gifts of nature.* Love, nonetheless, came to Carrie without seeking it, as if the seed were predestinedly sunk and waiting to flourish.

She admired Hubbard's Roycrofters, who made hand-hewn furniture with squarish lines that sold for spikey prices. "The cheap article, I will admit, ministers to a certain grade of intellect," went a typical Hubbard pitch. "But if the man grows, there will surely come a time when, instead of a great many cheap things, he will want fewer but better commodities. Our motto is: NOT HOW CHEAP BUT HOW GOOD."

Many historians credit Hubbard with creating a market later captured by more sophisticated designers and architects such as Greene & Greene and Frank Lloyd Wright. Some see in Wright's romantic dress and adoring students at Taliesin, Wright's home in Spring Green, Wisconsin, echoes of the Fra of East Aurora. In later years, Carrie was to design her own home in Grossmont, California, after the fashions and designs of Hubbard.

Hubbard fondly called a building *The Chapel* where Roycrofters assembled to hear concerts, lectures, and debates. Carrie entertained here as a regular, and the attentions showered upon her by Hubbard were great and large. Travel and intimate get-aways she enjoyed much to Carrie's retrospective remorse, because it betrayed her down-home values, but she was irretrievably lost in Hubbard's allure.

"The human heart is a hospice for out-of-nature indiscretions," Carrie breathed aloud to herself. She was intoxicated with Hubbard's potions of verbal elixirs. Although she had experienced immeasurable losses in her life, what was determinable was not so much what she had lost, but rather what she had remaining, and she would transform these into the richest of treasures.

Although Elbert Hubbard was not entirely beloved in East Aurora in his lifetime, Carrie, forever grateful for all the breaks Hubbard bestowed upon her, saw none of the characteristics others viewed. On the contrary, Carrie saw a splendid man and a splendid place where seekers could come to improve themselves, a bright oasis in the desert of humdrum and a solid woven fabric of deliberate purpose. She saw in Hubbard somewhat of a savior, the thought always surprising her.

Alice, Hubbard's wife, exercised enormous authority over the day-to-day workings of the Roycrofters, and thus remained acquiesced to Elbert's wandering eye. Bertha, Hubbard's first wife, divorced him when she discovered he had fathered a child by Alice. Gossip traveled on the air itself in East Aurora. Carrie breathed deeply at the information that friends were all too willing to convey to her. In her opinion, ridicule was offered by misdirected, finite minds.

Hubbard marketed himself as a cracker-barrel sage and the products his workers made as prominent contributions to the American Arts and Crafts Movement. With his long flowing hair, flannel shirts, and sturdy brogans, Hubbard liked to pose as the wise fool and free spirit locked in combat with local obtuseness. To his critics, he replied, "Every knock is a boost, and the leader of the orchestra is always one who has played second fiddle."

Carrie was locked in amazement at his simplistic, philosophical renderings, the portrayal of which was removed from self-conceit.

Hubbard's ambitions grew beyond having an outlet for his writings. If the world did not accept him, and by now it did not since Alice Moore had a child by him in 1894—he would create his own, *Roycroft*. In 1908, Hubbard divorced his wife and married Alice Moore, who was a schoolteacher and had long been an advocate of women's rights.

***

It was the same year that Carrie met Hubbard. She observed that he was a straight shooter with his people, and his infatuation with Alice as a vortex into which he was drawn, having the same ideologies as she did. Whatever his personal life, she viewed this Godsend of a man as dedicated to purposes as altruistic as patriotism.

The grounds were an exhibit of design and flow. Low, stonewalls surrounded the campus, and wherever there was a wall, flowerbeds of early spring crocus to late blooming asters and chrysanthemums ran chasing alongside. Shouts of competitiveness rang from a bowling green in front of the Inn, and squeals of laughter lifted from slides and teeter-totters inhabited by children. There were musical salons on the weekends, and a summer concert series, and these activities were free to the workers and everyone else in the village. As summer drew to lovely autumns with bright and still days, Hubbard continued his concerts as late into the year as weather permitted.

The Philistine, a magazine of modest circulation, and cranky enough to expect to remain so, became a national voice. As a writer, Hubbard is best remembered for the series of short biographies he called *Little Journeys to the Homes of the Great*. For the March 1899 issue Hubbard wrote *A Message to Garcia*, a famous motivational essay about a young man in the Spanish-American War who unhesitatingly followed his superior's orders and delivered a dispatch against fearful odds. The paean to blind acceptance of duty, and honoring loyalty and resourcefulness, took the country by storm. Hubbard sold some nine million reprints of this essay in his lifetime. Many sales were to company presidents who distributed them to their employees.

Subscriptions to *The Philistine* jumped from 2,500 in 1895 to 100,000 in 1899; they reached 126,000 in 1906 and 200,000 in 1911. The New York Central Railroad ordered more than a million reprints of **A Message to Garcia** and Hubbard was a household name. His publishing efforts made him a wealthy man, and he used his profits to support his Arts and Crafts Community…and his philandering, from which Carrie, in the end, was not spared.

A PERFECT DAY

The man must have rendered her senseless. The enigma of how and why was unsolvable. Her attraction to him she viewed not as a tragedy but as sustenance. As time drifted from one year to the next, Carrie doodled on her manuscripts. ***Love is never lost. If not reciprocated it will flow back, soften, and purify the heart.*** (Washington Irving)

She gnawed at her bottom lip in consternation, knowing her loving relationship with Elbert could never translate beyond what it presently offered: stolen time together and aching hearts upon parting. She reprimanded herself harshly, but the flame burned and she flew into it like a Midwest moth. In the privacy of her home, the conflicts that warred in her mind brought varying stages of barely-concealed modes of disbelief, anger, and love.

A PERFECT DAY

CHAPTER TWENTY

The fire ignited in Hubbard's presence led Carrie to forget there was cold weather marching around outside. Everyday inner warmth danced in her heart. In the early spring of 1909, she tackled a second Iowa concert tour and entertained in every important town in the state; however, her concert wardrobe was constantly a problem. She was concerned over the importance of the concerts in Marshall Town, especially as it was a testimonial for Hubbard, and she had nothing fresh and new to wear. Somehow, it made a difference to her what he thought of her. Her heart clutched with the magnetism she felt for him dating back to their first acquaintance in Iowa.

Confronted with her stage wardrobe, Carrie was able to say, "Even in the worst of times, I never looked shabby. I had learned to turn my old dresses inside out; had learned how to put a damp cloth over a hot flatiron and steam a piece of old velvet so it looked almost new; learned never to cut a piece to trim a hat if it could be utilized later for a belt; learned how to revive a tired ostrich feather with the dull side of a knife—all these things kind poverty had taught me, and I used some of my knowledge every day."

Searching through treasures of former days, she found two, beige, lace curtains and two yards of off-white satin, and went to work making a dress. There were shiny satin inserts into intricate lace down the long skirt front and capped sleeves of lace. She worked feverishly to cut and sew the garment and featherstitch and embroider thousands of French knots in every spare moment for four weeks before finishing her last knot just an hour before the performance. Standing critical in front of a mirror, she found the dress of beige and white complemented her fair skin, her blue eyes, and her blonde hair. She wriggled her eyebrows, incredulous at her prowess as a seamstress.

While the gown brought pleasing compliments, one columnist's words were to smart for years…"a plain angular woman who wrote plain, angular songs, and set them to plain, angular music."

Carrie took a deep troubled breath. "That's your penance for being blatantly proud," she admonished herself aloud.

It was through a Twentieth Century Club Charter Member from Bloomfield, Iowa that she was taken to hear Hubbard in lecture on his shop and work. In conversation afterward, Hubbard offered to sit with Carrie in the next two days to discuss *I Love You Truly, and Just A Wearyin' For You.*

He said, "Carrie, do you know your objectives?

"Certainly," she answered with an overt confidence that left her quaking inside. "I'm looking for a gate that leads from Chicago to New York, where, I'm told, the greatest opportunity for starting original things can be found. Yes. New York is where I want to entertain." She prayed that her germ of ambition did not sound too aggressive.

"Well, that's quite easily arranged," Hubbard smiled deeply. "If you care to come to the Roycroft Shop and give us a concert, I'll give you twenty-five dollars and your transportation to New York City and back to Chicago, and you can stop for a visit at East Aurora."

"Yes. Yes, I'll do that." Carrie felt wonderfully calm, even though she knew the trip would be braided with emotion and speculation.

She arrived at the station in East Aurora and met by the

A PERFECT DAY

two Elbert Hubbards: Bert, the son was a young man the age and size of her own son, Fred, and he was his father's partner, too. This was before the Roycroft Shop had impressive buildings of its own, but was built in the yard adjoining the Hubbard home and was called *The Gymnasium*. That was the only large room connected with the Roycroft Shops. There, Carrie viewed massive, heavy tables laden with books ready to be shipped.

She performed in the evenings at the Roycroft Shop, and such wholesome applause she had never heard. Everyone enjoyed it. Hubbard gave a speech before she performed. "We have a genius in our midst, and she has honored us by appearing here." His features had grown soft and benevolent.

"It was just as though I really *were* of great importance. In those days, my voice was full of sadness, and it brought tears to the eyes of other people. Therefore, unless I could see my audience affected, as I was accustomed to seeing them in small drawing rooms, I would have been disappointed and felt that I was not giving the performance my best effort.

"On this night, I saw tears in the eyes of my friend, Hubbard, and I felt that I was singing as well as I ever did. In the first issue of *The Philistine* after my concert was an article written by Hubbard. It was the first publicity of any importance I had ever had, and I felt the coverage was the beginning of my being known to the world."

> Art, at least, is a matter of the heart, not the head; and this fact was brought home to me strongly a few weeks ago on hearing Carrie Jacobs-Bond. Here is a woman who writes poems, sets them to music, and signs them in a manner that reveals the very acme of art. Her performance is also gentle, spontaneous and unaffected so as you think you could do the same

thing yourself—simple, pattering little-child songs set to tunes that sing themselves. In some ways, they search out the corners of your soul. You think of the robin singing at sunset, calling to his lost mate from the top of a tall poplar in days of long ago. As a reader and singer, Carrie Jacobs-Bond is as subdued as a landscape by Cazin and is as true and effective as a sketch by DeMonvel.

Carrie spent a week in the Roycroft Community, where every waking hour was spent with Hubbard. At the end of the week, Elbert asked Carrie, "Would you be interested in accompanying me to New York City to the first Philistine dinner that had ever been planned?" It was a question most cordially voiced.

"They're giving it for me," he explained. "I'm taking Bert, and would be happy to have you come along."

"Yes." Her answer was swift and spoken from the heart. What a mistake it would have been for Carrie to decline that wonderful invitation.

Later, she told Fred. "That night at the Philistine dinner that began at seven o'clock with dozens of red-jacketed waiters hustling huge trays of crisp salads and flaky rolls, then came a second invasion of the red-coats with entrees of Cornish hens, wild rice and vegetables. Just when you thought you could eat no more, there arrived triple-decker Black Forest cake drizzled with chocolate sauce. There were munchies and speeches lasting until three o'clock in the morning.

"I sat with Edwin Markham on my right, the American poet known for, "The Man With The Hoe," (a poem of protest against the exploitation of labor), and Bliss Carman on my left, a Canadian poet noted for his ebullient nature poems, including

A PERFECT DAY

the collection, *Low Tide on Grand Pré* (1893), with a hundred other brilliant men and women.

"I heard them laugh at Mr. Hubbard and say what seemed to me to be the most impudent things, while I thought him so fine and wonderful. I wanted to get up and tell everyone how terrible it was to abuse him. Everyone had said just what he or she wanted to say, and had laughed except me, and Mr. Hubbard's face did not change at all. He just looked on in the amused way that in time I came to understand. He really was having the time of his life, and I did not know it. Bert seemed to enjoy it more than anyone else did, for every little while he gave his father a sly glance.

"Well, by and by, early in the morning, the toastmaster said, now we will hear from Fra Elbertus, and we did. He did not use any jokes, but oh, how he did answer every jest. I knew from that hour that he did not need any special champion. He was perfectly able to take care of himself."

"I'm glad that you went, mother. What a unique experience." Fred warmed to read the excitement in his mother's eyes.

***

Whenever she went to New York after that, Carrie always went via the East Aurora route. No matter what time of the day she arrived—Carrie often went when she had only a few hours to stay— Hubbard would send word to the many shops providing work for hundreds of people.

"Carrie has come, and she's going to sing for us."

The shops closed and all the workers came to the music room established next door to where *The Gymnasium* used to be, and she would give a concert. No longer did they have to shove tables together and lift the piano. There was a fine platform with a magnificent Mason and Hamlin grand piano, comfortable chairs, impressive surroundings, and a ceiling frieze painted by a handpicked Roycrofter.

"Later," she indulged to Fred, "I gave there the most interesting program I've ever given anywhere. I sent word ahead, and preparations were all made. As it was apple blossom time, Hubbard decided that the concert should be out of doors. A platform was built around the great apple tree that stood in the middle of the Roycroft grounds and the piano was brought out doors. One lovely afternoon I sang with the apple blossoms falling down on the audience and on me—sang as hopefully and as freely as a bird sings because it was an ideal place for music, and I was among true friends."

"You know, mother," Fred interjected, "poverty does many things for one, but the greatest thing it does is show you your friends."

"I was so poor that I *knew* who mine were," Carrie replied. "I may have had some disappointments in life, but never through my friends. That is one of the advantages of being poor. Almost everyone can have friends if he can give something, but when you have nothing but yourself to give, and friends stand true, that means everything."

Fred nodded his head. "True enough, how very true." Touched by his mother's inner thoughts spoken aloud, he busied himself with filling orders.

It was at Roycrofters that Carrie learned that ambition was not aggressiveness. Ambition was a spur that guided her long struggle with destiny. It was at Roycrofters that she felt fulfilled by Hubbard, as if he were heaven's own incentive to make purpose great and achievement greater. In addition, no achievement was greater than Hubbard's love harbored in Carrie's heart.

CHAPTER TWENTY-ONE

Basking in Elbert's love, Carrie grew in mental strength and confidence. Not any longer struggling, she acknowledged that she brought as much to their relationship as he. However, opposed to Hubbard's robust health, she found it difficult to forget her frailties that caught up with her from time to time.

Carrie recalled vividly, when, six years ago, she had been ill for many weeks at a Chicago Hospital. It was just after Christmas, and her physician and friend, Dr. Alexander Ferguson, advised her to move to a warmer climate.

"It's absolutely necessary. Your rheumatism and neuritis are debilitating your daily life, and will only grow worse in the Chicago dampness."

A climatic move was an uncustomary domestic and business dishevels, but she took an engagement with the Santa Fe Railroad, an entity giving her transportation and expenses to Los Angeles in exchange for her singing in its reading rooms and employees' recreation rooms. When she reached Los Angeles, she took a similar job, for board and room, at the old Hollywood Hotel. There she met Geneva Johnstone Bishop, a famous Chicago singer with whom Carrie appeared on stage at Bishop's concerts.

She found that the arrangement paid her well by giving her attention and additional contracts. For six years she went west in the winter by Santa Fe and spent two months at the Hollywood Hotel. One result was, according to later stories, that a plaque was placed on a hotel piano there saying Carrie Jacobs-Bond had composed *A Perfect Day* with the help of that particular piano in that particular place. Carrie often said that story and numerous others were not true.

***

Carrie held her breath, when, in the autumn of 1908, upon opening the daily mail she found there an invitation from President and Mrs. Theodore Roosevelt to entertain at the White House. They were also going to have the pleasure of Joel Harris, better known as Uncle Remus, to accommodate their guests. A swift and unrelenting net of heat encircled her heart with delight.

Fred smiled as Carrie hustled about the Chicago apartment gathering her wearing apparel. She chose the beige, lace dress that she changed only slightly since the last time she wore it in Marshaltown, Iowa; she added a scarf and sash of royal blue chiffon.

"Perfect," Fred praised, charged up with his mother's appearance in high places. "I'll hold down the fort here."

"When God made you, he was showing off, Fred." Carrie's eyes were alight with renewal and enthusiasm.

At the White House, Carrie sat at dinner in an agony of nervousness. Behind her, she saw a portrait of Abraham Lincoln. The picture gave her courage. She thought, *You were plain and angular, too, but nobody seemed to mind.*

Mrs. Roosevelt cued Carrie. "Mr. Harris is shy and will listen to your renditions from another room." Her gentle hand patted Carrie's shoulder.

Carrie played *Captain of the Broomstick Cavalry*. When she glanced up, she saw Mr. Harris come into the room, and as he approached the piano, he said, "I came in because this is the kind of music I can understand." He sat down close to the piano.

A PERFECT DAY

One other song she sang that night was one that had these words. *It ain't so much the doing as the way the thing is did.* As she sang these words, President Roosevelt came over to the piano and laid his hand on hers, briefly stopped the music, and said, "Mrs. Bond, you will never say any truer words than those." There was an edge of steel behind his delivery.

As she said goodbye to them that night, Mrs. Roosevelt explained the President's comment. "Ted was terribly hurt today by the act of a friend. It was not the thing that was done that hurt, but it was the *way* in which it was done."

"I have so much enjoyed the evening," the great man said. In a few days, she received an autographed picture of President Roosevelt that remained one of her most prized possessions. He hand wrote one of his most famous quotes: "Far and away the best prize that life offers is the chance to work hard at work worth doing."

Was this memento really for her, the introvert lost soul from Janesville, Wisconsin, the down-and-out pauper off the cold streets of Chicago?

Carrie's stomach flooded with warmth.

A PERFECT DAY

CHAPTER TWENTY-TWO

It was at this time that Lulu and Esther Fairbanks of the prestigious Fairbanks family became her companions for the rest of her life. Lulu and Esther were daughters of Newton H. and Lucy Fairbanks; Newton was the brother of Charles Warren Fairbanks, a lawyer, political leader, U.S. Senator from Indiana, and Vice President of the United States under the Theodore Roosevelt administration from 1905 to 1909. The friendship with the vivacious girls and their mother was struck because of Carrie's visits to the White House. The likeness of Lulu and Esther to their mother, Lucy, was striking. They had the same uncontrollable, curly, red hair, gem-bright green eyes, fair skin peppered with freckles, and lightning smiles.

She found it most interesting that Charles and Newton came from a long line of New England ancestry, just as she was. In 1636, about a dozen years after the town of Boston was settled, a ship from England brought to the colony one Jonathan Fayerbanke, his wife, 4 sons and 2 daughters. The Fayerbanke family became well known in the early annals of the Massachusetts colony. Jonathan's descendants occupied the house in which he lived near Dedham until recent years, when it became the property of the Massachusetts Historical Society.

Carrie was surprised to learn that Warren and Newton were eighth in descent from Jonathan Fayerbanke, and it was all documented. She, too, could trace her heritage to many grandfathers, and of New England ancestry, in Vermont.

"Jonathan learned the wagon-maker's trade, and emigrated

to Union County, Ohio, where years later, Charles and I were born, Charles in 1852 and myself in 1862."

"That's the same year I was born," Carrie offered, brightening. The commonizing birth year brought instant camaraderie.

"My earliest recollections date from the log cabin in which Chuck and I were born," Newton went on. "The small building occupied a space on the edge of a farm of 216 acres in Union County, Ohio. We were typical country lads, grew to six feet tall early on making us a little awkward in our movements. We couldn't gain a pound if we wanted to, so we stayed pencil slim and slow of speech. We were, however, sincerely devoted to the task of getting through college and becoming for Charles, a lawyer, for myself, a capitalist owning foundries and manufacturing plants."

Carrie found that the mutations of life and the politics thereof never broke the closeness of the two men, or lessen it. In temperament, they were much alike.

Charles Fairbanks, while Senator from Indiana and Chairman of the Joint Commission for the settlement of the Alaska boundary from Canada, was the man for whom the City of Fairbanks was named in 1902.

While Charles was negotiating boundaries, the Newton Fairbanks established in Ann Arbor, Michigan. Subsequently, Esther was born in 1885 and Lulu in 1888. While yet very young girls, Charles gave them a tinted photograph of Mount Rainier in the state of Washington and Mt. McKinley, in the state of Alaska. The pictures were held most dearly by Lulu who kept them in her school geography, constantly admiring them, and promising to some day settle in Seattle. She kept that promise, arriving in 1916 at 28 years old, and after graduating from Michigan State Normal School in Ypsilanti. She accepted a position on the faculty of the Whittier School. *I do not feel fulfilled in this teaching position,* she wrote to Carrie in Chicago.

Although Carrie was old enough to be the mother of Lulu and Esther, the friendships flourished with no age differential.

One sometimes has to reach beyond daily doldrums to find a true calling, Carrie nurtured in a letter of response to Lulu.

Lulu did abandon the teaching profession to become the audit clerk of the Port of Seattle. From the purchasing desk, she moved to the export and import department, a work she found particularly to her liking. However, she resigned her position to go to New York to become the circulation manger of the Independent Woman, official organ of the National Federation of Business and Professional Women's Clubs.

The New York adventure was short-lived, however. Seattle loved Lulu and Lulu loved Seattle. The city refused to fade from her mind and again beckoned her to take over the circulation management of the Alaska Weekly Publication. It was at this time that Esther joined her to work on the magazine.

Carrie was not surprised when Lulu became president of the Seattle Business and Professional Women's Clubs, but was deeply impressed to find that the spunky redhead took over the presidency of the Washington State Federation of Business and Professional Women's Clubs, which she was instrumental in organizing. Carrie wrote to Lulu.

> My dearest Lulu,
>
> Congratulations on your presidency of the BPWC. How wonderful for you, and a prized reward for your organizing skills. Today is not yesterday. I change. You change.
>
> How then can our aspirations, if they are always to be the finest, continue always on the same plain.

PEGGY DePUYDT

I know that you must have found the change in your lifestyle a burning decision, yet so needful. You need to remember that nothing, which you have left behind, is ever lost.

A PERFECT DAY

CHAPTER TWENTY-THREE

While Lulu and Esther were yet students at Michigan State Normal School in Ypsilanti, in 1910, Carrie wrote, while visiting in California, *A Perfect Day*. Carrie was lodged at the Mission Inn at Riverside, California, and wished she had the company of the two, combustible redheads. Life knew no dull moments when in their company.

She had driven up Mount Rubidoux to see the raging, orange, and pink sunset. Upon returning to the Inn, she quickly wrote the words without change. She had spent a memorable day with friends under a precious sky dotted only with trailing, wispy clouds. That same evening by moonlight, she took a drive into the Mojave Desert with nature-loving friends. Without realizing that she had memorized the words, she began singing them to a tune.

"My friend, Helen Hawks, a tall, slim woman with a broad smile and tender eyes, sat next to me on the drive. In her kind home I had spent many happy days; her loving interest had encouraged me to write several songs."

"Carrie, you have another song, haven't you?" Helen said.

"Well," I replied, "Perhaps I have. The melody and the lyrics flow together as if pre-conjoined."

Carrie stayed in the Hawks home that night, but did not go to sleep, and finished the song before morning. The words were written at the Mission Inn. The tune came to her in that car in the desert. Finally, it would appear, she put the words and music together in the home of Mrs. Hawks, the location of which is not clear.

This song brought her more thrills than any other did. It was the largest enduring popular song in American history. More than five million copies were sold. Sixty different arrangements and excellent sales of *A Perfect Day* necessitated another move, this time to the Colonnade Building, downtown Chicago.

***

By World War I in 1917, *A Perfect Day* had hit its zenith. *I Love You Truly*, still ranks next to Mendelssohn and Wagner as the most frequently selected music for weddings. Famous songs do not spring out of empty lives. To appreciate, at its full value, the healing happiness of a perfect day one must have known sorrow and hardships, discouragements, and loneliness. Carrie knew them all.

I love You Truly had become famous because of its extensive use in wedding ceremonies. The song was slow to catch the public's fancy, but now ranks with *A Perfect Day* and was used on many radio programs. At least two, well-known orchestras of the era had it as a theme song. Carrie has a room named for her on Author's Row at the Mission Inn.

***

The stories concerning this song and its maker are legion—some sentimental, some jesting, many of them fanciful rather than factual.

Possibly the best of the comic yarns about the song pertains to its nightly playing on the Mission Inn chimes.

A woman Inn guest gushes:
"Isn't it beautiful?"
Her philistine husband says, "What?"
This exchange is repeated several times with

variations until the exasperated husband exclaims, "Wait until those damned chimes stop. I can't hear a word you're saying."

***

Carrie's homeport was yet the Hollywood Hotel for her winter health. It was there that she received an invitation to perform at Long Beach, California. She was just leaving the dressing room for the stage when a rip appeared in her homemade dress.

"Good grief, Helen, (Hawks)" she groaned. "Would you pin it?"

When she emerged onto the stage, the pin popped and stuck into her shoulder. As she went to the piano, she did her best by squirming to make herself more comfortable. The pin did not move. Determined to keep on with her performance, she did just that, the pin doing battle with her shoulder.

The next day, one of the critics wrote:

> Her songs were very enjoyable, but her rendition of them unique: she has some peculiar and unfortunate mannerisms, which will probably wear off as she becomes more experienced in concert work

***

Winter ran its course, and summer in Chicago turned into autumn in a burst of flaming hardwoods and Midwest warm days/cool nights. The pungent smell of fallen leaves and dewy damp was as familiar as her memories of The Davis House, the grounds, and the cemetery where Grandfather Davis was buried. Smells, sights, and sounds always were a source of intrigue and vivid memories, which inspired melodies, words, and sentiments.

Carrie brightened from her thoughts of a rapidly receding summer when David Bisphan of England planned a concert at Studebaker Hall. "I'm going to sing fifteen of your songs, Carrie." He watched her with interest, waiting for an enthusiastic, if not surprised, approval. "I want you on stage."

"My songs? My accompaniment?" She considered this invitation for some time—possibly five seconds. He skin shivered with goose bumps.

"Of course I will, David," she said, astonished and overwhelmed with the invitation.

Bisphan, a man of medium height and slight build, was long a fan of Carrie's, and when he opened his mouth to deliver a song, he grew to six feet tall with gargantuan lungs.

Carrie was dubious that he was really going to do fifteen of her songs, but she bought one hundred tickets, and went about town selling them to friends. She sold near fifty.

What was she to wear? The question created a growing amount of angst. Among Carrie's acquaintances was a woman who previously lived in Janesville, Miss Morisey, who had moved to Chicago several years earlier. Carrie yet called her *Miss*; there were some people in one's life that never shed their titles. She was touted as a well-known dressmaker so Carrie contacted her. Morisey, no bigger than a puff a wind, wore her eyeglasses on the bridge of her nose. Peering over the top of them in conversation, she appeared as if she were in constant scrutiny.

Carrie shared with her the story of the one hundred

dollar investment. "As a result, it troubles me to ask if you would accept a down payment and trust me for the balance."

"Yes, certainly. Don't you worry your head about it, Carrie." The most adventuresome thing that had ever walked into Morisey's life was Carrie Jacobs-Bond. Besides, Carrie had put Janesville, Wisconsin on the map, and Morisey was proud.

Her fragile frame jumped by living life vicariously through Carrie. Morisey designed and sewed Carrie one of the most heart-melting dresses Carrie had ever owned. The accomplished dressmaker put twenty-five yards of material into the creation. It was the color of spun gold, all tucked, fluted, combined with lace, and quite magnificent.

Previously, Carrie had made her own hats, but felt she should go to a milliner for this one, and she did, taking pieces of the dress with her and two, splendid ostrich feathers.

The concert was set on the Sunday night calendar. Friday night Carrie picked up her hat. Something told her on Sunday morning to try on the dress and hat and see what she was going to look like in the evening. The dress was uptown becoming, but, oh, the hat.

"I can't wear this hat," she exclaimed to Fred. "What in the world am I going to do?"

"Mama, you look like a duchess all the time; you'll think of something," he said with a generous dose of "uh's" and "um's," while hiding his head and laughing. "Come to think of it, Mama, you look like a *duke* in that hat, the way it is." A roar of laughter tore through him, inducing Carrie to see the funny side of the situation.

While expecting the worse, Carrie's eyes were snapping with ideas, and improvisations. The creative juices were on a tear. "I can do this," she said excitedly, but I wish that Lulu and Esther were here to lend me a hand; they are so inventive."

"You have to remember that those two young ladies would wear you out if they were here. That's what they'd do." Fred shook his head in frustration.

In an outrageously rash moment of extravagance, she had previously bought some lovely pink velvet roses never previously worn. It was about ten o'clock in the morning and she began to manipulate the hat. All she had to work with were pieces of lace and silk, and the roses. She had no frame, no wire. Nevertheless, huffing and sighing, it did not demand much time to remove the wires from the existing hat, and with some buckram and pasteboard, she made a frame that looked like her.

Fred almost strangled on complimentary words. "Good Lord, mother, the new hat is more attractive than the store-bought creation."

"You were right Fred; I don't need Lulu and Esther to help me dress, for heaven's sake."

At concert time, the autumnal equinox moon had risen clear of the buildings, and beyond the shadow of them, the street was as light as a mid-winter scene, thus a magical omen. The front steps of Studebaker Hall climbed in a sweeping reach to the main entrance, dwarfing Carrie, and making her feel small.

Her light-heartedness quickly shrunk when she found that of the fifteen songs that Mr. Bisphan was about to sing, not one was done in the original key. She had to transpose them all, and do it as she played. Her anxious child's look melded into confidence once she sat at the piano and found herself vigorously attacking the ivories in a mental photograph of the new transcriptions. How quickly she converted from the dominant major keys to the more sorrowful minor keys, and all were dancing pictures in her head.

The hall was packed, and many were turned away. She now wished she had never spent the hundred dollars, because the tickets would have been sold anyway. After the last song, there was such applause as she had never heard; consequently, she did not raise her eyes because she did not think any of the applause was for her. Part of Carrie's character was to submit to humility. It was always her nagging nemesis that the sufficiency of her merit was to acknowledge her merit insufficient.

A PERFECT DAY

Mr. Bisphan, shrunken to his normal size after singing, asked her, "Are you not going to stand up, Mrs. Bond?

She burst with gratitude, stood and bowed. He then sang *A Perfect Day* for the first time it was ever sang in concert by anyone but herself. In smiling silence, Carrie accompanied him to an explosion of overwhelming applause.

The next day, Carrie paid her bill at Miss Morisey's, who hovered about her like a mother duck. "In most things, success depends on knowing how long it takes to succeed," Morisey said. "You've paid your dues in terms of time."

"Why Miss Morisey, what nice insight. You're right. Time is the promise of the bud into the blossom. It's the cushion of the cocoon into the butterfly. I'll long remember your nice words."

Being invited for a warm cup of sweet tea was reward aplenty for Carrie, the stimulating conversation a bonus.

A PERFECT DAY

CHAPTER TWENTY-FOUR

The Bisphan Concert was to remain in Carrie's mind forever as her first, full-size recognition. Pumped up by the recent success, she proceeded to publish about fifty songs, among them *A Book of Seven Songs, A Book of Eleven Songs,* and a twelfth book waited in abeyance.

Carrie's music had universal appeal. The songs ranged from love songs, songs of optimism and philosophy, lullabies, and songs of nature to sacred and semi-sacred songs, convivial, and encore songs, dialect songs and special songs for mothers and children numbering more than three hundred.

Within her manuscripts, she poured words of love generated by her memories of Dr. Bond, and her adoration of Hubbard. It did not matter where she traveled, or the number of accolades thrown her way, Hubbard remained indelibly carved on her heart.

Although mentally she acknowledged Hubbard's characteristics of womanizing, emotionally she accepted him for what he was and for the undivided time he allocated her when together.

On her concert tours, she continued to make stopovers in East Aurora. Oftentimes, she never got off the train. Instead, Elbert boarded, and they traveled on to New York

City where they became lost in the flux and flow of life, love, and togetherness.

The train had its own rhythm lulling Elbert into thoughtful trance. "A woman who can always love will never grow old...in years or in boredom," murmured Elbert time and again, his eyes intense.

Whispered endearments never grew old and solidified Carrie's assurance of love. She floated on a diaphanous cloud.

"There are many loves, Elbert—the love of a mother, a wife..., and a close friend," she added reluctantly, not wanting to include the word, **mistress**.

"Yes, of course you're right, but these loves safeguard many charms. Serenity and peace is written in your face, Carrie, an after-spring, and you will know an after-summer as well."

Elbert disciplined his love until it became an unconscious art. In the street, at a fine dinner, in the lobby of the busiest hotels, he practiced being professional. Kisses for Carrie were showered on her behind doors, behind the doors of separate accommodations. Then Hubbard's admiration and love exuded from his every prose and posture. The beneficence of his lifetime of work would move in a large sweep to Carrie's favor, and Carrie's favor would move in a large leap from her normal characteristics of morality. She felt like warm mercury in his presence. Nonetheless, sometimes she resented his knowledge of her flesh and her vulnerability, but not enough to back away from the heat.

There are times when sanity plays no part in one's life and the time she spent with Elbert was one of them. Brains could not stand up against the muscles that moved under his clothes in a way that made Carrie feel quite warm. Feeling his skin next to her skin never became old. Feeling his heart pounding against her breasts as they lay in age-old repose, Elbert's head tucked into her neck, eclipsed all worries; all worldly cares slid into a vacuum, and she and Elbert were alone in a delicious world.

"You're my wonder of wonders, a delicate fairy, a moon

goddess, a gossamer wing," Elbert whispered. "I love you, Carrie."

"Yes," she said, her voice sounding like the rustle of velvet. She wanted to stop the wonderful words pouring from his mouth, but she could not; she had been in denial of a soul mate too long.

"You must know that I die with the waiting and the wanting of you," he said, his throat tight.

Carrie smiled softly. "And I, you, Mr. Hubbard."

Although financially independent now, Carrie's name was on the safety deposit box into which Hubbard plowed large sums of cash.

A frown crossed her face, drawing her brows together. "That's not necessary. My composing and publishing business is financially solvent, and I enjoy a multitude of pleasures."

Nonetheless, Carrie enjoyed the intrigue of having a lover. What's more, never more would she have to endure the pain of poverty, or tramp through parboiled streets in peasant clothing to sell her music, or through blasts of bone-rattling wind off Lake Michigan, wearing threadbare coats. She could sink these memories into her best-forgotten cellar of memoirs.

***

As if to underline in bold her happiness, Mrs. Frank MacKay of London invited Carrie to come to London and pay all her expenses plus a hundred dollars. Fred advised Carrie of the invitation by cablegram, while she was on yet another New York City rendezvous.

In her suite, she read the message on a day, which dawned all aglow in vibrant blue and swashed with transparencies of white, as if applied with a fine sable brush.

"Sail? To a foreign country, Elbert?" Her voice squeaked with excitement, inviting encouragement.

"You must do that; you've hit your stride, Carrie. Not many artists are acknowledged world-wide." He wished to keep his reputation for instilment of confidence intact. But praise and accolades for Carrie were forthcoming without a second thought.

"Would you come with me," she asked with her eyes as well as speaking softly. Perhaps her fear of traveling alone on such an odyssey was overbearing her reasoning.

"To leave my Roycrofters right now is out of the question," he said sympathetically. "What with new orders, new apprentices, and another building going up, I'm sorely needed at home. At another time and place, I'd shed the whole community for an ocean voyage with you. This trip is simply bad timing." He reached out and drew her to him, smoothing her blond hair, and breathing hard with the mental struggle. "I'll miss you terribly, Carrie."

Carrie was irked beyond reason; all the while knowing he spoke with the veracity of a responsible overseer. Well, he would not find her in a state of brooding annoyance. She loved him for what he was, and not for what he was not.

Carrie negotiated the long ocean voyage without incident, and was impressed to find that MacKay lived in a grand mansion belonging to a Russian Prince and located on Grosvenor square. Mrs. MacKay, exquisitely statuesque, was one of the most popular American women in the Royal Set in the early decades of the twentieth century.

On the designated day, Carrie was shown to the drawing room where she was advised that Mr. Caruso was singing on the program, also. She was struck with terror to sing in the same performance as the Italian tenor, one of the greatest opera singers of all time. She breathed deeply and stood tall with dignified elegance hoping the stance would make a statement. At least it was a present fear; it was less dreadful than the wild imaginings she would have had, had she been pre-informed.

She wore a white lace dress for the concert, the material for which had been given to her by a friend, but she had made it herself. The lace was bountiful as well as beautiful so she did not feel as homemade as usual for one reason or another, and she enjoyed the delicious feeling. On her ears and around her neck she wore pale blue topaz in fine gold settings, a gift from Hubbard. A radiant luster would be added to her natural talents tonight. She was in a zone...on top of the world.

The delicious feeling lasted only until she had time to survey her surroundings; she saw a picture she would never forget. She gasped in hesitation. There were shimmering lights, garlands, and masses of flowers festooned around the ceiling and balustrade. Carrie, having walked up the magnificent white marble stairs, now beheld the music room, a bower of beauty with a swathe of flowers around the ceiling. Grand rose trees were in bloom and arranged so that their sprays ran over the doors and windows. At the end of this room was a stage banked for about three feet from the floor with white, pink, and blue hydrangea blossoms. A gleaming gilt piano was in the center of the stage, and in the middle of the music room placed about four feet apart were exquisitely carved gilded chairs.

The superb ambience astounded her. How she wished Hubbard were in attendance for support. Feeling acutely uncomfortable, she never needed him more, or felt less self-assured. *She's a plain, angular woman, who sings plain angular songs,* danced in three-quarter time through her stage-struck mind. The hurting words held the subtly mocking cadence of *nah, nah,*

nah, nah, nah, nah of kindergarten days. Although she knew it was an artless comparison, she could not shake it.

Carrie wondered why the seating was placed so far apart, but when she looked at the audience, she discovered that the chairs were arranged so the magnificent trains of the women's gowns could be spread out properly to show their beauty. She looked down at her own gown. It was the finest she had ever owned, but reflected on its simplicity compared to the women of the court. Richness reflected in every movement of the gathering audience.

Her eyes brimmed with tears. She took deep breaths. Carrie reminded herself that her riches consisted not in the extent of her possessions and extensive wardrobe, but in the fewness of her wants. A clutching longing reasserted itself for the presence of Hubbard who always made her feel as if she were a crown jewel, a finely set latticework of diamonds that fused their affections.

When had her independence metamorphosed into a reliance on Elbert? It was the longing of the human heart for another. It was the flower needing the warm sun, the tree needing spring rain.

Lights from massive, crystal chandeliers made the women's jewels shine like stars in fairyland. Carrie blinked, adjusted her eyes. Mrs. MacKay was magnificent in white satin with three ostrich feathers in her hair and the most gorgeous diamond ring Carrie had ever seen. She had been given to understand that this was the gown in which MacKay had been presented to King Edward and Queen Alexandria. Carrie found herself gratefully sunk into the nearest chair until her performance.

The only recognition Carrie received at the concert was from the late Joseph Choate, Ambassador from the United States to the Court of St. James. Aside from his words, the evening slipped away as a most terrible experience. Why had she not been worldly enough to realize the Big Me — Little You attitude of a monarchy? The cold intelligentsia of court habitu, and their stereotyped mannerisms were affectations beyond Carrie's precepts. She had gone from deliriously happy upon arrival to hurt feverishly upon leaving, the experience disappointing and unnerving.

Afterwards, she settled into a small, one-horse shay, and for fifty cents, she was driven home to Russell Square where she climbed four flights of stairs to a cold, cramped room. This too, she would rise above. It reminded her of the abject years of denial in the walk-ups in Chicago. The adversities visited upon her at that time lay as heavily as any hardship she had ever known. However, she realized that the greatest affliction of life is never to be afflicted, and to know the satisfaction of principle derived from that condition. Wearily, she massaged her temples.

Still, she had an excellent write-up in a British Newspaper.

> Anything like a true English grasp of the American variety of humor has been many times declared impossible; especially has American dialect humor been adjudged incomprehensible to the British intellect.
>
> By at least one American humorist has this attitude recently been declared mistaken, at least as regards dialect humor of a certain kind.
>
> Mrs. Carrie Jacobs-Bond, songwriter and composer in London, found the supposedly stolid Britishers just as ready to laugh at and with her quaint stories as to appreciate the pathos and sweetness of her love songs, or keep time to the stirring measures of her children's melodies. Particularly among the men and women of

the London clubs did she meet with appreciation and encouragement of most inspiring order.

Mrs. Bond, who crossed the ocean in May to sing at a musicale given by Mrs. Frank MacKay, was agreeably surprised at the ready comprehension of ideas and thoughts essentially American everywhere received.

The Color Line, a Negro song monologue, was accorded enthusiastic applause in many quarters. The famous tenor, Caruso, who also took part in the MacKay program, was among the first to offer felicitations. The duchess of Somerset, Mr. And Mrs. Forbes Robertson, Lady Alexander, Lady Bancroft, Olga Nethersole, David Bispham, Sir James and Lady Bryce, and Mr. And Mrs. Cheatham-Tompson also succumbed as readily to the wit and humor, and to the pathos and tenderness of the Chicago writer and composer, and with them laughed a host of other notables and society folk of all kinds and varieties.

Such are the ways of the world, thought Carrie. She needed press even if the event heralded in the newspapers was not what she had experienced.

"What startled me," she wired Fred and Elbert, "is the first impression of imperiousness in royal circles. While their eyes shine with attempted courtesy, one feels no commonizing electricity."

A PERFECT DAY

CHAPTER TWENTY-FIVE

Upon Carrie's arrival in her homeland, American Actress, Margaret Anglin, a cool sophisticate, bold and unconventional, who marcelled her hair and wafted a cigarette holder, sponsored Carrie for three recitals at her theatre, the Bijou, in New York City. Although Anglin was polarized from Carrie's conservative manners, Carrie felt the comfort and hypnotism of being home again. These concerts netted her several hundred dollars, and she gained worthwhile publicity, including plenty of press from *The Philistine*.

Hubbard had paced with concern until Carrie's return. Although Ms. Anglin sent her personal publicity man to Carrie, and had him write about all her musical affairs, Carrie's coverage by Elbert was the uplift of all time.

She now started incorporating the sketches of the *My Old Man* series to vary her program and remove it from the monotony of piano renditions. Her writings about the Old Man were figments of her imagination. She knew no individual such as the old-fashioned man, but she felt his presence as if his soul was crying out to be recognized, to be heard.

She did know her son, Fred. It was at this time, when her career was soaring that she found Fred consumed with deep depression and had to have complete rest for two weeks. Carrie empathized so deeply with him that she felt a thunder shake her. She had never seen him look like this: in his eyes, the blue fires of intelligence had been doused, seemingly forever.

"Allow your mind to fly, Fred. You can find peace through

an endless variety of imagination. It's a luxury for your mind," advised Carrie, who had been down the black path of morass countless times, her mind muddied, and the devil wanting her soul.

Fred, although striking to look at, tall, blonde, and athletic, viewed her out of vacant eyes, his muscles constricted like ice.

To spare Fred additional stress, while he was gone, she moved again to a space of 5000 sq. ft. in the old Colonnade Building and had it all organized when the old Fred emerged from his damp den of emptiness as a young lion ready for the hunt. Fred reminded Carrie of the materializing butterflies she so much enjoyed in Grandfather Davis's gardens—Frank's explanation of the difference between Monarchs and the Southwest Queen butterflies. A deluge of debilitating recollections followed so many pleasant thoughts. She would not dwell on a painful past, however. Her path was now onward.

***

Growing, growing, growing, they moved to another unit of the Colonnade Building where they occupied a unit of 8000 sq. ft. The new orientation perked Fred with fresh enthusiasm. The unexplainable metaphysics of the human mind were testy, if not downright unsettling. Although the volatility of Fred's mind was an enigma, Carrie moved swiftly through the ensuing days with many measures of applause for her son's flagging, genetic nature. She prayed his new placidness would not evaporate.

By 1911, at age 48, Carrie had developed the support and friendship of many influential, powerful, and famous people, including French actress, Sarah Bernhardt. Carrie admired Bernhardt's self-assurance and flamboyant style of acting: relying on lavish decors, exotic costumes, and pantomime acts, during which her great, dark eyes rolled with comedic intent.

A PERFECT DAY

Margaret Anglin, a close friend now, again arranged for Carrie to come to New York for appearances with the Vaudeville group. The early winter show season was commencing.

"You must do this, darlin'," Anglin said with a great wave of her cigarette holder, the smoke trailing behind effectively hypnotizing. "Your audience is waiting."

Again, Carrie incorporated the *Old Man* series to give variety to her programs. In the ensuing eight years, she would create fifty-nine compositions, not knowing how or why, but she warmed to it.

In her first appearance in New York City, she was on stage with Helen Keller, who after conquering deafness and in spite of being blind, lectured to raise money for the American Foundation for the Blind. Helen's courage, faith, and optimism in the face of such overwhelming disabilities had a profound effect on Carrie. Carrie underscored Helen's accomplishments as the same symbol that fulfilled *her* potential as well as others.

"Life is either a daring adventure or nothing," Helen often said. "I thank God for my handicaps, for through them I have found myself, my work, and my God."

Amen, thought Carrie. If it were not for the difficulties thrown into my path, I too would not have found my work, my God, and myself.

Remember only the good times, and you will always be happy, Carrie, Frank had told her, and he was so right.

Also sharing the stage was Ernest Thompson Seton, American writer and artist. He interpreted nature for children, as in, *Wild Animals I Have Known*, and organized the *Woodcraft Indians*, a precursor of the Boy Scouts.

Carrie signed a contract for three months. In poor health, her own depression continued to be blight, but every consideration was shown her. She was allowed to work every other week. What snowmelt is to rivers' flow, thoughtfulness was to humanity. Though it is trifling, scattered along life's pathway, the benefits are inconceivable. Carrie was able to maintain and her performances were energetic, especially if Elbert Hubbard was in the audience as he often was.

"A cruel vagary of fate it would be to keep me away, Carrie. You are my true hero, and my fool's fantasy, which I will entertain as long as I live." Dressed in loose-fitting jacket, ribbon tie, breeches, and brogan boots, Hubbard could be spotted easily in any crowd, and he ingested the recognition as if it were a life-sustaining victual. Carrie, in turn, ingested his endearments, her rampantly pounding heart rendering her as speechless as a tongue-tied adolescent. The sound of his voice coming from a closed throat thawed her cool, public exterior, and her mind drifted from amazement to amusement with this wonderful man.

The New York City theatre had its greatest audience at noon. It was really a playhouse for busy employees who came in at lunchtime. She played *A Perfect Day* with an orchestra, a real orchestra. She had never played with an orchestra in her life, and thinking about doing so without a rehearsal was more than she could stand. Then Hubbard would exchange courtesies putting her frazzled nerves at ease.

When she arrived at the theatre, to her horror there was a large sign hanging over the door: *Carrie Jacobs-Bond, The Grand Old Lady of Song.* Her shoulders slumped in outrage. Helen Keller was eighteen younger than she was, that is true, but Sarah Bernhardt was eighteen years older than she was. Neither was touted in such a manner...*Grand Young Lady of Verse, or Grand Old, Old Lady of Improvisation.*

Extremely upset about being dubbed with the debilitating label, Carrie convinced the manager remove it, but he thought of her as another Gladstone, who was known as the **Grand Old Man**. Gladstone, at that time, was about thirty years older than she was, and that is what she found infuriating. Besides, Gladstone had been the Prime Minister of Great Britain, who championed Home Rule for Ireland, was a political engine, and favored fine wine from French Chateaus. Carrie viewed herself as simple, domestic home brew.

After a few years in Vaudeville, Fred heard her telling the **Grand Old Lady of Song** episode, and he related the same story to her friends. "Yes, the funniest part of the story was that the sign had been taken off the front of the theatre, but on the draw curtain, every night from that time on, just before mother's act came on, the words were flashed: **Carrie Jacobs-Bond, Grand Old Lady of Song**.

Finding humor in given situations was a gift from Fred's celestial angel. Carrie was sure. He knew how to chuckle deeply and with lightning speed, especially if the stories were of his mother.

Carrie's humor handling life's vicissitudes was to be tested mightily in the ensuing months.

A PERFECT DAY

CHAPTER TWENTY-SIX

While yet in Los Angeles in 1915 on an extended recuperation period, Carrie, upon an inexplicable urging, decided to go east and visit The Roycrofters in East Aurora. This last visit was April 26, just four days before Hubbard started on the fateful journey that was to carry him to his death.

Carrie had come unexpectedly again, and word was sent around, 'Carrie has come, and she is going to sing for us.'

"Are you on vacation, Carrie?" Elbert inquired softly. "Do you know how desirable you are, and how much I've missed you?" They stood on the green, green campus under the memorable apple tree.

"No," she said watching him with a sense of wonder. "Something prompted me to visit the Roycrofters so you wouldn't forget me." She smiled, lifting her eyes coyly.

"I wouldn't have forgotten you in a million years...Never... No way...Ever. I carry a place for you forever right here," he said scooping her hand and putting it over his heart.

His fleeting look spoke a compliment. Carrie's insides waxed aquiver studying the brilliant amber chips that ruled his dark eyes.

For the program, she wore a peplum jacket of maroon velvet over a peppermint, barbershop-striped skirt. Although the day was bright and sunny, Carrie wished that it could be one month later so she could repeat the matchless apple blossom day of time past. Instead, she gave the program in the *Chapel* and included the *Old Man* series, which she half sang and half spoke. *Captain of the Broomstick Brigade* was presented for the many employees' children present. Not wanting to be intrusive or create undue gossip, her stay was brief, just a few hours. She popped up her sun umbrella and was hurrying away, anxious to say goodbye to Elbert, but he could not be found.

She located Bert out on the campus. "Where in the world is your father?" She sensed something then and hung on his reply.

"I'm afraid he doesn't want to say goodbye to you," he answered roughishly. "He left the music room with tears in his eyes, and the last I saw of him, he was going on his horse in the direction of his cabin. He called over his shoulder: 'Say goodbye to Carrie'."

Carrie's heart tugged. Her relationship with Elbert was the best that could be maintained in light of his divorce and subsequent marriage—both of them recognized their plight. As the afternoon sun beat down with real heat, Carrie dejectedly walked away. Not even the wind could find its way to her sorrow. The dismal barking of dogs was answered amiably by a robin's song. The air hung empty with no other sounds, like the hole in Carrie's heart that she would never allow to be filled by anyone but Hubbard. The awaiting train stood glinting in the afternoon glare, its heavy sides heaving with escaping steam. Elbert's face continued to spin before her. She wanted all of him desperately; she wanted none of him logically. But, who loves with their mind?

Hubbard later wrote:

> The Roycrofters hear many good songs and stories, but nothing more pleasing has ever occurred in our Chapel than the recent performance of Carrie Jacobs-Bond.

✻✻✻

A PERFECT DAY

Hubbard's fame and fortune, his bunkum and blarney, went on unabated until the month of May, when he and Alice embarked on a trip to Europe. Hubbard hoped to speed up the peace process, he told the press, "By having a word with the Kaiser," a statement so true to his strong self-image.

Elbert and Alice Hubbard went down aboard the British Steamship, Lusitania, May 7, 1915, when a German torpedo ripped through its hull. Avalanches of condolences were sent to his son, Elbert Hubbard II. Death suggested that Hubbard had attained the status of a cultural messiah. His children received more than forty thousand letters of condolence; Carrie received a knife to her chest.

At her office in Chicago, she wrote in her diary.

> The next time I went to East Aurora, it was to attend the funeral services for Elbert and Alice Hubbard, where hundreds of friends gathered to show their love and respect. It was a time of appalling grief. We all stood with bowed heads, and tears streaming down our cheeks beside the outstanding memorial stone placed in the garden of the Roycroft shops to remind strangers of the man whose friends could never forget him, friends to whom no marker was needed to remember his many kindnesses.

Carrie's grief knew no beginning and no end; it grew exponentially daily.

"No, no, no," she exclaimed in funereal denial, her head on her folded arms, resting on her desk. Then she sat in silence, trying to conjure up scenarios that made some sense.

"Why, why, why?" She asked herself, edging her nerves further.

She scoured her soul with what-ifs that may have changed Elbert's fate. What if, long ago, she had insisted on marriage? What if she had pursued him to his cabin in the woods? Would the rendezvous have changed his mind about the sea voyage? Her exhaustive mind searching was degenerating, and she knew she could not allow herself to lapse into the spirit-killing crater of depression. She would remember the happy times as she had done after her father's death, her mother's death, grandfather's death, and Frank's demise. Although repetitious, the wounds gaped as new slashes each time. She clung to Fred trembling. How much longer could she survive in a world that sometimes seemed to be too cruel to be endured?

A few months later, an exquisitely bound book was sent to Carrie from the Roycroft Shop. It contained the original manuscript of a story that was found among Elbert's treasures; the script he had written about her evidently after the last recital at the Roycroft Shop.

> Carrie Jacobs-Bond was along Roycroft way, and as usual when Carrie came to East Aurora, she sang for us. Carrie does not pretend she has an operatic voice, so she sings and talks, but she certainly can play the piano, and Carrie has personality. She is young. Just my age. Time has tempered her, fate has buffeted her, destiny has dashed her dreams, but she has cashed in all her experiences, so today you behold her. All her actions are regal, graceful, gracious, chartered with honesty, illumined by intelligence, flavored by success, and that is all success is good for...Just to flavor. The think in its pure state is nauseous.
>
> Carrie played and sang songs of her own, and one of these songs was *A Perfect Day*.

A PERFECT DAY

When I hear that song, I think I hear the notes of a robin singing in the tree of my mother's dooryard, years, and years ago. It must have been a perfect day when *Perfect Day* was written, for her song has been more widely sold than other piece of music since Gilbert and Sullivan launched *Pinafore.* If you will agree not to mention it, *A Perfect Day* has passed its five million mark, and has brought its composer thousands and thousands of dollars. Not too bad for a lone, lorn widow.

***

That same winter, Carrie again served the Santa Fe Railroad and journeyed west. After returning to the Hotel Alexandria in Los Angeles, she wrote the following poem in memoriam of Hubbard.

> I once had a garden
> Where sympathy grew.
> I plucked a soul
> The soul was you.
> And then further on
> Where the flowers were few,
> I looked for hours
> Thru the damp and the dew,
> Till at last I found
> Where devotion grew.
> I plucked a heart,
> Twas the heart of you.
> And still further on
> Where life's flowers grew,
> I stood for hours

In the damp and the dew
Till at last, I found
Where my ideal grew.
At last, I found it,
Twas my twin soul—you.

✼✼✼

    Carrie's flair for writing was equal to Hubbard's. In the genre of poetry, she, indeed, outstripped him. The inevitability of their attraction for each other was due to their symbiotic talents and cultural pursuits. From these elements, there spread a deep intimacy, the kind only lovers can hold in their heart.

    Carrie, who had fought depression the greater part of her life, determined now to wrap her heart in a leather gauntlet that not even a desert thorn could pierce.

A PERFECT DAY

CHAPTER TWENTY-SEVEN

Her heart swaddled, and her affairs becoming financially enhanced, she determined to stay at the Hollywood Hotel for a while, and leave Fred in charge of business in Chicago. In addition, what would it hurt to indulge in an uncharacteristic whim? She needed a divergence to keep the ghost of Hubbard at arm's length, the fete a daily struggle. The sensual indulgences she had known with Elbert would now morph into corporal indulgences by pampering herself.

She wrote to Lulu and Esther in Seattle. "It is so nice to have both of you closer now and settled on the West Coast. We must visit often. You need to be the first to know that I am going to invest in an Electric. Can you believe that?"

In no time at all, Carrie had a response from the outrageous redheads. "Yes, we can believe that you would do that, and think that it is quite wonderful. Being unadventurous is boring, boring, boring. Be assured that we will be visiting you soon."

✷✷✷

With expendable income, she purchased her first automobile in 1916, one of those electric machines with the big top that could be put up and down, and bold electric lights on both sides. It was a surprise for Fred, who was coming to California, and she was practicing every day. She intended to show up at the station to meet him, meet him with pride of purchase, and prowess of abilities.

The June day was extraordinary, the gardenias hanging in

fragrant abundance on roadside trees when, for the first time, she drove downtown. More than a year after Elbert's death, the grip of his passing was loosening, but would never slip away entirely. Waves of grief would encompass Carrie at any given moment at any given place. She shook her head to release Hubbard thoughts and was crossing one of the busiest streets in Los Angeles when a police officer held up his hand indicating for her to stop. Not being comfortable in the crowd, she did not stop just where she should have, and her electric went over the crossing by about ten feet.

Putting her hand over her mouth, she croaked, "Oh my God."

The police officer rushed up to her in uniformed drama and ordered, "Back up." The leather bill of his cap reflected the sun, hid his eyes, and accented a bullish chin.

Carrie sat bolt upright and looked back, the ostrich feathers in her hat bending and stretching. She knew with all certainty that it was going to be an impossible thing for her to do, to back up with any assurance of being able to stop before she hit someone.

"I can't," she protested. To her chagrin, the words came out whiney.

By this time, a sizeable crowd was collecting in curiosity.

Finally, the police officer said, "You will back up," he insisted, "or I'll take you to jail."

By this time, the jail seemed like a haven to Carrie, so she rejoined, "Get in the car; I'll take you there."

She did, expecting of course, to find a kind judge sitting on the bench waiting to hear her story, a credible account of purest circumstance. Carrie figured that she had probably saved someone's life by not backing up. She never had been in jail

A PERFECT DAY

before, and upon arrival found that she was to stay there until 2:00 p.m., because that was the time the judge came in.

"Well. What are you going to do with me now?" Carrie asked weakly, her gloved hand nervously clutching at a wee, beaded bag.

"You can bail or stay here," the police officer responded.

Carrie's bail was $5.00; she did not have that much in her purse. "Can't you allow me to leave my machine?" She did not remember that it took ten cents to get to Hollywood on the streetcar, and she was going to be penniless plus tax by the time she got out of this predicament.

"No." the police officer declared.

"I happen to have on a diamond ring. Would you consider this?"

"No."

With that, a kind-hearted police officer from the back of the room stepped up and said. "Madam, I'll lend you five dollars until this afternoon." His eyes were crinkled with amusement, yet embracing a measure of empathy.

How often Carrie wished she had the name of that police officer. It seemed they were all joking with each other about her plight. The poor police officer who had brought her to jail had probably never had the least idea of doing such a thing, but he could not do anything else with the crowd laughing as they were.

After accepting the bailout, she thought she had better telephone for a lawyer. She knew only one in Los Angeles: Carrie called the office of Albert Stevens, a milquetoast man who sputtered spontaneously when he was stressed. He must have thought Carrie had been arrested for some terrible crime, for he arrived at the jail breathless to see what he could do for her. He tried not to let Carrie see him smile when she told him.

"Now don't be upset," he advised. "Just get in your Electric, drive home and forget it."

Carrie drove to the home of her friend, Helen Hawks, the same gentle woman who had befriended Carrie numerous times since her arrival in Los Angeles, and indeed, had entertained Carrie in her home when Carrie found the words for *A Perfect Day*, which fact Carrie would never forget. In the throes of disgrace, Carrie told Helen about the scandalous thing that had happened to her, and stayed with her until evening.

When Carrie arrived at the Hollywood Hotel at 7:00 p.m., the front desk attendant said, "Mrs. Bond where have you been all day, and what in the world has happened? Reporters have been waiting for hours but finally got tired and went away. What is it all about?"

Only then, did she babble, "Mercy sakes, the newspapers, the newspapers!" Carrie wished that she could vanish into nothingness. Sure enough, the next morning in large letters in the Times was a cartoon of a fighting woman in an Electric with a hand as big as the car held up in front. There it was, **Carrie Jacobs-Bond Arrested**. In crushingly small type, the reason was stated. Carrie was cut to pieces with an agony akin to dying. She wished that she could feel the magic touch of her grandfather, healing words from her mother (maybe), reassurances from Frank, a light quip from Elbert, or humor from Fred. Anything. Anything at all, she thought, searching for an anchor.

She called her friend, Helen, and said, "Would you go to Grossmont with me. I'm leaving in the morning."

"For how long?" Helen asked, not being one that cared to be out of the city for any measurable amount of time.

"I have no idea," Carrie told her. "I just need you to come."

"Well," she said, "I can get away for a few days."

A PERFECT DAY

Carrie, herself, hid away for two weeks.

Back in Chicago, Fred, as he was riding the bus to his office, opened the Chicago Tribune, and saw the headlines: *Carrie Jacobs-Bond Arrested in Los Angeles.* He was so excited, he could not read; he could barely breathe. He handed the paper to the man who sat next him, and said, "Would you mind telling me what this article is all about? I don't feel well."

The stranger read the story of the poor mother in disgrace.

Fred laughed until his sides were sore. Oh, how he laughed.

He may have thought it was funny, but it was many years before the incident looked so funny to Carrie.

Of course, Fred wired a sympathetic message, but he immediately appreciated the value of the publicity of his mother's dilemma to The Bond Shop. It was not until 1922, when he and Carrie were the guests of honor at The Advertising Club of Los Angeles that Fred revealed he had been responsible for all the publicity she had received. He told the story of how he had obtained permission of the Chicago Tribune to reprint that story, and how he had copies of it sent out everywhere.

Subsequently, Carrie and Fred received letters from England and quantities of mail from the within the U.S.A. Many letters asked for money, asked to buy for them pianos, and other trifles. By the time the story had been published a few times, the editors had made Carrie one of the richest women in America, and the consequence was the flood of letters with their impossible requests.

In later years, she was heard to say, "I'm acquainted now with the absolute need for publicity, but I don't like it any better than I did twenty-five years ago. Of course, the publicity I had was of an innocent nature and funny, probably much funnier because I took it so seriously."

A PERFECT DAY

CHAPTER TWENTY-EIGHT

To fight depression, Carrie traveled abroad accompanied by Esther Fairbanks, whose "boss," Lulu, at the *Alaskan Weekly* gave her a leave of absence. In 1917, while the whole world was at war, she booked concerts in Europe and the near East. While entertaining in Jerusalem, a city quaking and besieged not only by war but also by dreadful oppression of its people by the Kaiser, she had the occasion on a bright moonlight night to hear the marching feet of soldiers. After a late evening of entertaining, Carrie took to her hotel room. Dressed in fuzzy bathrobe and slippers, she looked down from her fourth-floor window. There she observed twelve military men marching along, singing *A Perfect Day* unaware that its composer was above them. Her breathing quickened and she hugged herself at the wonder of it all. "Come see, Esther," she said in awe.

"You composed the song in the Mohave Desert, and here we are thousands of miles away, only a stone's throw from the Syrian Desert, and your song is reverberating around the world," said Esther, her red curls bobbing as she shook her head up and down.

***

Carrie's tour took her to Turkey in July 1917. For centuries, the ancient city of Istanbul was known as Constantinople, and still was at the time of Carrie's tour. After the defeat of the Ottomans in World War I and the subsequent creation of the Turkish Republic, the City was known as Istanbul. Although it is no longer a capital city, Istanbul is still the cultural center of modern Turkey. Carrie found the city straddles the Bosporus, a narrow strait that divides the continents of Europe and Asia—a strategic location that has made it the largest city and seaport of the Turkish Republic.

Dressed for warm weather, Carrie wore a white eyelet gown and carried an aurora borealis scarf over her arm when attending a Turkish wedding, which was held at the Blue Mosque built by Sultan Achmet in 1616. What a surprise she had. Amidst all the colorful pomp and grandeur, she found an Islam Turkish man whistling ***A Perfect Day*** when he welcomed her. Something primitive within her stirred a prideful acknowledgement of creativity, but her country upbringing settled the stir with built-in defenses against the devil's sin of arrogance.

Esther squeezed Carrie's elbow in silent admiration.

***

Yet on tour that same summer, she performed in Edinburgh, Scotland. Fascinated with the ancient city, Carrie studied everything from its geography to its architecture to its cultural aspects. She found that Edinburgh lies on the southern shores of the Firth of Forth, a long arm of the North Sea.

Not surprising, her concert was given at the church of St. Giles in Parliament Square on High Street. The church was historically famous, for this is where John Knox, the Protestant reformer, often preached. Although the concert was well received, Carrie felt diminished in the hanging atmosphere of history.

Having a desire to shop while in such a celebrated place, Carrie and Esther traveled to New Town, which is connected with the old Edinburgh by bridges, and the Mound, an artificial causeway. On the Mound Carrie found Scotland's two, most

A PERFECT DAY

famous art centers—the National Gallery and the Royal Scottish Academy. Making some irresistible purchases, she gave the clerk the address for mailing them.

The young man, snappy and alert, asked, "Do you happen to be the Carrie Jacobs-Bond who wrote *Poor Little Lamb?*"

"I am," Carrie answered, and was so pleased not to hear *A Perfect Day*.

He replied, "Oh, I have sung THAT song for years."

What kind of powerful undertow was she caught in? The song was gathering the whole world into its heartfelt melody and sentiment. She felt a kick of pleasure to be in this historical country while the world was at war, yet to be recognized for a peaceful contribution.

"I'm not surprised at the global recognition," Esther said.

Carrie had turned to Esther for companionship, and was inordinately pleased by her reinforcement, as if value was added, an extra piece of cake, a dollar found on the pavement.

***

Pleasures multiplied when, in England at Epsom Downs, a municipal borough 15 miles southwest of London, she found that the name *Epsom* salts comes from its mineral springs. She searched her memory to recollect if she had ever had such lessons in historic value on her visitations to various cities in the U.S.A.

She visited the thoroughbred race tack which was a flat course made exclusively of grass. In the United States, Carrie knew the famous races were known as the Belmont Stakes, (1867), the Kentucky Derby (1875), and the Preakness Stakes (1873), collectively called the Triple Crown. Now she learned that in England, they are known as England's Gold Cup at the Royal Ascot (1807), and the Derby at Epsom Downs (1780).

As she and Esther stood at the empty Epsom track in 1917, she could almost hear the cheering crowd, the heated narration, and the pounding of horses' hoofs on turf.

It was late afternoon before she arrived back at her hotel, and she found that dinner was being served picnic style on the campus. Stepping into a pair of suede culottes and a white shirt, she was ready for the occasion. In queue for the buffet, she heard her song being played. There, across the green, she saw a crippled soldier playing on a coronet.

"If I had felt any better, I would have been comatose. Of course, I had to go thank him. As I stepped out of that line, three other people stepped out and followed me, one of whom was Thaddeus Rich, the concertmaster of the Philharmonic Orchestra, completely out of character wearing a pair of loose trousers and an open-neck shirt."

"Aren't you Carrie Jacobs-Bond?" He asked his voice tense.

"Yes," she turned hesitantly, then recognizing Rich. "Would you tell me true, if you were ever second fiddle in the orchestra?" Rich, round-faced and clean-shaven, always reminded Carrie of a pumpkin.

He laughed, recognizing the lexicon adage. "As a matter of fact, I was. I really was!"

During that trip to England, on a rare, star-spangled night in London, Carrie and Esther attended James Barrie's play **Shall We Join The Ladies?** Her song was referred to three times in the play, and one verse was sung. Thousands of miles from home, and carrying a yeoman's load of sorrow, her mouth twitched and broke into a smile. She was so uplifted that, at that moment in time, she could have spoke of many things, *shoes and ships and sealing wax, of cabbages and kings* came to mind.

***

A PERFECT DAY

While in Vienna, Carrie wrote in her diary.

I find that Austria is a small, mountainous country in central Europe, and is at the center of a great empire and one of the great powers of Europe. Its position at the middle of Europe makes it a center of trade, transportation, and culture. The Republic of Austria occupies the eastern end of the great mountain ranges of the Alps, and, very surprisingly to me, the high ranges of the Austrian Alps are glaciated.

The city of Vienna has retained a style that reflects its elegant and ornate past. For tourists and contract concert entertainers such as me, Vienna still has the trappings of an empire: Imperial Palace, or Hofburg, a great cathedral and other stately churches, government buildings, a university dating from 1365, and palatial hotels. I had the honor of entertaining in a magnificent opera house, and the audience was delightfully receptive. Such a heartfelt response I have had rarely, and from such musically educated listeners.

After all, Vienna is the home of the great Strauss Brothers, Johann the Elder, Johann The Younger, and Josef and Eduard. I must remind myself that I was only ten years old when the Strauss Brothers gave concerts in New York City and Boston.

Very impressively, the city is built on the slopes of the Vienna Woods, which descend to the Danube River in a series of four semicircular terraces. The awesome beauty is a magnet to all, but I could not live here because the average yearly temperature hovers only around 51 degrees, and the rainfall, heaviest in the summer months, is approximately 26 inches per year. My rheumatism and neuritis would flair up even worse than it does in Chicago.

This August morning at dawn, I heard, beneath the window of my empirical hotel, boys singing *A Perfect Day* to a marching beat. I looked out to see fifty or more sun-browned youths of about fourteen years marching like soldiers down the street. I knew they were Austrian boys on their vacation. They wore uniforms of brown leather knee pants, white shirts open at the throat, green woolen coats, sandals, and knives thrust into their leather belts, hats of fancy colors with jaunty feathers sticking up, and carried long, Alpine sticks. On their heads, those jaunty vibrant caps said howdy-do with every nod; they looked like shaving mugs to me, only larger. In about an hour, the boys returned, singing like soldiers who had won a battle. They were camped nearby and had been to a lake of icy water for their morning bath.

Tomorrow they would march again to some lovely spot, perhaps to climb a few miles from here. Thank God for youth, the pillars of tomorrow.

***

Carrie returned to Hollywood and Esther to her job in Seattle. Carrie found that *A Perfect Day* was used often during the First World War. There was a cartoon in the Stars & Stripes Newspaper that depicted a horrible trench in which a young soldier was holding a skillet over an alcohol flame so small you could hardly see it. In the skillet were an egg and a pathetic piece of bacon. In his other hand was an umbrella that he held up in a futile effort to ward off a downpour of rain. Notes were flying out from under that umbrella, and he was singing *The End Of A Perfect Day*.

The ironic play on her song left her anorexic because of the sympathy she felt for those in the trenches. Carrie was greatly surprised and grossly ashamed when she considered the debilitating lives of the doughboys compared to the advantaged life she lived. Some would never again know the comforts of home and all the bacon and eggs they wanted. The thought was weary and filled with frustration.

Her face showed drawn eyebrows, disbelief, anger, and empathy.

During the war, not all the depictions of A Perfect Day were pathetic. One evening that same year, Carrie was invited to a dinner at the beach in Los Angeles. She was slightly late, and as she arrived, she heard the last strains of *A Perfect Day* and good-hearted laughter. She was intrigued but somewhat embarrassed about going in, thinking that someone had written another parody on her song.

"When one has written a song and sung it to ten and twenty thousand soldiers, one is apt to view it a trifle seriously," she declared.

Everyone wanted to tell her at once what had happened. "This dinner is given for an Austrian musician composer who knows little of America's popular music. When your song was sung, Carrie, he stood up. When he had been standing for a few minutes, someone asked him, 'Why do you stand?'

"He answered, 'Am I the only one who stands up when your National Anthem is being played?'"

"Dear God in heaven," she cried, her tone struck with disbelief.

***

While all around her the world hung locked in a cloud of deadly war, she found promise, she found life. About the greatest thrill of all was when she sang in Washington D.C., and saw her name in electric lights for the first time, electric lights blazing down the street and reflecting on the pavement. She said to her nurse, "This is too much publicity; it's going to kill me."

However, the next night she told the chauffeur, "Be sure to drive up to the front of theatre. I want to know if I have been successful enough to warrant the lights being kept on."

Later she confessed to Fred, "That goes to show how proud we are, after all. You give the singing fat lady money, comfort, and catering…the lush life and she wants more. It's absolutely reprehensible."

The most impressive occasion that the song was sung was one time that she missed, but Fred did not. The intensity of the apex moment spoke volumes, and the description remained indelible in Carrie's soul. It was on the real Armistice Day, November 11, 1919. Fred was in New York; the town was wild with joy. At the Vanderbilt Hotel, he looked out the window when he heard men singing *The End of a Perfect Day*. They were forming a serpentine line, each man with his hands on the shoulders of the man in front. Thus, they started down Fifth Avenue. Back and forth, they went from the Plaza Hotel to 59th Street, and on the Washington Square. Fred joined the singing crowd, and had the exquisite joy of mingling with 100,000 people who were all wildly happy, and above all the din, thousands of people were singing *The End Of A Perfect Day*.

Carrie, upon hearing the story, said, "Did you sing, Fred?"

A change spread over his expression. "No, mother, I cried," his voice catching coarse.

A PERFECT DAY

CHAPTER TWENTY-NINE

Thanksgiving, 1920, came and the weather churned wicked. Old man winter arrived in Chicago shattering the autumnal routine. Everything from freezing rain to blinding snow sloughed off Lake Michigan. Carrie longed for her California friends, sun wrinkles and all.

Instead, she found herself in her Chicago office on Michigan Avenue, Walter Gale reclining in a buttery-soft, leather chair across from Carrie's desk. Together they mulled the tremendous strides made in Carrie's publishing business. There was a real sign on the boulevard. Joe Bidwell, his lightning smile revealing gleaming teeth, orchestrated seventeen employees sending out songs—perhaps as many as four hundred thousand a month.

Gale, threads of silver now mingled with dark hair insistently falling on his forehead, (his left hand pushing it back), laughingly said, "Would you like to sell another tenth interest in the Bond Shop?"

"Yes, I would," Carrie said, surprising even herself.

"What would you give?

"Would you consider eighty-five hundred dollars?" ($98,770.00 today)

A long, searching moment went by while the offer floated around Carrie's mind.

"Agreed," said Carrie, her breath becoming shallow.

Without a word, he nodded his head and drafted a check.

"What are you going to do with the money, Carrie?"

"I'm going to buy a home in California, something I'd hoped to do for many years."

Carrie, now fifty-seven years old and weary of the Midwest winters, longed for the warm sun on her rheumatic body.

***

She bought an existing home at 2042 Pinehurst Road, Hollywood, at that time, a suburb of Los Angeles in which there was no more than fifteen hundred people living. She named her new home *The End Of The Road* and opened the California Bond Shop, closing the Chicago Bond Shop, and thankful to shed the bitter winters in which the wind prowled and temperatures dived.

When Carrie moved to Hollywood, it was a bump of a village consisting of horse carts and dirt roads. There was one crossroad, Vermont Avenue, a shortcut from Los Angeles to Hollywood. It was not so short, as it was rough and bumpy, but always indulging because of its lovely trees.

The three months she spent at the Hollywood Hotel every winter for several years, probably saved her health, and certainly planted in her soul an enormous love for California.

Her standard Christmas card was of the three wise men, their reflection shimmering in a desert mirage.

> We all would like to send a gift,
> No matter if 'twere small,
> But sometimes, just remembering,
> Is the dearest gift of all.
> And so I am sending just a thought
> To journey down your way,
> To say "God Bless You, Loyal Friend,
> On Merry Christmas Day.

***

A PERFECT DAY

Carrie took sightseeing trips, leaving the Bond Shop in the capable hands of Fred.

Between the 1920's and 1940's when passenger steamers ran between Seattle and Alaska, Lulu rode them to gather stories. On several of Lulu's trips, Carrie joined the younger woman, now in her thirties. Wound up to see new country, they left Pier 48 in Seattle, sailed north through Puget Sound and on to Alaska.

"By the time we got to Seward, Lulu knew everybody in Ketchikan, Wrangell, Sitka, Juneau, Haines, Cordova, and Valdez, which, I found soon enough, was a typical trip for Lulu. Then she'd sashay through the territory to Fairbanks, which in those days was larger than Anchorage and the other major towns," said Carrie. "No one was a stranger to Lulu."

"If any Alaskan needs help at any time of the day or night, she is there to aid them. She's a marvelous person." Thus, spoke Carrie of her frequent guest at *End Of The Road*.

"I anticipate that Lulu will serve as chairman of the Alaska Committee for many years to come. She has a vested interest in each Alaskan and them in her," Carrie advised a journalist. "Each Christmas she helps take a collection for the Pioneers of Alaska living at their special home in Sitka."

Carrie faithfully read Lulu's column about Alaska and Alaskans for many years. It appeared in the Alaskan Weekly newspaper, which was published in Seattle. The weekly was crammed with interesting Alaskan news items and many people in Alaska and the Lower States subscribed to the periodical.

Carrie never tired of the spectacular beauty of The Land of the Midnight Sun, Alaska: Glacier Bay north of Juneau famous for its vast ice fields and fjord-like bays, the awesome Mendenall Glacier, the autumn salmon run, majestic Mt. McKinley at 20,320 ft., quaint villages, and great forests teeming with wildlife and white spruce, Alaska birch, black cottonwood, balsam, poplar, and aspen.

She experimented with all cuisines: baked salmon served on a bed of rice, surrounded by a cream sauce, fish eggs on twice-baked bread, flounder stuffed with onions and nuts, and pies oozing with fresh-picked wild berries.

***

Alaska was not to be the limitation of adventures. Carrie toured California like a sponge, soaking up all the varied and interesting sites the state had to offer. "For anyone who has the appreciation of what it means to wish all one's life that you had something," she said, "having never seen the thing that you wished for, and suddenly to find it twice your dreams and to live to see and own all the several things on that spot, it's indescribable."

For those who can appreciate such a moment, Carrie told the story of her first get-away-from-Hollywood house. All her life she had dreamed of a valley surrounded by voluminous mountain peaks and a way off in the distance, so far away that you could not hear the beating of the waves, she could view the wonderful ocean. Her wishes had not been extravagant, but had they been, the spot she found to build her home upon would have met all the requirements, but the view could not be bought for millions. However, she thought that a home could be built for $1,700.00, ($1,723,800.00 today), and it was.

She wanted medieval-looking metalwork on the doors, like the Roycroft Village of Elbert Hubbard. She would have her portals emblazoned with a vintage Hubbard motto: *The love you liberate in your work is the love you keep.* She envisioned the Arts and Crafts, which Hubbard espoused, the austere, rectilinear furniture, Spartan but still looking modern and working as well in urban lofts or Western cabins as it would in the tasteful interiors Carrie mind-created.

Her heart turned over with loneliness for Elbert. She still could not accept he was dead, and remembered how his mouth moved against her hair, treasured endearments whispered hoarsely, his perfect decorum and cool exterior when in public. She rubbed her arms in agitation. In his memory, her dining room would have a beamed ceiling, oak table and chairs, and a chestnut sideboard. She would not forget to add the color with wallpaper, textiles, art glass, and pottery. The home would embrace the memory of his reassuring voice. Yet, she shuddered at the thought of raising strutting peacocks and peahens in the true tradition of the Roycroft campus.

There were so many striking places between Los Angeles and the place that she was going to build, that Carrie determined that she would have fun in spite of her troubled life. In her diary, she wrote.

> Come along with me. We'll just skip along and stop but for an hour at the old Mission at San Juan Capistrano. Now for about fifteen miles we'll drive along the most scenic road on the ocean beach, and the first thing you know we'll be at the foot of a mountain that seems perpendicular, but it isn't.

How she wished that Dr. Bond or Hubbard could be at her side for viewing such grandeur; they would feel like lords of the manor. Of the two men, Dr. Bond would puff up with the new sights, sounds, and smells of the ocean side; he was the adventurer in time and space, and Hubbard the dreamer of arts and crafts. She would maintain these moments as memory-treasures.

Putting on a little more steam, (her diary read,) we fly up the side of the mountain, and stop; we gasp for breath. On a mesa, before our unbelieving eyes, stand the famous Torrey pines that have weathered the ocean's storms for no one knows how many hundreds of years.

The beauty of the scene cannot be fully grasped. It takes some time to realize all we view. The elasticity of the mind expands to meet the challenge of such grandeur.

Below, about five miles, is La Jolla, a lovely quiet spot with its remarkable coves and its caves, and the mysterious White Lady, and high up on the banks the most unusual houses built by Mrs. Heinrich, a far-sighted developer and architect. Beyond all the delightful scenery is San Diego with its Point Loma, the Coronado Beach, the vast protected bay, and the grand Pacific Ocean with its Mexican Islands all gleaming in the sun. Our minds and bodies are intimately inseparable in this setting. Time stands still, and peacefulness overcomes us as if water were gliding in gentle folds over rounded boulders in the stream.

When Carrie arrived in San Diego, she met two people who later in life became near and dear to her: Colonel and Mrs. Ed Fletcher. A retired military man, Fletcher dabbled in real estate, and bought up what was considered undesirable land. Fletcher carried a walking stick and was a very proper gentleman.

Fletcher and his wife took Carrie on a journey to a quaint place called Grossmont. This mountain was owned by Fletcher and was one of the dreams for which he was often darkly laughed at.

A PERFECT DAY

"Twenty years ago," Carrie related, "I heard him say quietly, his eyes intense, that some day there would be a theater on the Helix Mountain and, 'Mrs. Bond, you'll look right down into a lake from your lot.' People smiled tolerantly, but we now have a 6,000-seat theater on top of the Helix, one of the most astounding sights I have seen, and I do look down into a sparkling lake from the east room. So, after all, it doesn't pay to laugh at a dreamer, especially a practical dreamer for they are the people that make the world splendid."

CHAPTER THIRTY

Carrie and the Fletchers took a long breath and started to the top of the mountain location called Grossmont. They traveled around and around its sides, first up then down, and around again for several hundred feet and finally reached the summit and faced the ocean.

"How can I tell you of the glories of that sunset," she exclaimed brightly. "Think of some of the most glorious colors you've ever seen in your whole life, and that's about one-half as amazing as this was. Tears welled in my eyes, and I said, 'Well, here's my spot. The only place in the world that I have ever wanted to live.'

Fletcher, after a second's astonishment, grinned.

That spot was for sale, Carrie had money enough to buy it, and she did. Her friends thought that she had lost my senses. For four years, she built a house every day on that spot, only in her mind, of course, because she had to earn the money first.

She refused to allow herself the indulgence of Hubbard's beneficence. Using the money would be akin to admitting that she had been in the keep of a man, albeit a wonderful one. It would be the end of her scrupulous self-image, and the beginning of acquiescence to yet other unacceptable circumstances. She ran her hand over her eyes as if to close that chapter.

One rewarding day she had saved enough money to build, and took the journey again. With a string, a stone, and a few sticks, she measured out the distances of her new home.

"It had a room 40 ft. by 29 ft., because that was the space

between the boulders. On each end where there seemed to be a vacancy big enough for a room, I added one. There are two lean-tos in my home. For the real muscle, I called contractors from La Mesa."

One side of Carrie's home greeted the sunrise, the other with a soothing, smiling porch, looked down on the sunset. Then, of course, there had to be a few windows, so in the room that measured 40' X 29', she installed twenty sliding windows. The wicker furniture was painted the soft green and gray of eucalyptus leaves. The cretonnes she added were of soft pinks, yellows, and lavender of the euc bark, and in the eucalyptus-green, tiled fireplace, she burned big eucalyptus logs. Sometimes Carrie spurred on the fire with a stick of orange wood to make it sound extravagant, and lying back, she dreamed.

Hubbard would have thought her a pilgrim, but not lacking in entrepreneurial flares for designing her own home. He would have admired her inventiveness in choices of arts and crafts and natural scenery, and how she adapted the home to the location almost as if God had placed it there.

The house boasted all the modern improvements, water, gas, and electricity. "But when I have company, we sit in the candle light," Carrie stated humbly. "All we have to do in such a setting to return to reality is look down into the green and brown valley of El Cajon with small villages scattered here and there, where the train comes and goes sixteen times a day. We do not hear the wheels or smell the smoke, but in about a fifteen minute walk, we can take a train to San Diego."

Carrie did not blast any of the ancient rocks where the home nestled between wind-shaped granite. She called her Grossmont home, *Nest-O-Rest*, and dedicated a song to it, naming it **A Little Cottage in God's Garden.**

A PERFECT DAY

I have a cottage in God's garden
Upon a mountain high,
Away from strife and turmoil
And all life's dins and cries.
Away from cares and sorrow,
And all earth's tears enroll
In God's garden where I am free to go.
There's a cottage in God's garden
Where my tired feet may rest,
And really will my soul and spirit be there blessed.
The wild birds chant their carole and wild flowers bloom galore,
Out in God's lovely garden,
How could I ask for more?

When Carrie built her home on the top of the mountain, she decided to have an art gallery, and so she built her windows as if they were picture frames and looking outdoors was visiting the art gallery. In her art gallery, she had a magnificent collection, but it was not a private collection. The pictures were for everyone who would look. She felt this particular window innovation was Hubbard-inspired because of their bold individuality. At her fireside, Carrie was struck by the riches of nature she observed through her windows on the world. If she could create songs of particular charm, how much greater was God's creation of nature with a divine rotating-of-the-seasons foundation.

"Here I come every year with a dear friend or two, especially Lulu and Esther, and Tom, my sweet-voiced canary, and my faithful dogs, Mike and Pooch, to rest and to seek from the sky, the mountains, and the rocks the relationship to the songs I would sing, and I find it here, even as I find spiritual and physical re-building, also"

For *Nest-O-Rest*, she wrote a stylized invitation card that she used without exception.

> Will you come to my little
> Nest-O-Rest
> Out in the lovely southern West.
> You can look in the valley's wondrous heart
> And make of it yourself a part,
> You'll bless the things
> God gave to you,
> When you look at the mountains'
> Strength against the blue.
> All this is yours—at
> Nest-O-Rest—
> Out in the lovely Southern West.

***

After World War I, Americans enjoyed a period of economic growth that produced a popular faith in lasting peace and prosperity. The austerity of the war gave way to a general relaxation of standards, which had profound effect on the social, sexual, and cultural values of Americans. A new feminism arose in 1920, after women gained the right to vote, and the advent of mass-consumption made available silent movies, radios, cars, and other consumer goods. The popularization of jazz music and introduction of provocative new dances, (the Charleston and the Big Apple), typified the spirit of the exciting and contentious decade between the end of the war and the 1929 stock market crash, which is often referred to as the Jazz Age, or the Roaring Twenties.

A PERFECT DAY

The stage was set for more than a decade of combat between the "Wets" and the "Drys"—those determined to keep drinking and those determined to enforce the law. The new mood of the Jazz Age was in complete contrast to the moral earnestness of many Americans who were determined to stamp out vice.

In February 1920, Carrie read with amusement in the Chicago Herald Tribune, (she read it faithfully by subscription), about the Whiskey Rebellion in Iron River, the treasured village where she had lived so happily with Dr. Frank Bond. Oh, God, how her life had changed after Frank died. She buried her face in her hands. *Don't go there, Carrie*, she half whispered. Enjoy today, the present, and all life gives you.

It seemed the Rebellion had commenced because the Revenuers had seized homemade wine, used exclusively for the Italian dinner tables. Because of the many Italian patients to whom Frank had administered, Carrie was aware that the homemade, **Dago Red**, was practically a religious ceremony in the Italian community. She reminded herself that she must one day go back to Iron River and visit her many friends. She had learned by trial and hardship that great friends were few, and few friends were great. The small, northern Michigan village held some real troopers she numbered among her friends who were great.

***

Fred, now married, moved to Lake Arrowhead, California to launch his independent experiments in living. Cognizant of Fred's genetic inclination to depression, Carrie found the distant move troubling. Her unuttered protests were sometimes groaned aloud. "It's a rash move. It's too far." She fought bouts of puckishness about his absence, but realized that was the way of things. Birds flew the nest, acorns fell from oaks, and whales dropped their young, all sharing in the evolutionary rotation of life. He had two daughters of his own whom Carrie rarely saw because of the prohibitive distance. At that time, people seldom traveled more than twenty miles from home.

Carrie wrote *The Hand of You* one day when she was lonely for Fred. She found in the moment an opportunity to cut him adrift and, at the same time, find the preciousness of him in her solitude. His endearments and dedication throughout their struggling years were irreplaceable. When his melancholy swallowed him rendering him as soil left in fallow, brambles sprang into his personality as if his only nutriment was burned-out desert. He had to fight against this condition just as she had waged a fierce war with herself to overcome the malady. Even at her worse moments, the thought of Fred needing her triggered a response: "Be there in his hour of need."

'With determination, she made every moment count with the business, instead of counting every moment in a sea of indecision. Carrie trusted that Fred's responsibility to his wife and daughters would be challenge enough to keep his head above water in the rushing stream of morose. Yet, she missed his silly grins, his germane euphemisms, (the Step Inn for the state sanitarium and Opulent Atoll for Catalina Island), and his outrageous ability to make her laugh.

※※※

Lulu, as well as Esther Fairbanks, was now long-time friends of Carrie's. Lulu encouraged Carrie to write the song *The Golden Key* the theme song for the Federation of Business and Professional Women's Clubs.

THE GOLDEN KEY
I found a golden key one day

A PERFECT DAY

Upon the path I trod,
And it unlocked a golden door-
The door that led to God.
And as I looked inside, I saw
`These words upon the wall,
"Your God is Love and Love brings Work,
There's love and Work for all."
No idle life can happy be
We all should do our part,
Should work awhile and play awhile
With all our soul and heart.
For all who do their work with joy
`Grim toil can live no more
And in their hand, they will find the key
That opens every door

***

In the company of the loquacious and lively Lulu, more than twenty years younger than Carrie, she lived in a whirlwind of travel during the Roaring Twenties. She dressed in the clothing of the day, and the days clothed her with the giddiness of the times. She disproved the old adage that the defects of the mind, as those of the face, grow worse as we grow old. She had made heaven of any hell she had lived through, her face growing smooth and serene, and her eyes gentle.

A PERFECT DAY

CHAPTER THIRTY-ONE

Fueled by travel, Carrie took the high road by not living in the past.

It was 1922, and the Teapot Dome scandal was a great embarrassment to the Harding Administration. In exchange for a $200,000.00 "loan," Secretary of the Interior Albert Fall granted development rights in the naval oil reserves at Teapot Dome, Wyoming to Henry Sinclair, head of the Mammoth Oil Company on April 7. Fall also organized a similar deal with Edward Doheny for rights to the Elk Hill oil reserves in California. When a Senate committee uncovered the improprieties, Fall resigned from the cabinet, was prosecuted, and served nine months in prison.

President Warren Gamaliel Harding, in an effort to bring credibility to the White House instead of cunning, held invitational concerts at the capital. 59-year-old Carrie was among the first entertainers to be invited. Her music being much admired by Harding, he had always had the Marine Corp Band end its concerts with *A Perfect Day*, his favorite song.

A year later, Carrie was in Washington again on her way to Europe. She sent a message. "I am in the city and would be delighted if I could see the President and Mrs. Harding. When I had previously been in town, I spent a happy evening with the Hardings in concert."

Later that same day, she received a return message from them: "Please come to visit the White house and bring your friends, Governor and Mrs. Yates, with whom you are visiting.

A concert will be given this evening after the dinner for the Supreme Court Judges."

As Carrie and party entered the room, the Marine Corp Band was playing *A Perfect Day*. She was introduced to Judge Taft and his wife, with whom she spent a few moments prior the concert that was to be given in the Blue Room. She wore a navy blue coatdress adorned with wide white collar and cuffs. A matching, cloche, felt hat hugged her head; her short-bobbed, golden curls peeked out from beneath the small brim.

Entering the Music Room behind President and Mrs. Harding, Carrie sat directly behind them. They were handed programs for the concert and the last number to be sung was *A Perfect Day*. It was not done in her honor because they did not know that Carrie was in Washington when the program was printed.

Before the last group was sung, Mrs. Harding said, "Mrs. Bond, would you mind singing something for us?" There was a twinkle in her eyes that effectively posed the appeal as a must.

Carrie's head turned, sweeping the room uncomfortably. Mrs. Harding's request was unexpected and Carrie would have preferred not to, instead she said, "I don't see how I could refuse such a pleasant request." When the program was ended, she again was requested at the piano where she sang a group of songs.

After completing her concert tour, she returned to Hollywood and shared with Walter and Cora Gale, (now Hollywood retirees), her deep sentiments in regard the White House visitation.

"I never ceased to be glad that I did oblige the Hardings with a few songs, because it was my last meeting with President & Mrs. Harding." Her voice was low and lacked the lightness she wished to project.

On Harding's final tour of the country, destination Alaska,

A PERFECT DAY

the president appeared tense and worn after having delivered eighty-five speeches along the way. On his return from Alaska, he fell sick. At the Palace Hotel in San Francisco on July 29, he collapsed and died four days later of an embolism, August 1, 1923.

He and Mrs. Harding were scheduled to visit Carrie at her Hollywood home during this tour. Her remorse was beyond the limits of courteous bereavement, and it did not escape the Gales notice. Walter and Cora found they were helpless with their kind solicitations. "Everyone can master a grief but he that hath it," thought Walter, remembering his Shakespeare.

After this year, her number of compositions decreased.

***

September 1923 saw Carrie again on concert tour. She loved autumn in the east; the air was sweet and clean as after a rain. From Chattanooga, Carrie wrote to Esther at the Bond Shop in Hollywood, where Esther was assisting Fred.

My Own Dear Esther:

I think of you every day and I have dreamed four nights of Penny. She is always just escaping something, and I have dreamed of her twice. That dog has a certain charm—no getting away from that.

I do hope you are not homesick and lonely. I am not at all well, but guess it is tired more than sick and I am spending the next week in a rest cure.

I appreciated your precious little letter. I wonder if you found my checkbook. If so, send it on. I haven't it with me.

I think I shall be home without fail the last of

October. I am mighty homesick and I do not expect I shall do any visiting at all. Pardon this short letter and know that I am,
Devotedly yours,
CJB

October 1, 1923
From the Hotel Pennsylvania in New York City, Carrie wrote to Esther at 1770 Highland Avenue, Hollywood, California, where Esther was housed.

My Very Dear Little Friend;

You are so good to write me such nice, newsy letters, but my son, on his last visit to the shop, said you are growing homesick. If you are too homesick to carry on, inform me at once, and I will see what other arrangements I can make, because I shall be away another month, I am sure.

How good you are to that little dog; it is wonderful. How homesick I am for him. He is like a ray of sunshine and I know you love him too.

My dear girl, sit right down and write me a long letter telling me some more news, and pat little Penny and tell her I hope she will turn out to be a nice, house-broken pet, and she ought to be ashamed of herself not to have been nicer all the time. I appreciate the clippings very much.

Now, goodbye. I would write more but time is short, and I am a busy lady.
Warm regards,
CJB

A PERFECT DAY

October 4, 1923

On letterhead stationery, from Boston, Carrie wrote again to Esther at the Bond Shop.

Dear Esther,

I guess we are being even better acquainted through our letters. I find myself most hungry and heartsick for you. I think of you as something home there that loves me, and I am so glad that you and little Penny are having so much pleasure together. I do not know how much you pound and play with her, but I do hope my little dog will have some hair left when I return. I really have no time to write you a long letter. I can only say that I am the busiest woman you ever knew: music, playwrights coming to see me, the title pages, new music, radio concerts (three within the next week,) besides the dear friends that I know who live in New York.

I have a piano in my room and have written a new song since I came, and I know that I shall not be able to get home until the last of the month, but I am doing the best I can to hurry things along because I am homesick.

Thank you for finding the book and the pictures, and I know you will tell me that you fixed the things on my desk. I know that I will not know how to live with my desk in order; confusion is such rest to me. When I get back to my desk and look, I will say, "Well God and Esther know where they are, but nobody else does."

Write me often, dear, and know that in my heart

there is a place just filled with Esther.
Devotedly, CJB

***

After her east coast tour, Carrie enjoyed a prolonged respite at Nest-O-Rest, where Esther popped in and out solicitously.

At a point during this time, she followed with interest the Scopes Trial, also known as the "Monkey Trial," of July 10-21, 1925. John Scopes, a Dayton, Tennessee high school biology teacher, was charged with teaching the Darwinian theory of evolution in violation of state law. Clarence Darrow, Scopes's lawyer, challenged the religious fundamentalist views represented by Prosecuting Attorney, William Jennings Bryan, but Scopes was found guilty and fined $100.00 ($1003.00 in today's monetary market.) The disputed law stood until repealed in 1967. Bryan, a three-term losing presidential candidate, died five days after the trial's conclusion.

Putting this information into perspective, Carrie believed that the Bryan death seemed an undue punishment for challenging such a frightful concept as humans being descendants of monkeys, for heaven's sake. What was that man, Clarence Darrow, thinking of?

***

Rested and spirited, she booked another European Concert Tour in 1925 during which Esther joined her, Lulu pouting because she was too entrenched in her work to accompany them. That same summer, after the Monkey Trial, she was sitting in a restaurant at Monte Carlo at an ocean-side club. A bulging moon had begun its ascent into the clear night sky, creeping slowly from old gold to resonating silver. The picturesque resort, on the sunny Mediterranean coast at the foot of the Maritime Alps and near the boundary between France and Italy, was a playground for the world's rich. Parisian shops and many hotels and restaurants served its guests. Carrie resided in a villa on this leg of her tour.

Why was she not surprised to find that the theater in Monte Carlo's finest building, the Casino, or Gambling Hall, was home to the Monte Carlo Opera? She observed, however, that the Casino fronts the sea and is the center of social life, and thus quartered the culture of the small monarchy. Carrie played at the Opera, and felt right at home in the unanticipated setting. Nonetheless, she never could shed the fit of nerves that seized her at Mrs. McKay's mansion in London. Since that time, she had memorized and practiced a Hubbard adage. *If pleasures are greatest in anticipation, just remember that this is also true of trouble.* With that thought in mind, her anxiousness disappeared in a vapor with all the noise of a puff of smoke, so strong an influence had Elbert Hubbard been on her self-confidence.

After an early-evening performance, she and Esther took a table to be by themselves quite near the orchestra, which played *A Perfect Day*. After it was finished, Carrie mentally wrestled with "dos and don'ts," but finally quarried up enough courage to approach the director.

"Do you know me?"

He said, "Why no ma'am."

"I'm very glad," she told him, "because I wrote that song and thought you had played it for me." She smiled proudly.

"We play it almost every day," he said.

The incident prompted them to reach beyond social banalities to a level of harmony in which they both turned an ordinary evening into a smashing entertainment success for the club patrons.

※※※

Carrie could not resist booking into Jerusalem again where

she stayed in the American Colony Home. It crossed her mind that this was a completely new adventure for Esther, whose eyes danced with excitement. Why was the moon so eerily bright in the desert? It shone like a great steel ball against a black velvet sky. Moving away from the window of her suite, she heard the marching feet of soldiers. She returned to the window, and saw twelve military moving in unison singing *A Perfect Day*. It put her in mind of similar incidences in previous places. Her head came up in brief surprise and a deepening smile grew on her face as well as her heart.

In idle curiosity, in the morning, she said to her host, "Did you hear that music last night? Those soldiers singing?"

"No, I didn't," he responded.

"Well, it seemed very strange, but they were singing one of my songs *A Perfect Day*."

"Did you write that song?" He said eagerly. "Will you autograph a copy for me?"

"Gladly, but I have none with me," Carrie replied.

He brought out a worn sheet of *A Perfect Day* and told Carrie the story.

Two American boys were billeted at the American Colony Home, and every evening during their stay, one played and the other sang *A Perfect Day*. When they were well enough to leave, they had left the song as a token of their gratitude. It was all they had to give."

Carrie's heart was pumping madly when she autographed the dog-eared sheet music.

***

As late summer melded into autumn, The Pasadena

A PERFECT DAY

Tournament of Roses Association contacted Carrie in Paris to write the music for a poem for the pageant of 1926.

She received the rhyme the day before she sailed back to the United States. As hard as she tried, she could not find the inspiration. She heard no tune. After seven weary days and nights, she became panicky. For the first time in her life, she knew she had declared her intention to write a song in a given time, and she was drawing a blank. Flickers of disappointment traveled her face.

Upon arrival in New York City, she sent for a piano and shut herself up in her room at the Pennsylvania Hotel hoping to sluice away the blankness in her mind. She scarcely closed the door when she heard in her mind a waltz that was later published. In less than half an hour, she was ready for dictation. Down the hall, Carrie heard the maid humming the melody after hearing it played repeatedly.

The Tournament of Roses did indeed use the song for their pageant, and Carrie rode in an open car with the Parade Marshall, Col. J. G. Mygatt, and Tournament of Roses President, Harry M. Ticknor. The year 1926 saw the first local radio broadcast of the Rose Bowl Game, announced by Pasadena sportswriter and ex-Olympic track star, Charlie Paddock, and Carrie experienced the thrill of being part of it all, when, for so many years, all she had been was part of nothing.

Of the occasion, Carrie said, "Immediately behind our car came the Rose Parade Queen, Fay Lanphier, and on a lovely float bedecked with flowers, twin palm trees, trailing vines, and a flower waterfall all made of live plants, pods, and seeds. The queen was a glowing young lady; I was an angular and plain aging woman, and at this point, was willing to admit the truth of the critique."

Carrie reflected that when she was the queen's age, she had

been married, married and dedicated to her glorious new son, Fred, the gift of a lifetime—a trove of love and laughter, she thought. That is what he had added to her life.

Fred was her treasure to whom she had passed the depression gene. Yet daily he had to be curried and groomed to sustain a healthy mind. Carrie's features were overtly composed with the thought, but covertly drawn by concerns.

A PERFECT DAY

CHAPTER THIRTY-TWO

Although anxiety for Fred found her sighing heavily, memories of the Rose Parade stayed joyfully locked in her cerebral trunk. Carrie absorbed herself with the Bond Shop knowing that the business kept Fred's mind occupied. When in need of fulfillment, he returned to Hollywood from Lake Arrowhead. The Bond Shop in 1925 was in a very Charles Dickens neighborhood: attached buildings, steep roofs, and mullion windows. The shop boasted a red and white, candy-striped awning with fringes. Above the awning, there hung a sign that read, *The Bond Shop*.

The Bond Shop in Hollywood was the realization of all her goals. From the time Carrie had the first Bond Shop in the hall bedroom in Chicago, the idea she had in mind was that of a lovely English building with the sign *Bond Shop* over the door, and that is what she had. Inside there was a cheery fireplace and a counter with cases for sheets of music behind that. On one side of the counter, there was a door that opened onto a stairs that led to a blue text room, which was her private office.

"I just wanted to feel I had an office," she said. "I had no need for one, for my son had always done the real business for the Bond Shop. But this office, I really wanted."

Behind the Bond Shop, there was a fine office for Fred with lovely old furniture and a dear little spinet to decorate the Bond Shop proper. There was a large space behind the store for stock and wrapping, and all the necessary accouterments for shipping and receiving. The biggest space was the hole in Carrie's heart because Joe Bidwell declined to move west.

"When we moved everything from Chicago to Hollywood, I saw my dream come true. However, alas, within three months the publishers found many faults with our supply being so far from demand, so we agreed to take over publication and distribution of the Bond compositions.

"I never asked anyone what I should be doing. I knew my greatest gift was music, but I did not know the terrible difficulties that lie before me to earn a living. If I had known that I was to stumble for years on a road filled with stones, my tears would have overlaid the dust I was constantly making. I do not mean real tears, but aches in my throat. I wonder if I would have kept on walking.

"Walter Gale understood that I was profligate with money, and anyone who came to me with a sad story, stranger or not, would get whatever I had to give. I was put on a monthly budget until a sufficient amount had been saved to guarantee enough to care for me in my old age. I considered the plan a priceless investment."

***

One year before Luther Burbank died, (1926), Carrie had expressed a desire to meet him. Not knowing that she was speaking to a friend of Mr. Burbank's, the friend arranged a meeting. Shortly after that, Carrie received an invitation from Mr. and Mrs. Burbank naming a time they would be glad to have her come.

She had heard about the Plant Wizard from Lancaster, Massachusetts. His first successful vegetation was developed through selection. He found a potato seed ball and planted its 23 seeds in a special plot. One seed produced many large, firm potatoes. Burbank replanted these and reaped a small harvest of fine potatoes, still known as Russet Burbank. He sold the rights to the potato for travel fare to California. Settling in Santa Rosa, Burbank decided to experiment with plant growth. Eventually he established a nursery garden, greenhouse, and experimental farms that became famous.

Carrie drove to Santa Rosa early in the morning, having stayed overnight in San Francisco. The 400-mile drive had taken four days, but she found it to her liking, every mile. The trip was one of those rare and beautiful tours one finds from southern to northern California. The sun was a mammoth shiver of white light in a blue, blue sky.

Mr. Burbank's modest home was reached early in the afternoon. As she came into his parlor, the first thing she noticed was one of her verses on his piano.

"Mr. Burbank, that is one of mine," she exclaimed, so pleased to see it in his home.

"Did you write that?" His head turned quickly.

"Yes, yes I did."

"No," he said. "I didn't know that. It's been in my house for twelve years."

These are the words.

It's not so much about the house that anyone can see.
It's not so much about the ground
That call the bird and the bee.
It's just folks that live within,
And flowers that bloom without,
That call the bird and bee.
And friend, that's what we care about.

After giving him a short recital, Carrie was invited to view the garden with Burbank. As they walked along the path to the poppies, he picked one, and it seemed to Carrie that at that moment there was only one thing he thought of or saw. Buried deeply in his thoughts, he was hearing nothing.

"Are you all right? You look...Errh...strange," she said with overtones of angst.

"Do I? I'm sorry," he replied.

Way down in the heart of that poppy he found the tiniest little speck, and it caused him to blurt excitedly. "Yes, it is time."

He looked at Carrie and apologized. "You see, if I could only teach someone when it's time, all the things that I have worked so hard to find could be handed on. I have been offered a fine sum to go to Stanford to lecture, but you see, Mrs. Bond, it is not possible for me to tell them how. I only know when I see it, and what I see I cannot explain."

How interesting, thought Carrie. Here was a man who could not explain the hows and wherefores of his greatest abilities, and yet, could be invaluable to the world of horticulture. Juxtaposed, there was Elbert, who never saw in the depths of a flower its reproduction processes, but was successful in seeing into men's souls and encouraging them to flower in their abilities. Could Elbert have explained how he did this? Could he have verbalized what cultivated a man's mind to bring out only the best, the purest of results? Had Elbert produced hybrid brains at Roycroft by exposing his employees to the best of associates as Burbank exposed his seeds to better germinations? Carrie thought not that Burbank was unequipped to communicate his boundless knowledge, but that Hubbard dealt in a different commodity, with fewer unknowns. Every human has abilities, and these abilities are his identity, separating him from other men. Another's identity cannot think your thoughts, speak your words, or do your works, thus Carrie recognized that although Burbank was arid in the world of communication, he was drenched in the workings of the genetic structure of plants, a virtual wizard.

Everyone has his or her quota of God's gifts, Carrie thought. Burbank's gifts would live on forever, whether or not he managed to lecture at Stanford. She wondered if he was lonely in his private world of research. Alone, yes, Carrie determined, but not lonely. She shook off the faint sadness she felt for Burbank, and smiled instead at the goodness in life that goes unnoticed.

A PERFECT DAY

CHAPTER THIRTY-THREE

Three years slid by in all-consuming work at the Bond Shop until the historical Stock Market Crash of October, 1929. The market collapse was the signal for a widespread economic breakdown. Trade fell off as credit tightened, and people with cash feared to spend it. Overstocked merchants and manufacturers were forced to close down or to discharge employees. Workers displaced by new laborsaving machinery swelled the army of the unemployed. Widespread bank failures took the savings of hundreds of thousands. Mortgage foreclosures swept away people's businesses and homes. Added to the suffering of Middle Western farmers, a severe drought occurred in 1930. The unemployed were forced to turn to public or private charity when their savings were gone.

Carrie had to lay off six of her employees, then ten. It broke her heart with empathy for those who were faithful and dedicated to her and the shop. Walter Gale had invested large sums of Carrie's savings in the Gale and Blocki Drug Company and this proved to be a saving factor. In good times or bad, the demand for drugs never diminished, and the Gale & Blocki firm stayed afloat through the density of the Crash and the lean years that followed.

***

That same year, Carrie at age 66, found her personal life crashing down around her. On a stormy night in December, at her End-Of-The-Road home in Hollywood, she watched for hours the ominous darkness driving out of the west, the ocean churning. Distant rumbles of thunder rolled through the sky. Then the darkness widened like the giant spread of wings encompassing the total skyline. Absolute stillness settled over the Hollywood hills. Thick darkness was torn by violent blue-white streaks of lightning and cracking thunder. The giant wings loosened a torrential, driving rain.

In the midst of the fierce storm, there came a steady pounding at her front door. Who in God's name would be out on such a night? There loomed a police officer standing under the protective overhang of the roof. Her hand went to her heart. It hurt to breathe. Confusion etched deep lines in her face.

Fred had been found in his cabin at Lake Arrowhead dead and seated beside the Victrola with the record of *A Perfect Day* run down.

Carrie stood mute for what seemed like hours before thanking the police officer for his kindness and solicitations. She carefully grasped the arm of an overstuffed chair and softly slid into it. She knew without a doubt of Fred's suffering. Although the medical community called his malady an incurable ailment for which he had overdosed to shorten his life and end his torment, she was flooded with a visceral feeling of his deep hollowness. To add to her woes, the wind blew as if it was driven by a hellish fury, battering her home and rattling the windows. She breathed deeply in a slow, measured rhythm to calm herself, but a creeping headache went from a dull throb to a painful thump.

Carrie mulled through rolling tears. Memories of Fred wafted through her mind. Fred, at nine years old, holding her hand in a strange city. Fred, at fourteen, taking a taxing position at the U.S. Post Office. Fred's brilliant graduation from engineering school. Fred's devoted management of the Bond

Shop, his marriage resulting in two beautiful daughters. His irreverent humor through thick and thin. His was the melody she heard in the rushing wind. Her blessed child, who had lent encouragement in her darkest hours, was gone. Yet, she was not there for him in his last hour of need. She choked on her sobs.

Fred had been successful, but he believed his business prowess was impossible, and by believing found the way to make it so. Not of a nature to have a compelling ambition and egotism, he slipped easily into the mopes of hopelessness.

Carrie was aware that his marriage had aborted through despondency, and had been strangled from the onset by Fred's downtrodden imagination. She reviewed the vexing times of their mutual despair and rejection, and yet they picked themselves up repeatedly, and held the course. She had learned life's lessons in controlling her own despair by understanding that it was a sure step to failure and abandonment of her child, who needed her, but Fred could not. His volatile, earthy strength of mind and spirit had reached its lowest curve.

This latest disaster in a life of disasters numbed Carrie like none other. Was it his death or the denigrating manner in which he died that plagued her soul? A swelling in Carrie's throat worked its way from its inception in the cerebrum to her quivering mouth. Could she have done more? Should she have stepped into his married life like some wicked witch of the north, and given advice? Surely, death was inevitable, but was it possible that something so natural, so necessary, and so ubiquitous as death, should steal such a young life, only 45 years old? Life was just too harsh to handle sometimes.

Rain ran down the windows replicating Carrie's tears. In bereavement, she wished him back so dearly. The night was filled with terrors, guilt, remorse, nausea, and irreversible longing. Had she ever felt so devoured by emotional turmoil? It was too horrifying to dig up thoughts of the people in her life that had gone to their rewards. She held her aching head, sucking in the saturated ocean air sweeping up the mountainside.

She would write. She would write while the fireplace threw long shadows. She would write while thunder echoed in the Hollywood hills. As a cleansing, she would write to the beat of the rain on her roof.

TO MY SON
ON HIS LAST BIRTHDAY
So many years have come and gone
Since first you came to me
That as I look, the past seems dim
Yet through it all, I see
My little baby's precious face
And touch my baby's hand.
And feel a little beating heart my own can understand.
When you came dear—my other self
My very life apart—you bound yourself
With bands of love—around your mother's heart.
I wonder if you really knew
You've been the world to me,
That every moment of my life
Yours is the face I see—
That every joy you've ever known
And every sorrow too—
Has touched the very soul of me
For I am part of you.
I wonder if you can believe
That I would gladly give
My very life and every hope through death
That you, my son, might live.
For now I know in all the world

A PERFECT DAY

> That I can never find
> A son gentler or truer
> And no one half so kind.
> We shared our burdens—every one
> Those glorious struggling years
> "Twas you alone brought happy days
> And wiped away my tears.
> (All this is what I think of you
> No matter what I say)
> So, Dear God, Bless my only son,
> On this, his last Birthday.

Upon finishing the poem, lightning lit the room as if ten fireplaces were at play. Carrie never fancied herself a superstitious person, but the timing and the brightness soothed her soul, as if Fred was acknowledging everything she wrote. As if he were telling her not to be sad, or disconsolate, or unfit for the happiness she gave in life. Indeed, God wanted Carrie to be comfortable, and of service to others. All this was rendered in a split moment in time. How radiant and consoling the thought. It was Fred's gift to her—and a gift from her angel...*to light, to guard.*

She was lightened, but she knew Fred's death had not been a dream, and she was grounded by grief and heavy with heartache.

She called Walter and Cora Gale, her childhood friends from Janesville who had stood by her during the worst of times. With their bolstering, Carrie—first tentatively, then eagerly—returned to her poetry and music. She produced songs, she made personal appearances, and she kept up a huge correspondence with friends. Time and loyal associates were the healers, but memories would never be erased, treasured memories.

CHAPTER THIRTY-FOUR

Although bogged-down busy, for three years Carrie struggled with life. It hurt to live. A long time ago, her mother ragged about the insufficiencies of life, and the loneliness a woman suffers, loneliness without resolve. The sentiment only served to drag her down.

The country, as well as Carrie, was in a deep depression. Conventional wisdom has long blamed the Great Depression on the stock market crash and other flaws in the national economy. Therefore, Carrie considered it reasonable for the federal government to do something about the worst economic crisis in the nation's history, and in hers.

Daily scanning the newspapers, she was pleased to find President Herbert Hoover immediately taking an active role in trying to engineer the restoration of prosperity. Then, later on, his successor in 1932, Franklin D. Roosevelt, adopted Hoover's policies and added many new ones. These included a sorely needed new labor law, new farm policies, a Social Security program for retired workers, bank regulation, trade policies, public works programs, and many other initiatives. Unemployment in 1932, the bottom of the depression, was at 25%. The situation seeming hopeless, Carrie nevertheless supported and applauded the new policies and would help re-elect Roosevelt three more times.

The murk hanging over the country matched Carrie's miserable state of mind. In the three years since Fred died, the thought of him was never off her mind. When Carrie hit bottom in January 1932, a repetitious, clear-weather pattern lay over the coastal city.

The Los Angeles Times reported:

> Los Angeles, where she lives, set aside a week as a tribute to Carrie Jacob-Bond's work: January 7 to January 14, was declared, ***Bond Week***.
>
> Because of a nervous breakdown, Mrs. Bond will sail on January 29 for Hawaii in search of better health.

※※※

Carrie on this trip wrote:
YESTERDAY, TO~DAY AND TO~MORROW
(Under the title was painted five wild roses)
"Yesterday" was a child I knew
Whose hair was gold and whose eyes were blue.
"To~day" is a maiden fair to see,
From childhood grown to maturity.
"To~morrow?" Ah, yes, "to~morrow" shall be
The fairest one of all to me.
For she is the mother whose hair is white,
Whose love has followed on day and night.
"Yesterday" was ambition strong.
I shall climb the ladder and not be long.
"To~day" is a spirit knowing true
That the TOP is reached by JUST A FEW
Who climbed the best, who did it well …
Who never fainted when strife was strong
Whose hearts were brave when the task was long.
We all shall know these three words well.
"Yesterday," "To~day" and "To~morrow."

A PERFECT DAY

As every heart and every tongue
Knows life with its joy and sorrow,
The "Yesterdays" are of the past...
"To~day" alone is here...
But "To~morrow is something we cannot see.
It may be a smile or a tear.

***

Upon her return from Hawaii, Carrie took her doctor's advice and concentrated on a relaxed social life instead of exhausting concert tours. The months drifted away meaninglessly until on a misty, umbrella day in Seattle, June 23, 1932, Carrie was recognized by friends.

Dateline Seattle

> Honoring Mrs. Carrie Jacob-Bond, noted composer who is visiting in town, Lulu Fairbanks and Esther Fairbanks entertained last evening with an informal dinner at the Washington Athletic Club.
>
> In complement to the honored guest, the orchestra played several of her compositions during the dinner hour.
>
> An official photograph was taken. She is seventy years old, fabulously fair, butterscotch blonde, and patently pretty.

(In 1986 an oil on canvas was painted from this photograph.)

Alone, although in a crowd, her heart beat with grief for her lost loves. Carrie scribbled the following lyrics on the back of the Program.

The tempest heats up in my soul, dear heart,

But I have you.
The world seems cold, and I am sad, dear heart,
But you are true.
How could I sing?
How could I smile?
Where would I go from day to day?
How could I live with you away?

It was no easy fete for Carrie to get a word in edgeways with the Fairbanks women, who were disposed to animated conversation and redhead reactions. Covering their hands with hers, Carrie shared with them a philosophical thought. "I am most fortunate. I have known poverty and grief and still have left my faith, my Lord, and you, my friends. I have been most fortunate because I have had my share of joys, more than anyone should really have. And more, I think of all the gifts that have been given me. In you, my fine friends, I place my confidence and will never be betrayed."

Tears sparkled, and chins quavered at the words.

***

Lulu and Carrie took another trip to various Alaskan cities via ferry. The Chinook winds were blowing a moist, warm wind from the sea.

Lulu was now 41 years old and established well as the journalistic courier of the Alaskan news. Over a cup of coffee, she explained to Carrie the deep regard she had for these people. "Uncle Charlie was instrumental in defining the Canadian/Alaskan boundary in 1903; it was then that the city was named after him, just a year after gold was discovered in Fairbanks. It was only a few years ago that Alaska's territorial flag was designed. I am so much tied to this land."

"I can understand that. These folks are pioneer souls, and

A PERFECT DAY

not afraid of breaking new ground, especially the fishermen. What do they catch beside salmon?" Carrie asked.

"Sea food, fresh, frozen, canned, and cured is a big business, also, but the Chinook Indians show the spunk it takes to survive in the fishing industry. They arrange their lives by the annual run of the salmon. In spring and summer, they gather along the Columbia River to spear them as the fish swim upstream in tremendous shoals. The Chinook then dry them and store them for winter food. This is no small fete for them because the average Chinook salmon weighs 22 pounds, but specimens weighing 70 to 100 pounds are also taken."

"I can see whey they call you Miss Alaska, Lulu," said Carrie.

Lulu's emerald green eyes focused intently on Carrie. Her voice sang with enthusiasm. "Well, you know the story of the root of my interest since I was in third grade: Mt. McKinley. It is higher than any other peak in North America. In addition to these ocean-ways that I travel, there is the Yukon River, one of the longest navigable waterways in the world."

"Look!" Carrie jumped up from their small café table on the ferry, all her senses charged. "Look," she pointed to the nearby shoreline in childish enthusiasm.

"It's a Kodiak, the largest of brown bears," Lulu said, also wide-eyed under her corrective lens eyeglasses that had thickened greatly from year to year. "They can weigh as much as 1700 pounds. Alaska abounds in wildlife: grizzly, black, and polar bears, moose, caribou, musk oxen, wolves, otter, walrus, seals and humpback and killer whales," Lulu said with a half smile, enjoying seeing Alaska through Carrie's eyes.

Therefore, Carrie's new adventures lured her away from the despondent isolation visited upon her after Fred's death. These new times served Carrie with constant personal reminders of all her blessings, blessings that cast away the dread of bad times, which were, she acknowledged, irreversible.

CHAPTER THIRTY-FIVE

In the ensuing four years, Carrie saw many changes in the country. President Roosevelt closed all banks in the United States and refused to let them reopen until they could prove that they had enough funds to cover their customers' deposits. "When you come to the end of your rope, tie a knot, and hang on," he said when announcing the plan.

Well, that was fine and good, thought Carrie, but how was he going to pull *that* rabbit out of the hat?

Back to back with bank closings, Roosevelt went one step further. In order to ensure that customers would never again lose their money, The Federal Deposit Insurance Corporation (FDIC) was established. The federal government, up to a certain limit, protected money in banks insured by the FDIC. How farsighted, thought Carrie. It was akin to locking the barn door after the horse was out, but a candle lighted is a flame of hope. She had lost nothing but some downtime during the collapse of the banking system, but her heart swelled with sympathy for those who were caught in the terrible undertow.

Prodded by Roosevelt, Congress created the Tennessee Valley Authority (TVA), a government program aimed at improving the lives of the people living in parts of the seven state area drained by the Tennessee River system.

Carrie had personal knowledge of the poverty life-styles of those folks. When she was on her last East Coast tour, she saw and learned more than she wanted to know. Her own life having experienced indescribable poverty, her soul went out to these folks. Now, because of the TVA, their living standards were raised and electrical power usage in the area increased by twenty times.

Subsequently, Carrie found a parade of sweeping national changes taking place. The 20th Amendment to the United States Constitution changed the inaugural date for the president and the commencement date for Congress from March of the ensuing year to January 1.

The 21st Amendment repealed the 18th Amendment, making it legal to again sell, manufacture, transport, import, or export alcoholic beverages.

***

What Carrie enjoyed was President Roosevelt's Fireside Chats. She listened to them, ears bent to her RCA Victor radio. Sometimes the message came through as if being carried in a seashell, but Carrie persisted in hearing what the noble president had to say about the Great Depression, and the New Deal.

"We look forward to a world founded upon four essential human freedoms. The first is freedom of speech and expression. The second is freedom of every person to worship God in his own way. The third is freedom from want, and the fourth is freedom from fear," the president professed.

She heard first hand of the Federal Housing Administration created to provide guaranteed bank loans for construction and repair of houses, upgrading the housing of the poor in rural and urban communities. Roosevelt always managed to calm her fears concerning the economic depression gripping the country and to reestablish her confidence in banks and financial institutions.

When, in 1935, Roosevelt was instrumental in getting the Social Security Act passed providing unemployment compensation and old-age insurance based on money paid into a fund by the worker and the employer, Carrie was amazed again at the far-sightedness of this wonderful man.

On the heels of this followed the Works Projects Administration, (WPA), providing employment to about eight million workers during the Great Depression. It was downright unbelievable to Carrie what these WPA teams accomplished: built schoolhouses, community centers, highways, sidewalks, and public buildings.

What other miracles was this magic man going to expedite? She shook her head. Now here comes the National Labor Relations Act to settle disputes between labor and management. The act also guaranteed the right of employees to organize and to bargain for better wages and working conditions. Carrie returned her full staff to work, but had no problems with bargaining.

While all these vehicles for betterment were taking place, the Boulder Dam was being built on the Colorado River as a Public Works Project designed to create employment for people who were without work because of the Great Depression.

Not a single effort by Roosevelt went unnoticed by Carrie. How it took her back to the days when she was welcomed at the White House by Teddy Roosevelt. Secretly she desired an invitation by yet another Roosevelt, but none was ever forthcoming.

***

By 1936, seven years after Fred's death, Carrie launched into a demanding life of concerts and whirlwind appearances. The crunched timeline was of immeasurable assistance in staving off sorrow.

On her own letterhead stationery reading *Carrie Jacobs-Bond, Hollywood, California,* Carrie wrote to Esther at 1833 13th Street, Seattle, Washington.

My Very Dear Esther:

I would not blame you if you never thought of me again. I have simply been too busy to write the kind of a letter I always expected to write to you—a nice long one telling you a great deal of news. Now it will have to be a typewritten one and not very interesting, I am afraid, as I have not been well.

I went to New York had a remarkable experience on the radio, and, in addition took a journey to Old Mexico. I have been very busy trying to carry out some new ideas in which I, too, may boost the nation's economy…like Roosevelt. Just as soon as I feel able, I will write and tell you all. But this is just to tell you I appreciate you remembering me with a lovely Christmas card, and also for holding down the fort while Lulu and I went tramping off to parts unknown in Alaska.

Enclosed, you will find a little card, which I think, is beautiful.

With love and kindest remembrances for all your family, I am,
Most sincerely,
CJB

***

April 11, 1936, on her personal stationery from Hollywood, Carrie wrote.

My Dear Lulu:

Your nice long letter received, and I am sorry I cannot reply in the same length and so forth, but that is quite out of the question. I have been doing a great deal of public work since I saw you and I have gotten myself into Mail Order business, a swamping added effort. It may, however, add to the availability of my music to rural areas so often overlooked by urbanites.

Roosevelt's good deeds have brought everyone under one umbrella with equal opportunity, and so shall I.

Your new Alaska caper is very cunning, and I wish I might go along with you but it, too, out the question at this time. I do hope you will ask me again as I would like to see more wildlife along the inlets. How very fascinating that was. I shall never forget the splendor of that lovely territory.

I have just received the same sort of a trip invitation from the Chamber of Commerce here. I went to Mexico with them in October and had a wonderful time.

Since I saw you, I have been to New York and made my radio debut, and assigned myself to work more than I should undertake. I am not so very well and all this excitement is very hard, but I am trying to do my work, my writing—and keep myself as quiet as possible in order to have strength enough to do so. How I miss Fred and the many burdens from which he relieved me.

I am so glad you have a car, and I know you are having a wonderful time.

I received a letter from Esther, also, and I wish I could answer it now, but there really isn't time. I know you will forgive me; I am the poorest letter writer in the world.

This brings my love for you all,
Most sincerely,
CJB

Carrie was surprised and delighted, when, in the spring of 1937, Hilda Benson, Carrie's Iron River, Michigan housekeeper from 1889-95, was in California visiting, and Carrie had a chance encounter with her. Hilda was driving along Pinehurst Drive with Mr. and Mrs. Carl Mansur, California relatives, when they stopped the car to allow an elderly lady to pass.

The lady approached the car. "Are you looking for someone?" She inquired.

Mansur, recognizing the beloved composer, introduced the two women in the car to Carrie.

"Hilda Benson? Are you from Iron River, Michigan?" Carrie glanced at Hilda doubtfully, scraping her mind for a mental picture of the beloved housekeeper.

"Yes, the same," Hilda nodded happily.

Carrie was silent, hardly a breath passed from her surprised mouth. "This is unbelievable, my good gracious, Hilda. It's fate that has brought us together."

The anxiety of a dubious reception from Carrie disappeared from Hilda's face. She nodded.

"I'm on my way to catch the street car to Grauman's Theater, "said Carrie.

Carl Mansur, an eager-to-please young man, waved Carrie to drive with them to her destination. "How extraordinary it is to run into you like this."

Hilda, a woman now grown old, squiggled in place. "It's our pleasure; I'm sure, Mrs. Bond."

"You must come to my home later in the week and spend an afternoon," Carrie invited. "We have so much to talk about." Carrie was more than willing to share old times and old happenings with the women. They never knew of her poverty-stricken days, when Carrie shared her hospitality with total strangers, and she had so little to give. From whom had Carrie received the greater amount of hospitality? From other poor, Carrie found hospitality in its perfection.

If she could share, now that she was rich, as altruistically as she had shared when she had nothing, her own woes were lightened and made insignificant. She had never forgotten the wonderful meals that Mrs. Benson had set out for Dr. Bond, herself, and Fred, not to mention the miraculous tables she set when the Bonds entertained: salvers of baked ham, scalloped potatoes, green beans, vinaigrette salads, warm biscuits, and desserts heaped with whipped cream. Worlds away, now. Worlds away. Great rivers had filled and flowed to the sea since that time.

A year later, Carrie responded to a letter she received from Hilda Benson.

> February 25, 1938
> Dear Mrs. Benson,
>
> Tonight, I have two platters, one holding my dinner, and one holding a thousand stars spilling from the California night sky.
>
> I hold also in my lap your kind letter. You must remember it is more than forty years since I lived in Iron River, and my life has been filled with a little of everything that comes to anyone who lives—and with it great sorrows. I have forgotten a many things. I do think it was so dear of you to speak about blessed Frank Bond's kindness, for there never was anyone in the world kinder than he was. I have lived in the memory of his life for all these years.

I am hoping to come to Iron River some day, and, if I do, I shall certainly hunt you up. With deepest gratitude for your remembering me, and for our unexpected visit last year here in Hollywood.
Sincerely,
Carrie Jacobs-Bond

April 28, 1938
Glenn Dillard Gunn, music critic of the Washington Herald, paid Carrie a memorable tribute.

> Carrie Jacobs-Bond, whose place in the history of American folksong is next to Ethelbert Nevin and Stephen Foster, was guest of honor last night of the
> National League of American Pen Women. She told them of the importance of little things that make up so large a part of life; how these daily and often unconsidered experiences really lie deep in the hearts of all; how it has been her fate to sing only of them.
> She let her hearers glimpse something of the struggle, which prefaced the hearing of her songs and said nothing of the triumphs that presently were won by these lyric fragments concerned with simple joys and sorrows and homely sentiment. She let them catch a few of the echoes that have gone 'round the world.
> Like Foster, Mrs. Bond creates melodies that all can understand and nobody can improve upon despite their simplicity. Again, like Foster, she can give these tunes, which the multitude finds irresistible, settings that are literate and meaningful.

***

A PERFECT DAY

The silence of the room pressed upon Carrie when she read the article. Ageing had made her vulnerabilities even more pronounced and her emotions fragile. Surely, she did not deserve such grand words. She buried her face in her hands finding overwhelming humility in the moment.

A PERFECT DAY

CHAPTER THIRTY-SIX

Given new life by the favorable publicity, on May 14, 1938, at age 76, after an absence of forty-five years, America's dear lady of song did again visit Iron River. She no longer saw a struggling mining village, but a bustling city affected radically by scientific and industrial advances.

Arriving on the evening train, she stepped down to a chilly evening, the moon only a cold slice in the sky. She was struck by the vast difference between now and the warm, June day when she had arrived in the village accompanied by Dr. Bond.

She registered at the Iron Inn Hotel.

Then, Monica Irvine, wife of Dr. L. E. Irvine, invited her to stay at her home as they had a downstairs guestroom and bath. At the Inn, Carrie had to climb a flight of stairs. Dr. Irvine was one of the several doctors who were successors to Dr. Bond to cover the health interests of the Village of Iron River. He was a large man, standing more than six feet tall, the top of his head covered in a mass of blonde hair as if glued there. Monica was tall, too, with a ready smile and witty tongue.

"The Irvines were wonderful hosts, most gracious and accommodating, and I loved the Irvine children. Of course, Doctor Irvine replaced Frank in my mind because the circumstances were so similar," Carrie commented to friends. "We've kept in touch since I went to Chicago, and later from Los Angeles."

An emotion outlasting time created a bright light in Carrie's eyes as she spoke.

Monica shared with friends. "Carrie sat down at our piano and played, never using copy. The makings of World War II were in the fire, and Carrie continually prayed for a better solution than death and destruction."

At St. John's Episcopal Church, where she served as organist many years ago, Carrie attended services with the Irvines.

"Will you play for the Communion Service?" The pastor, standing at the front door, asked with an irresistible smile.

"Why, yes," Carrie said, excitement in her voice. "Music is the fourth great material want of our nature: first food, second clothing, third shelter, and the fourth, a mix of music," she said counting them off on her fingers. "I can't think of a greater delight than to put music into your services."

It was a bit awkward for Carrie not knowing how the present organist would feel about the request from her pastor.

The parson led Carrie into the church, nodding to parishioners along the way. He did not leave her side until she was seated in a front pew next to the church organist who greeted Carrie with warmth, allaying all Carrie's fears of rejection.

Music always in her heart, Carrie felt as if she had never left when she slid onto the familiar organ bench. The congregation sang like an imperial chorus of a thousand voices.

That same evening she greeted over six hundred persons in a comprehensive program at the High School Auditorium On her right hand, was a large diamond in a plain silver ring setting.

She informed the audience: ". . . work is rewarding and to work hard is what we're here for." She recalled Hubbard's adage *Folks who never do any more than they are paid for, never get paid for any more than they do.* God had given Carrie love and work. Without her work, she was nothing now, because the closest loves of her life had slipped away, the thought never far from her mind. She struggled valiantly to know when to let go of a thing that was dead.

She played for the packed auditorium her most valuable collection, the three best-known songs written by her: *Jest A Wearyin' for You, A Perfect Day, and I Love You Truly.* Scanning the hometown audience, Carrie was never more cognizant that there is no more abiding happiness than the knowledge that one is doing the best work one can do, and that this work is absorbed by an appreciative market and thus supports one's own life. She understood much about human illusions and the hunger they created. She also knew the strength she found in realistic goals and successes.

She was most grateful when, after the performance, a white-haired man came backstage to shake hands. "I used to be the grocery boy at Fisher's store," he explained, "and I delivered groceries right to you door. I have a store of my own now," he admitted proudly.

"That is such a nice story," Carrie nodded, her blue eyes direct. "Man must work. That is certain as the sun, but to be successful enough to stay in business for years and years takes an extra kind of courage and determination."

The aged man expanded and grew with the compliment. "Thank you, "Ma'am. Thank you very much," he replied smoothly, feeling at ease with Carrie.

***

The next day dawned clear and cool again, perking her spirit, for she was to be honored with a tea at the Ben L. Quirt residence. There she found a warm fire cast a cheerful blaze, and the Quirt family dog established his presence in front of the fire, nose on paws, making canine-observations. The ambience reminded Carrie of Schneider and her childhood as well as Fred's childhood. If she were an easily spooked woman, she would have thought Schneider had been reincarnated; the dogs were amazingly similar. Her heart tugged remembering her three Schneiders.

The Carrie Jacobs-Bond Musicale arranged the tea at which over seventy women were present. The warm affair commenced at four p.m. and ended at seven p.m. with a farewell, *A Perfect Day*, being sung by the women guests accompanied at the piano by Carrie, herself, who felt she was bringing to closure her nightmare years following Dr. Bond's tragic death. No longer would it be lamentations or sad songs to celebrate the passing of a good man, but by joyous songs, for she was sure Frank had been numbered among the divine entrants to heaven.

In her brief speech to the Musicale, she announced her latest song.

"I wrote *A Long time Ago* about the City of Iron River. It is my favorite song," she said. "But please don't misunderstand as I love all my songs very much. I consider this song reminiscent and a companion piece to *I Love You Truly*.

"In the last twenty-eight years I've seen the motion picture industry grow from its infancy to the billion dollar institution it represents today. Many times I have appeared on programs sponsored by movie stars."

The statement caused her to use caution knowing these women would, in all likelihood, never travel to Hollywood or be privy to the close associations Carrie enjoyed, and she did not want to come off sounding arrogant. Arrogance was an unwelcome commodity in Carrie's life. The applause that answered her revelations more than mollified her personal concerns.

She continued more calmly, her striking blue eyes shining with stimulation. "I indulge myself in a measure of pride in a

A PERFECT DAY

bird garden I established next to my home in Hollywood. Every day I distribute the crumbs of a loaf of bread to my feathered friends, and at least seven bird families are represented in the hundreds of wild birds that visit the sanctuary."

Glancing around the room, she evaluated the varying degrees of attention and curiosity. All faces reflected her own enthusiasm leaving Carrie with a goodly amount of humility, her fingers braiding at her side as if comfortable only on the piano keyboard.

"My songs have been translated into several languages in practically every country in the world, if you can imagine. My songs…all over the world…it defies my imagination," she smiled, shaking her silver-haired head.

Carrie's quick mind kept coming up with anecdotes. "One day, I heard *I Love You Truly* whistled at my side on the street by a man whom I recognized as someone who had yawned through one of my recitals. Turning to him, I smiled, whereupon he recognized me."

"I felt so guilty thereafter," he shrugged, "that I invested in every song of yours that I could find."

Her old friends laughed aloud.

The sunlight streaming through the windows was like a gift for Carrie, giving encouragement and strength, which often were elusive in her later years, she found. The Quirt dog eyed her, but with lazy somnolence.

A Perfect Day, and I Love You Truly, did not have the chance that songs have today," Carrie said. "It took three and four years to introduce a song back in the old days, whereas today it requires only from three to five minutes because of the radio. When I presented my latest song *A Long Time Ago* on the radio from a New York station three months ago, approximately 7,000,000 listeners heard it!"

More applause.

The Quirt dog lifted an eyebrow as if in dull askance, sighed, and returned to his fireside doze, aloof, distant, detached, and imperious.

Mercy me, Carrie thought, how I am reminded of the slow pace of life I had with Dr. Bond in this lovely village. When she continued, her voice sounded far away as if stirring thoughts from layers and layers of gauzy memory.

"It disturbs me very much when my songs are put into swing or jazz arrangements. My more than 300 compositions are copyrighted; consequently, they do not undergo much of this treatment." The admission was a quiet statement void of any acclaim.

After Carrie's comments, the aroma of coffee drifted through the home bringing with it a down-home balm. Buzzing chatter dominated colored by the presence of a prestigious person. Carrie sipped the coffee, conversed, and had two slices of lemon layer cake. If she felt the esteem accorded her, she chose to not notice, gaining the goodwill of those with whom she conversed. She was like a fresh mountain stream flowing quietly, renewing completely everything along its course.

***

The next afternoon, the fickle sun came roaring down, a typical weather pattern in Michigan's Upper Peninsula, even in the month of May. She felt its warmth kindly as it reminded her of the last time she saw Elbert, when she walked to the train station in the quietude of a radiating sun, never to see him again.

Appearing before a student assembly, she spoke generously of the area. "I think Iron County is lovely with its fine roads, trees, and lakes. Countless changes have come over the west side district. The happiest seven years of my life were spent in Iron River. Coming back now is as being in Heaven," she admitted to the student body. "I'm enroute to my home in Los Angeles after a short tour through the east, where, in addition to concerts, I got to view the TVA Dam in Tennessee…an awesome endeavor. Once in Chicago, however, I couldn't help but turn northward last Thursday, and come to see the community that has taken the place of the Iron River I once knew."

The students, enraptured with a celebrity, especially a hometown celebrity, applauded the sentiment.

"The first thing I asked was that I be given time with the schools, if I could. I thought I could do some songs; I want to do what I can for all the children. I feel very much indebted to a great many people in this world," she confessed. "If you had written songs that had given you a comfortable living and if you had any conscience at all, you would feel that you owed something to the people who had made these things possible."

She observed an audience hushed but in unison such as could have been written into a quiet concert at the Philharmonic. This is exactly how she wanted her appearance at the Iron River High School to be, to delight the boys and girls who had heard her music, students whose parents knew her in the early days.

"Upon my departure from Iron River, the ten most eventful years of my life were spent in Chicago, a wonderful and attractive city. I predict that in ten years it will far surpass its present beauty. All destinations considered, I have a fondness in my heart for Wisconsin, the state of my birth, Michigan, where I lived with the dear doctor, and my final, adopted home, California."

Carrie's heart had been troubling her, and she suffered from shortness of breath. She paused. Her hearing was not good, but her love for people, her friends and those she knew only through the glue of her music, remained undiminished. It was as if the high school auditorium itself were a bulwark against poor health, and was infusing strength into the once uncertain young woman she had been...a radiating strength safeguarding her against the formidable odds of aging.

Carrie allowed her mind to wander, her thoughts blowing about like the dandelion down of old. She traveled back over the road and reminisced particularly about her earliest experiences in Iron River, cows wandering the streets with dogs barking at their heels, the old Ammerman Drug Store, the iceman, the life-saving Nollingberg Bakery, Nora Nash, and Hilda Benson.

The genial, white-haired lady came back to reality. Her audience was still there like the sun that comes out dependably after a storm. She made an appreciative study of the packed auditorium. How long had she mind-gapped? She must not give in to lapsations like that. Yes, she had to concentrate.

She wrapped herself in a smile and spoke softly. "I didn't begin to compose many songs until several years after leaving Iron River. It was the inspiration of my husband, the late Dr. Bond," she said, "and the memories of my days in Iron River that motivated me in the composition of songs that brought back old memories and permitted me to live over again the days of my youth.

I Love You Truly took approximately four years in the introductory stage," she stated. "It became popular after several reputed singers presented it. To date, more than 5,000,000 copies have been sold.

"I found one of my songs in a London music shop though my publisher listed no English sales. Today it is sold in practically every country in the world and has been translated into several languages.

"In closing, I would leave you with the words of an old

woman's experience, don't be afraid to work hard, and never give up, because that is just when success may be just around the corner instead of the poor house." Her smile was brighter than the auditorium lights coming up on a motley audience. She felt a deluge of emotions at that moment: gratitude, joy, peace, and fulfillment.

A warm breeze wandered over the manicured campus of the high school as she left, as if it, too, were pleased she had come home again. Her shoulders lifted in a vague feeling as if she had never left, the lank air kissing her face.

While at the Irvines, Carrie sent a message to Hilda Benson.

> My Dear Mrs. Benson,
> I was out on Highway U.S.-2, but not knowing your daughter's name, where you are living, I became lost.
> Please let me know where and when to see you, and I will try once more.
> With kind wishes,
> Yours Sincerely,
> Carrie Jacobs-Bond.

Hilda's daughter drove her to Irvine home on Sunset Lake in Bates Township for a visit with Carrie. The modesty of character exhibited by Hilda impressed Carrie. Hilda had a way of approaching all things peacefully and calmly; she assuaged Carrie's soul. The world could stop, and Hilda would handle it just fine, exactly as she had unleavened the pressures of serving dinner guests numbering twelve and more. Carrie never undervalued any person, for God was present in everyone and in everyone's work.

Long after Hilda left, her voice traveled inside the Irvine home, a hint of tears in it for the joy of visiting with Carrie, perhaps for the last time ever. Hilda's lifeline at 88-years-old was growing short.

A PERFECT DAY

CHAPTER THIRTY-SEVEN

Upon Carrie's departure from the Irvine home, her persuasion to travel never ceased to amaze the Irvines. On January 16, 1939, the Irvines received a telegram from Carrie.

I am in Chicago for a Columbia Broadcast with Edgar Guest, the Detroit
Free Press syndicated writer. He is immensely popular for serious verse in regard everyday life.
This brings my love for you and yours,"
CJB

***

On Monday, May 23, 1939, while Hitler was invading Rhineland, Austria, and, Czechoslovakia, an evening of song and story was held with the students and friends of the Radford School for Girls in El Paso, Texas. The occasion would always live in the Carrie's memory. Gathered on the lawn of the school on this peaceful Monday evening, Carrie heard the whisper of her footsteps over the mossy lawn, saw stippled sunlight through the branches of ancient creosote trees, and the streak of orange and beige as house finches flitted, always seemingly in fright.

"From a cultural standpoint, the Radford School for Girls is to El Paso what the Hollywood Bowl is to Hollywood," she said in her address, a definite reserve in her posture reflecting the dignified occasion. How vividly she remembered *her* school for girls, a bleak institution removed by eons from Radford.

Carrie, whose life had been rich with living, loving, and working, told the girls to bear in mind that, "We are only what we remember. If we remember only kind and warm things, that's what we are."

She read poems she had written about *My Old Man.* "He is, in my imagination, poor, kindly, sympathetic, and someone to whom people bring their sorrows because he never betrays their trust." Looking around at her audience, Carrie saw trust hanging on all her words. Trust always would be the virtue carried in their hearts. Innocence would disappear, reliability would sometime desert them, but trust would be their anchor. In the back of her mind hung the grave threat of World War in which these young women would surely be involved in one way or another.

She referred to her newly composed song *A Long time Ago* a sort of sequel to *I Love You Truly* written 38 years previous when her heart sorrowed with the death of her beloved husband, Dr. Bond.

There was humor and pathos in her talk, combined as if in a quiet melody. As a finale, Carrie sat at the piano and played *A Perfect Day*, probably her most beloved composition. As the program progressed, the green lawn of the school shadowed, and the dark sky overhead became gemmed with stars. A gentle breeze in the trees, and the flower-embanked stage were a perfect setting for the song.

Carrie, now 77 years old, was gowned for the evening in white chiffon flowered with orchid tints to match a corsage bouquet of orchids. She wore multiple strings of pearls as white as her hair, and diamonds sparkled on delicate sensitive hands. When she left the improvised, outdoor stage, a violet velvet wrap snuggled about her shoulders. Good-natured laughter and buzzing conversation drifted long on the evening air.

A PERFECT DAY

Subsequently, a classroom at Radford was named for Carrie, who had become one of the students' most cherished friends.

***

On June 14, Carrie wrote Lulu F. Fairbanks, C/O Alaska Weekly, Seattle, Washington

Dearest Lulu,

I suppose you will fall right back in your chair when you get this letter from your negligent friend, but really letters are my bugbear. All I do now days is answer all I can.

I suppose you will soon be starting on another journey. Maybe next year I can go with you, and tell you my great disappointment that it was out of the question for this year.

My youngest granddaughter is on her way to Sweden and will probably be having a grand time.
Kind regards,
CJB

***

The Irvines received on August 1 an invitation from Carrie to attend the Chicagoland Music Festival and stay with her at the Stevens Hotel.

> I have an outstanding suite of rooms, but am very alone. I don't trust the help. Would you come, Monica, to care for things for me? It is organized chaos here.

Monica met people, screened them, answered phone calls, even pressed the lovely aqua lace gown Carrie was to wear for the Soldiers Field appearance. Monica had butterflies to picture Carrie in such a color…the same as her eyes.

"It's such an exciting occasion, and Monica rises to it like the trooper she is," Carrie commented to friends.

An escort held out his hand to take hers, and Carrie was brought onto Soldiers' Field under spotlights where she heard 90,000 people sing *A Perfect Day*.

"The experience was one of the greatest of my career," she sighed with ecstatic thrill.

"In performance, she was incomparable," Monica said, "but arrived home with collapse threatening to engulf her. This is a woman in her seventies, not too strong physically, yet her love of people and giving of herself to the public drives her on to do so many things."

***

Back in Iron River, Monica, on August 28, had a telegram asking her to meet Carrie in Green Bay, Wisconsin, and Carrie would come north to visit at Iron River at Sunset Lake, but for a rest, not performing! While visiting, there was a frightening hurricane, which downed many trees. Carrie had just come in from a boat ride with Doctor Irvine and held the youngest daughter in her arms while they hurried to close the windows and doors.

"We could get inside the huge fireplace if things get too bad," Carrie said, her eyes not as comfortable as her words.

A letter from Chicago on Carrie's way home mentioned of the hurricane. *It was not too frightening. It was just another experience!*

She never did know why she said that, more for something soothing to say, she supposed, than for any other reason.

***

A PERFECT DAY

She *was* scared out of her natural calm by the fact that Hitler now had invaded Poland, and resultantly, France and England declared war on Germany. All the lovely lands in which she had visited, toured, and entertained would now smolder in the ruins of war. A picture of the World War I doughboy cooking one strip of bacon and a lonely egg in the pouring down rain buffeted her mind.

Later, she wrote to the Irvines telling of a trip to New York, Philadelphia, and out to San Francisco for the World's Fair where they had a day in her honor. ***A Perfect Day*** was the last piece of music they played.

> My voice was barely audible. I will treasure the sights and sounds of the fair for all eternity.

Monica could envision Carrie's eyes moist and full of rapture.

※※※

On November 16, a letter from Carrie, written at Nest-O-Rest in Grossmont, arrived at the Irvines.

> I came home so tired I could not think. My cook has had a bad accident, several old friends have died, and I see by the newspapers that World War II is well under way in Europe.
>
> I am picking up but I am terribly nervous, and I have about decided that I can never endure so much excitement again, as the fair, and so much devastation as another war. If you remember, I entertained in Europe and the near east during World War I. I think it is quite remarkable that I have lived through

it. It is only occasionally that I remember that I am an old woman, and I don't want you to say, 'Oh, no you're not old.' That is the way everybody answers me. However, nobody that has reached seventy-eight in August can be very far from being old. I don't mean I am so old that I am dumb, but I am too old to have much excitement or bad news. I might be able to stand up to a hurricane with you, but hearing 100,000 people sing my song would be more than I could possibly live through again, but wasn't it wonderful? It puts war in its menial place.

***

With a view of the ocean, complete rest, and quiet, Carrie again gathered her strength and wits about her. The morning fog hung heavily on the water, swirling as if fiercely protecting what lie beneath it. It was at moments such as this that the laughter withdrew from her eyes and she became preoccupied. Her carefully erected defenses tumbled like the walls of Jericho. Thoughts awash with Hubbard's voice, his mannerisms, his warm eyes, and his unqualified acceptance of her crept in with the fog. Seeking to extinguish her loneliness, she reached into her files and found a copy of *Preachments From Hollywood*, her syndicated column originating in the Los Angeles Times from 1928, and re-read it. Every word had been dedicated to Elbert Hubbard.

FRIENDLY PREACHMENTS FROM HOLLYWOOD

By: Carrie Jacobs-Bond

February 19 through 26, 1928
SENTIMENT

A PERFECT DAY

Way down the road of happy years
Through light of happy days
I seem to see your face aglow
Through all the golden rays.
And through the sound of waving grain
And through the whispering tree
I seem to hear your voice again
And you are calling me.
Oh happy road of years and days
Dear sound of grass and tree
I wish I were as much to you
As you have been to me.

Right now, it may be out of style to have sentiment but it will never be out of style long. Sentiment can never be taken from the soul of youth and old age. Perhaps there are a few years along in middle life when folks seem to lose their sentiment—when the dreams of youth are shattered and when the ripeness of older years is not yet realized.

What man, young or old, does not cherish the memory of the whispering tree where he first told of his love, or experienced his first kiss? Who does not recall now and then the scent of some sweet flower that takes him or her back to happy childhood days?

Sentiment is one of the priceless possessions of every generation. It should never be out of fashion, for it brushes away shame and pretense and carries us back to the deep springs of love and hope, and devotion. Yes, I believe there is a spot in every heart that responds to the memory of a sweet scented flower and to the whispering of a tree and says of some love done, "I wish I were as much to you as you have been to me."

While she was in Hubbard's arms, there was no one more exultant than she was, unless it was he. But deeply seeded was the knowledge that the thought was fallacy. Yes, he cared, he loved, but the caring love of Dr. Bond was faultless, and from her life's experiences, her judgment of human nature was pretty much right on target.

A PERFECT DAY

CHAPTER THIRTY-EIGHT

After several months' lapsation, in 1940, Monica heard from Carrie in February, July, August, and, more amusing, all at once from Jackson, Michigan where Carrie attended a festival and took part in the performance every night for eight evenings!

The Third Annual Cascades Festival at Jackson, Michigan, a 465-acre scenic wonder located at the southwest edge of the city, was like nothing Carrie had ever participated in, or, indeed, had ever seen. The colorful, ever-changing beauty of the far-famed Illuminated Cascades of the William and Matilda Sparks Foundation, Inc., proved to be an irresistible magnet to millions of enthralled visitors. Varicolored lights, changing with kaleidoscopic rapidity, flashed rainbow hues in gushing, tumbling waters and in the dancing jet plumes of spouting fountains.

Carrie read the brochure.

> The only construction of its kind in the world, Jackson's famous, $3,000,000, ($37,620,000 in today's dollars), Illuminated Cascades exemplifies the ability of man to duplicate the beauties of nature. Of massive concrete construction, the Cascades are 550 feet long, 60 feet wide and 84 feet high. The reflection pools of the Cascades contain approximately 350,000 gallons of water beneath the rippling surfaces of the falls and pools.

Lights of three primary colors: red, green, and blue, add to the six fountains to produce 100 different combinations of color in each hour's cycle.

On the convenient walks arranged completely around the Cascades with 129 steps along each side, Carrie strolled under her summer umbrella. Balustrades edged the outer sides of the walks with comfortable settees located at frequent intervals for the convenience of visitors. Thank God, thought Carrie. Her pulse accelerated at an alarming rate when she overdid herself. Nevertheless, her eyes sparkled with life and her cheeks glowed with high color with the stimulation of being a part of something so lovely.

In addition to the Illuminated Cascades, the Foundation also invited its visitors to enjoy the facilities of its picnic grounds, its rolling, 18-hole golf course, and its luxuriously appointed clubhouse built in the Tudor style of English architecture. Carrie felt right at home, for, coincidentally enough, the Charles Dickens structural design was exactly as she had designed her Bond Shop.

Carrie quickly found that Jackson, Michigan was more than a skyline of bricks. The silhouette of modern buildings and factories stood for every virtue of wise expansion, fair dealing, and confidence in the future. Solidly behind these structures were organizations of executives and co-workers whose civic pride and belief in Greater Jackson was unmatched with any community, save the Roycrofters Village.

Carrie knew that stone, brick, nails, and lumber did not make a city. It takes more than that. It takes faith, vision, hard work, and a spirit of community pride. Jackson, Michigan was built that way. *The art of winning in business is in working hard—not taking things too seriously,* Elbert had many times pressed upon her.

A PERFECT DAY

Certain localities, like certain people, have a definite charm and appeal that eludes analysis and definition.

What attracted Carrie was that the 1940 Cascades Festival was not a pageant, not a drama, but instead, this year an enthralling musical revue in the manner conceived by the incomparable Ziegfeld. Highlights of the 1940 production were born in the minds of Broadway's great...given life by the colorful cast, orchestra, chorus, ballet, and the magical resources of the theatrical realm. Superb music and inspiring beauty against the incomparable setting of the Illuminated Cascades were under the spell of summer nights. Of such was the 1940 Cascades Festival prompting Carrie to agree to a performance every night.

Unforgettable moments were these magical evenings! Over her breakfast coffee, she read in the program. *Wedding Night, starring the beloved Carrie Jacobs-Bond in a romantic bridal scene with a cast of 200.*

Her heart stopped beating for an instant. Never-Be-Anything, Carrie Jacobs, from Janesville, Wisconsin now was in a starring role in the Cascades? There it was in black and white. No walking up four flights of stairs as she had in London. *Au contraire*, she had uptown accommodations right on the grounds overlooking the golf course. Her gaze traveled from the lush fairways to her coffee cup. She could feel the silence grow heavy around her, but she would not allow it to be consuming. It was tricky, but she made a lightning switch to bright-eyed and light. She was too old for melancholy.

In addition to Carrie's tribute, there were eleven other super-colossal musical spectacles involving a cast of 1,000. There were ten huge stages in simultaneous operation, and a sixty-piece symphony orchestra and singing ensemble of fifty voices.

The symphony orchestra, Cascades Singing Ensemble and the dazzling bridal ballet augmented *Wedding Night*, a tribute to Carrie.

UNIT 1 - *At The End Of A Perfect Day* - Singing Ensemble
UNIT 2 - Carrie Jacobs-Bond and the Children's Chorus
UNIT 3 - Wedding Party—Featuring the brides and grooms of yesterday in the immortal, *I Love You Truly* spectacle.
UNIT 4 - Brides of Today—Flower Girls
UNIT 5 - Tableau...Long Live Love!

Carrie, at 78 years old, reminded herself that the secret to living long is to live slowly. It was time for her to toss out the anchor. She had climbed many a steep hill in her lifetime. Now on the far side of the hill, it would be outrageous for her to overdo. She filled her days with the attractions of the Cascade Festival, yet as soon as her performance at night was concluded, she disciplined herself to seek her bed. Carrie reminded herself of a match struck and burning enthusiastically until its energy was consumed, its flame guttering as her fireplace logs had so many years ago when she received Dr. Bond's proposal of marriage. The joy of that moment revisited was as a hot flood of rejuvenation in her chest, her very breath catching.

There was not a night that she did not pray for Frank, Fred, and Elbert. Bond would be 82 now, Fred 54, and Hubbard would be exactly her age. How would they look? Would they have aged well? Would it have made any difference? She loved them all dearly. The tranquility of their love lasted beyond time passages. However varied the courses of Carrie's life, whatever the phases of pleasure and ambition through which it was swept along, when in memory she would revive the times that were comparatively the happiest, those times were found to have been the calmest.

Peaceful was the backyard serenity of her home in Iron

A PERFECT DAY

River, Michigan sitting with young Fred and doctor, the towering white pines whispering as if in conspiracy to keep them sheltered and happy. Peaceful was the magical time in Hubbard's fragrant apple orchard with the soft fluttering of blossoms onto and around the concert stage, falling onto her hair, onto her eyelashes, giving a watercolor surrealism to the afternoon program, especially to Hubbard himself, who was deeply, and silently wearing his heart on his sleeve in admiration of his special woman. Peaceful was Fred's encouragement through all the bitter years of poverty.

Carrie savored repeatedly the sweet memories. It soothed her longing for tranquility. In the beaded string of Carrie's years, she found that her pearls of peace were not the result of perfection but from acquiescence not exempt from suffering. In all her losses, she had not expected the time for good-byes to come so quickly and be so final. Yet, she no longer wanted to explore the heavy sadness in her life; it flagged her energy. She would dwell only on successes. She had had enough of premature nights falling, engulfing her in gloom.

After the eighth performance of The Cascades, Carrie slept the sleep of the peaceful.

A PERFECT DAY

CHAPTER THIRTY-NINE

In late July 1941, Carrie wrote from Grossmont:

Dearest Lulu:

I presume you have thought all kinds of things about me, and I do not blame you in the least. It seems to me that I wrote you that we could not go on the trip, as my one granddaughter could not have the time. I do not know whether I wrote you; if I did not, you must forgive me for between the time of your letter and now, I have been at death's door again. However, I am picking fine now. I am very thin and don't like that very well because it makes my wrinkles so much worse.

Maybe sometime this winter you could come down to see me. I should be delighted to have you. I am freer to have company now, as I do not live such a hectic life as I used to.

This brings my love for you and yours, and do forgive a typewritten letter. I am not quite able to write.
Devotedly,
CJB

**

In spite of her weariness, Carrie was gone from her Nest-O-Rest home in Grossmont from August 5 to September 30, 1941, again going to San Francisco where *A Perfect Day* was sung, and she was accompanied by a symphony orchestra.

Overjoyed, she said, "200,000 people sang it in the dark!"

All this after the letter the year before to the Irvines in which she declared her ensconcement at home due to bad health.

In this same year, Carrie published her last song ***The Flying Flag***, but found her in bed most of the time. Being the tough character that she was, eventually she smiled, took a deep breath, and traveled again. Enthusiasms long submerged surged to the surface like a caprice current of air.

Whether it was a second wind, or the bizarre absence of self-preservation, whatever, but the weariness dropped from Carrie's eyes, and with a thud of her heart, she blazed on. It was as if she needed a last hurrah, and the arrow of stimulation pierced her brain. She had to stay active. Without hesitation, she joined the gathering of the Los Angeles Chamber of Commerce for the Twelfth Annual Goodwill Tour to Alaska.

A reporter wrote:

> Mrs. Bond was in a hurry. She said, "It has been a wonderful trip so far. I have never seen so much breathtaking scenery in my life as I am seeing in this vast country. That's all. I don't like publicity."
>
> She was off to Columbus Hospital to visit an old friend, Lucy E. Fairbanks, 77 years old, of 1833 13th Ave., who was ill. Mrs. Fairbank's two daughters, the Misses Lulu and Esther Fairbanks, and Mrs. Margaret Garred, met Carrie, at her request, and took her to the hospital.

Carrie threw her arms around Lucy as she greeted her. "Oh God, Lucy, why do we have to grow old so soon?" They had been friends for close to forty years, since the Roosevelt/Fairbanks administration.

A PERFECT DAY

"It's not by the gray of my hair that you know the age of my heart," Lucy murmured. "Come closer." Carrie bent over the bed, soothing Lucy's head.

"Let us respect our gray hair, Carrie, especially our own." Mirth danced in Lucy's eyes, eyes that had paled with age and walked a milky path sunk in bony confinement without benefit of the deco of youth.

"Your daughters inherited enough of your red hair to pass on for generations," Carrie said, while Esther and Lulu sparkled with every word.

Yet, Carrie's heart was heavy with a sadness she was not prepared to explore, and she would not. She had to believe that Lucy was a survivor, like herself.

After the hospital visitation, and an hour's rest, the three women attended a supper, where a hundred or more women gathered for a *Boost The Philharmonic Symphony* program at the Biltmore Galleria Hall. Carrie was dressed like a queen with a magnificent tiara in her hair.

A journalist, who had previously visited in Carrie's home, decided to say hello and interview her.

> Carrie remembered my visit and asked me to call again sometime. Miss Lulu Fairbanks of The Alaska Weekly was this journalist's reason for visiting Carrie.
>
> I begged Mrs. Bond to take me with her to that dinner, and she did. Mrs. Bond, however, was soon surrounded by a group of women in evening gowns, furs and diamonds too numerous to mention, and charming in their simplicity, so I had to get away from there.

***

Carrie's professional life surged away to carve out room for things polarized—a social life where she was held in high esteem for herself, and her lifetime of dedication to peaceful privacy. The two entities were as two streams in confluence, coming together; they mix and create a whirlpool, sometimes gentle, sometimes whitewater.

On November 14, 120 Southern Californians beaming with good will checked in at Union Station that forenoon, breathed deeply of Seattle's invigorating atmosphere for an hour and a half, reluctantly pronounced it good, and sailed for Alaska on the *Aleutian*.

"The ship was a far cry from the small ferries that Lulu and I used on our previous jaunts up the coast line," she shared with her nurse/companion.

As if in sudden realization of what she was undertaking, her eyes widened. Am I really doing this? Carrie, after the fact, wrestled with the decision. Her stomach did a slow, lazy roll; however, her senses soared and swirled with a spirit of adventure.

The ripple of the ocean liner sounded musical to Carrie, as if late-summer breezes were leaning the prairie grasses of the vast Midwest. Included within her mental concert was the enormous dome of blue sky with playful clouds folding and unfolding caricatures of the many features she had observed in the Wisconsin clouds of her youth. Harmonious notes jumped onto an empty staff of music creating a private symphony.

Encapsulated, Carrie needed nothing to enhance the magic of the moment. For her it was all here in the brisk air, and the performance of happiness in her heart. Once aboard the *Aleutian*, Carrie's chief concern was how she would get about from deck to deck. At 79 years old, stairways presented a difficult obstacle. Nonetheless, she smiled.

A PERFECT DAY

"I'll have my meals served in my stateroom." Relief leapt to her eyes, the deep lines from years of tension smoothed from her face.

She mulled all the times she had spent so happily with Dr. Bond, and then, with Elbert Hubbard. The awful fits of shyness as a child, superimposed by her mother, had faded as if they were non-existent, especially with Elbert, who had a magnetism and talent for putting people at ease. He brought out the best in her, and taught her the value of her own self-worth. After all these years, she recognized that she forgot much of what they talked about, but, at length, they learned all about each other.

One of the most profound thinkers of our lifetime had written a mourner at Elbert's funeral. She no longer felt weighty grief for either man, only love remained. Whatever one's loss, with the passage of years, happiness creeps back.

In her stateroom, she could hear the ocean skimming past the hull of the ship, and overhead, hear the bright laughter of deck walkers. Under her warm quilt, she sighed, her body in need of rest. Her eyes burned with fatigue. The last thought that crossed her mind was a memory of Schneider leaping up on her bed to snuggle in for the night, whenever he got past her mother, the three-headed Cerberus of The Davis House.

While Carrie slept, the devil's power was at work, and before she got back to Nest-O-Rest, the United States entered World War II resultant of…"an unprovoked and dastardly attack by Japan on Sunday, December 7, 1941."

A PERFECT DAY

CHAPTER FORTY

The ocean voyage, forever an indelible memory, assured Carrie of how pliant she yet was. Father Time was clicking, however, and a year later found Carrie ill at home in Grossmont, and on December 11, 1942, she reported to the Irvines, that she'd been miserable since last December when the whole world went crazy with war, and her body went crazy with rheumatics. Demanding more and more of herself, she acquiesced that her pliancy was stiffening.

Carrie took to her bed so tired and aching, she was shaking. A hired nurse, blonde and tireless, "Young Helen," at her bedside, Carrie sank back into an exhausted sleep of peace. The rewards of years of struggle, worry, cold, and disappointments came together with an amazing success that afforded her rest, plenty of rest. It was time to never assume, never pre-determine the mileage remaining on her strength odometer.

On a day when she felt invigorated, she wrote a letter to Mr. Walter Olson, president, Olson Rug Company, Chicago, Illinois.

> Over twenty years ago, I sent you a great bunch of old carpets, and rugs, which your catalogue said would be returned to me in any of the desired colors, for about half the amount of money. I doubted that a little bit. As the carpets were no use to me the way they were, however, I thought that I would see what would happen.
>
> In the most remarkable space of time, I received

one of the most serviceable rugs I have ever had in my house.

Since then, you have made five more for me, but the first one is still in fine condition, and I am proud to have them on my floors.

About the colors, they have never faded. One was light green, two were blue, and two were taupe. I think that is quite a record, don't you?

Most Sincerely,

CJB

Wave after wave of pleasure washed over her when, ensuing to her letter, the Olson Rug Company asked her permission to use the letter as an endorsement. She agreed.

***

That same year, The Christian Science Monitor featured Carrie after an interview at End-Of-The-Road.

> In a lovely garden, *Just as God-made it*, in the heart of Hollywood, one of America's most beloved characters, now eighty years old, does not sit and dream of the past and sort over her memories. She is much too busy for that—and busy with things that concern today's problems and the cataclysmic events that engross the human race. She still writes songs with life that reach the far corners of the world.
>
> During the last few months, she has written two stirring songs that have to do with the war effort *The Flying Flag*, and *Somebody Waiting For Me*. She is donating the royalties of these songs to the American Red Cross and the U. S. O. for the duration, so that anyone who buys them directly helps these two groups.
>
> Mrs. Bond shares a deep and obsessive love for

A PERFECT DAY

humanity.

"This caring is a product of my own unhappiness and lack of self-confidence as a child, when I was instilled with a brutal nonchalance for others," she said.

***

On June 23, 1944, in a letter received by the Irvines, she wrote that she'd been very ill, unable to write and in bed for four months.

On September 17, a letter came from End-Of-The-Road in Hollywood.

> My wonderful nurse is with me, and I am making plans for disposition of my belongings. I would like to offer you, Monica, one of my desks. I know that I will never travel again.
>
> How I have taken such delight in the early morning sunshine of this wonderful home.
>
> The air is crisp, and the dew shimmers on the mountain flowers. Over the ocean, a gauzy cloud of mist swirls as if it were a living entity.

The crescendo of her self-admission thundered in her ears upon drafting the letter.

***

October leaped into view bringing moisture-laden air that hung limp and clinging, sometimes chilling Carrie to the bone just looking out her window on the world. The war news held promise. General MacArthur reclaimed the Philippines just as he had promised, and the Japanese navy was destroyed.

***

Into her life was to enter a tangible delight. A young man by the name of Mark Hanold of Iron River attended a radio broadcast while in military service in California and selected for an interview.

"Do you know anyone in the area?" He was asked.

"Yes, I know of Carrie Jacobs-Bond, the composer. She lived in my hometown at one time." Carrie happened to be listening and before he left the studio, she had him paged. "I'll send my car for you to bring you to my home. We'll have a fried chicken dinner."

Carrie found the young, copper-haired man serious and quite grown-up for only eighteen-years-old. After that visit, he saw her frequently, going for drives with her in her chauffeured car. Other times she asked him to drive. During one call, they sat in her garden in which she took special delight at her Hollywood home.

"I love to sit among my flowers and watch the sunset and follow the motions of the humming birds that come to get food. I set out special concoctions for them everyday, and manage not to waste a single, fleeting day. I know that my life is almost over, Mark, but I feel no fear. I am deeply religious. Death is merely the opening of a portal that will reveal the road home."

Mark, biting his lip uncomfortably at Carrie's delving into her demise, was nodding, mostly listening while Carrie reminisced.

"I know that you're going overseas," she said. "Make sure you and your cohorts meet your enemy on your choice of surprise. Choose carefully the position to fight from."

After he deployed (to the Philippines), Carrie wrote his mother, and made a recording for her. Mark Hanold

A PERFECT DAY

remembered her as a personable, kind person, interested in everyone, with an all-consuming enthusiasm. He remembered the silver radiance of Carrie's hair, and the attaching moments of their conversations.

***

December 10, 1944, Carrie wrote Lulu Fairbanks from End-Of-The-Road.

Dearest Lulu-

Just a word of love because there's so much mail I'm frantic trying to answer it.

It seems to me your timely letter was just about the nicest Christmas present anybody could have. It suited me to perfection.

I am sorry your mother is not well, and that you have been sick. I bet you're all right now—both of you.

I am going to visit my granddaughter in San Antonio the twentieth. I shall be gone for two weeks. After that, if you want to fly down and see me, I shall be happy. Only let me know a little while ahead.

With a heart full of love for you and yours.
CJB
P.S. I helped elect Roosevelt to an unprecedented fourth term of office!

January 1945
Well, dear Lulu:

I was glad to receive your letter, but very sorry to know you were sick, and very glad to know you are better.

I do not seem ever to get well any more. I think I shall be around, and the next day I am in bed, where I am tonight, having had another bad spell with my stomach. Nonetheless, dear friend, and of course you know you are among them, I hope you are all better now. I don't know how anybody can perk up with such a world to live in, when you think of all we have that is good and treasured that has to be ruined by hate.

However, the weather is perfect down here, and the birds sing in the garden just as if there were no troubles in the world. I try to think what a lucky old woman I am that I have a home, and feel sure that I shall be dead before the war is finished. I do not know but that it would be a very nice way to have it end. I Think I would like to go before the crash comes. I don't worry about it at all, and I don't think very many people do. I think we all know it is serious, but, someway, I don't expect to be bombed the way everybody thinks we are going to be—everybody that lives out East.

I think I would just as soon live on the shore of the Pacific as to be where they are sinking vessels outside New York City. In fact, I don't know of any real safe place, do you? If you do, let me know, and I will try my best to get there. I haven't any blackouts ready, sand piles, or long hoses, but I talk about having those things every day. I don't know who is going to win, the Japs or me.

I am sorry not to write a better letter, but we have been trying to get the writing desk clear tonight, so all the letters have to be a little short.

Did I send you a picture of my sweet dog—little

A PERFECT DAY

Peter Pan? If not, I will send you one. The precious thing died about three weeks ago with the most vague, puzzled look; it just about broke my heart. He was the loveliest animal I have ever known, and I was not the only one that thought that. Once more, goodbye, with love for you always. I hope your mother is better.
CJB

February 15, 1945, Letter to Lulu.

Dearest Lulu:

I am so distressed to hear your mother is sick. Please give her my love.

At last, I can truthfully say I am improving instead of deteriorating. Last night, for the first time in a year, I had dinner with some friends. I stayed all night, had a perfectly wonderful time, and expect to do it sometime soon again. Obviously, I have been too closely confined. The doctor wants me to get away, and I may possibly, but can't say at present, as I have no clothes to wear. I am so thin, that everything just about falls off me.

I am returning the letter you sent. It is very nice. When I get well enough to have my clothes fixed up, I hope to journey some place, and I think it will be Chicago. The friends with whom I spent the night last, Walter and Cora Gale, were old friends from

Chicago. I had just the nicest time; we did not even mention the war.

I do hope and pray your mother will soon be better, Always, with love,

CJB

March 6, 1945 Carrie writes. Miss Lulu Fairbanks, Alaska Weekly, 2100 Fifth Avenue, Seattle, Washington.

Dear Lulu:

I am so distressed to get your letter about your precious mother; I see before me her freckled face. It is all too terrible, but all we can do is what I have always done, trust in God. If they have to live and suffer, just try to make the best of their going.

I think of you often. I am not very well, but of course, I am gaining, but it is terribly slow. I don't have a nurse anymore. I just have to get along with other help. I had a very faithful one, Helen, who lived with me for seven years, but she is not able to come to do my work. She comes to stay with me, however, and I am very fond of her. I have a nice little girl to help do the work, so we are getting along all right.

The weather has been rainy but it is comfortable in its own way, and I am very, very happy in many ways.

I often think of you, and always with love. I know you will excuse a short letter, because there is so much to do and so little time.

With love for you and yours, and especially your dear mother,
Affectionately, CJB

Some day, Carrie promised herself, she would consider another trip to Seattle to see her dear friends. She stared fixedly at the morning sky, studying its soft blue, the same color as her eyes. A healthy wind from off the ocean whipped at her windows and bent the early-blooming daffodils in her garden. What a lucky woman she was.

A PERFECT DAY

CHAPTER FORTY-ONE

There was a soft rain falling on the roof when Carrie read the Los Angeles Times headlines announcing the death of President Roosevelt. As fate would have it, only a month after Lucy died, he expired after suffering a stroke in Warm Springs, Georgia. Perhaps Lucy joined Carrie's beloved president, whom, Carrie was sure, rested in a special place in heaven where Lucy could find him. Carrie's thoughts tumbled as if they had wings of imagination. She wondered, do people talk to each other through their minds, in heaven? Are they spirits, or flesh and blood? The answers were a conundrum never to be solved by anyone, Carrie determined.

One month later, May 7, 1945, a week after the death of Adolf Hitler, Germany surrendered to General Eisenhower, supreme commander of Allied Forces in Europe. Carrie had seen much history written. She sat in her garden under some trees, pulled her rheumatic knees up, wrapped her arms around them, and put her head on her arms, dwelling on the end of the terror, the hellish number of heroes sacrificed, for what? Until the next maniac surfaced?

**

On the Tenth Anniversary of the First Chicagoland Music Festival, Carrie, just turned 83 years old, was invited to return as honored guest, and she did. It was August 1945. The Japanese had surrendered in the Pacific after the United States dropped an atomic bomb on both Hiroshima and Nagasaki, and Carrie's lifeline was becoming short.

She sat and cut clippings from the Chicago daily papers about the horrific destruction of the bombs, and so she would have something in words to tell about what happened to her the day before. She still did not understand why such honors had come to her, and at the same time as the end of the awful war. Her room was filled with flowers, gifts, letters, telephones, and folks, for the last three days, and she did not understand why it was she was still able to think. Everyone was so kind. People looked at her with pointed curiosity, which made her recall that strangers had always been kind to her.

Carrie cultivated in her mind where she was. Within moments, she determined that she was almost on the identical spot on Michigan Avenue where the last lovely Bond Shop was. She was on the twenty-fourth floor of the world's largest hotel, The Stevens. The lodging faced Lake Michigan, the banks of which she knew forty years ago, and whose winds pierced her frail clothing. The Great Lake shoreline was, at that time, just a little beach with the Illinois Central Railroad swishing by, black smoke spoiling everything, and such a noise!

Today Lake Michigan had moved out about a mile; she shook her head in disbelief. With a bewildering glimmer of delight, she viewed the most magnificent park with glorious buildings, great fountains, fields big enough for hundreds of people to stand and watch a ball game, ample tennis courts, graceful statuary, and all free to anybody.

Someone pressed a cup of cocoa into Carrie's hand. At sunrise this morning, she lay abed and saw the wonderful dawn happen way beyond Lake Michigan, and it seemed to her, the world. Then, later, she observed the rush of thousands of people coming to town to work, and all day long until sunset. She could no longer see that happen due to her failing eyesight, but she could see ten million lights come on, all in little rows marking out the boulevards. She laced her fingers and leaned back against the side of an armoire in wonder and amazement. Every little while a red light flashed, and all the traffic went one way. A warning light of yellow, and then the green light, and the other line was taken. All night long the changes happened, keeping Carrie dumbfounded, as she never slept very well anyway.

Resultantly, most every morning since she had arrived, she pulled on her wrapper and sat by the window watching the few late home-goers whirl down Michigan Avenue and the other drives, faster than most anything she could imagine, and she wondered what it was all about. It became apparent to her that she must have been living in a different time dimension at her End-Of-The-Road. She believed she belonged here as if she had never left, therefore she did.

Into her room, there came half a dozen friends to cheer her on her way to the Ball Room of the Stevens Hotel, where she was to be given an honor for something. She could not imagine what, because nothing she had ever done deserved such a reward. She had thought that Dr. Bond's undying love for her and Elbert Hubbard's everlasting attraction had cured her of the self-effacing nature printed into her character by a reticent childhood. The timidity that had disappeared in their presence quickly reared its head and paralyzed her from facing the throng that greeted her. There were twenty-six hundred people attending breakfast! Her irresolution framed a thousand horrors, each feeding on the other. She must stand resolute and, **_Do what she would do when she should do it._** Shakespeare's words were a comfort, and sustained her for days.

In the evening ceremonies, Carrie led the procession. Dizzy and overcome, she could not see, but intermittently somebody touched her shoulder and pointed. She marched to a strain of music she could hardly hear, with all those people following her, her face a mask of uncertainty.

There were fifty people seated at Carrie's table. She sat at the right hand of the speaker, Maxwell Anderson, an American Playwright, and her dear old precious friend, John

Tinny McCucheon, sat next to her. Living in the same generation as Carrie, John was a cartoonist, war correspondent, president of the **Chicago Zoological Society,** on staff at the **Chicago Tribune,** and won the Pulitzer Prize for cartoons in 1931.

On the left side of Maxwell Anderson, was George Ade, another of Carrie's generation, a U.S. journalist, writer, and playwright, who was known for his humorous tales of urbanized country people. He wrote for the **Chicago Record.** However, he was best known for **Fables in Slang** and sequels, which portrayed city life in country vernacular.

"There Ade sat looking as sober as somebody who had just been to a funeral," Carrie quipped to a friend. Deep runnels ran down the sides of his mouth, but there was a soft, warm, lively look in his eyes. Carrie suspected that he was probably chuckling inside every minute. She was stunned when they both gave her their speeches, two more precious things for her to put away and read when she arrived home.

"There were fifty important people at our table. I don't mean to say there are ever any more important than anybody else is, but they were all people who had done something outstanding, or the head of something, like the University of Chicago.

"The whole hall was decked with bountiful flowers!" Carrie exclaimed. When the band struck up pomp and ceremony, a lovely blond girl, not shy but confident, was heralded on the stage, and with a graceful wave of her hand she thanked everybody for being so nice to her. "Oh, she was lovely!" Carrie said, almost holding her breath. "As the young lady led the procession, accompanied by soldiers in full dress, they approached the table where I sat. I did an unheard of thing. I threw my arms around her and gave her a smacking kiss. I see, however, by the morning papers, the smacking kiss was what she remembered of yesterday, so it paid to take the chance."

John McCutcheon had introduced George Ade, and he had made his speech. While Carrie, for the first time in her life, had written what she wanted to say, John and George Ade took out their notes, typewritten copies of what they were going to say, and she knew they could read every word.

Carrie thought of her hen scratching that no one could possibly recognize. "I looked at it, and I couldn't read a word myself!" Her eyes rounded in shock and her body felt numb with realization.

Just about then, Edith Mason began to sing *A Perfect Day*. Carrie had always been a little deaf, but she was stone deaf after the rendition. "I didn't hear a sound of applause. This time, however, I thought, *Well, I am not only blind, but I am deaf, and I wonder when I get over on that platform if I am going to be dumb.* The old doubts and reservations of early adolescence came crunching back to nest ominous and shapeless, like a cloud of immense portent. *Do what you would when you should,* she repeated to herself. The silent message waxed more eloquent than kind words could ever have done.

Carrie was led away across the platform, "While the audience sang almost as well as the Community Chorus in Hollywood," and she found she was on the stage. Her eyes stung, and she lowered her head. She had to firm her chin and carry on. The resolution, mandated as it was by the occasion, burst upon her in a flash of pride that shored up her wretchedly churning thoughts. She prayed to God to free her mind and loosen her tongue.

The panic that she was witnessing was a sudden desertion of her normal self and an enemy. It was a spooked stampede of her self-possession, a rout of gigantic proportions. She thought of the warmth and beauty of her garden at The-End-Of-The-Road, her three-story home on the hillside there, and thus managed to calm herself. She lulled herself with thoughts of her bedroom, two floors up from the street. Opening onto her garden in back, she envisioned the plot of ground that offered a place to walk and sit in quietude. Calming and bolstering was her fierce concentration on home and those who had loved her in the past, for herself, for her graciousness, for her altruistic lifestyle. The ferocious winds of doubt calmed.

"I have written my speech, but I can't read it," she confessed stalling to contain her flyaway emotions.

A murmur of encouraging laughter arose from the audience.

"So…from here on I think I'll tell you the story of my life, from the cradle to pretty near the grave, because I think I am either going to die tonight, or at least, sooner than expected."

Again, there prevailed whispers of supportive amusement.

"I'll begin with my grandfather more than eighty years ago coming from Chester, Vermont, and heading across the United States in his caravan, with his family of six, my father being the sixth member, with all their household furniture, piano and all, for two houses. With the Civil War simmering in the south, grandfather stayed north and drove through Chicago. When he saw this place, he said, 'Too windy and marshy for me! I'm going to Wisconsin.'

"So the caravan with the tired horses, to say nothing about the tired folks, went farther north to Janesville and was perfectly charmed by the village. Divided by the Rock River, thousands of acres of prairie were waiting for a good farmer like my grandfather. In about two years, I was born."

With confidence and eloquence, she continued until the speech was ended, as if the chronological events were sturdy Italian Cypress in a city park hedgerow.

"I didn't hear any applause," she said later, "but they said there was some, and I didn't see anybody stand up, but they say they did. The spotlight was on me, and something happened to my heart. It didn't stop beating, but it did an extra something that it never did before.

"I didn't cry. I waited until the morning when I sat alone in my room, ate my breakfast, and thought it all over; then I cried. I wasn't crying because I was unhappy. I was just crying with amazement, for I still don't see what I have done to deserve so much. Nobody could have had more done for them than I have had."

Carrie, as she had sat at the guest dais received flowers sent to the table, notes, and letters, before she went up to the platform. While she was yet at the microphone, they gave her a remembrance.

"And what do you think it was?" She said, smiling. "It was a replica of the delicate wreath I have always used on my music, only it was four feet high and made of ivy and pink roses, just as near as they could make it like my music." Carrie took a deep breath to save hold on her courage and composure.

"The spotlight was turned on Edith Mason, a Chicago Operatic Soprano, and me again, and Mason sang *I Love You Truly*. It was the cue for another spotlight to be focused from the gallery, and there was the most special picture you could ever imagine: a divine bride and groom," Carrie related. "They say she is the loveliest girl at the University Campus, and she looked perfectly lustrous. It was quite a minute before the people realized the full meaning. They were still looking at Edith Mason who was singing *I Love You Truly* to me, but finally they looked up and saw this lovely picture. It was a startling idea."

While the audience sang *A Perfect Day,* Carrie was escorted across the ballroom once more followed by a magnificent birthday cake in honor of the Tenth Anniversary of the Chicagoland Music Festival. Carrie looked pleased, more than pleased; she sparkled, when on top of that cake was another wreath to represent her title pages.

It took her back to when she hand painted dishes and sold them for sustenance. The wild rose was always a part of her artisan work, her manuscripts. She could almost feel the cold creeping into her bones again as it did in her one room that was kept barely heated. Icy fingers crept across her chest as she relived the pandemic of poverty for which a cure eluded her for so long.

Emotionally fragile, tears slid unnoticed and unchecked down her creased cheeks.

A PERFECT DAY

CHAPTER FORTY-TWO

Carrie's longed-for End-Of-The-Road greeted her kindly upon arrival in California. Her garden, never disappointing, offered multiple varieties of humming birds sipping nectar from delicate hibiscus and lantana.

During these hours of relaxation, and, at age 83, Carrie offered Monica Irvine a mirror and candlesticks to go with the desk she had previously promised, also Dr. Bond's picture, and a picture of Carrie with Fred. These items were never received. Monica banished her preoccupation with ownership of these precious mementoes believing that Carrie was too ill to see that the instructions were followed.

In October, the desk did arrive, and, later, in November, a brief note written by Carrie's secretary conveyed kind thoughts to the Irvines.

Most of Carrie's remaining time was spent at End-Of-The-Road in Hollywood. There she indulged in the pleasure of the sun-lit patio with a tiny, tinkling waterfall that activated or remained silent, as Carrie wished. Long, lazy hours were consumed there with Carrie's gifted hands busy over needlework, and her cherished wirehaired terrier, tiny blind Michael, taking turns on her lap.

When Carrie was tired, there were lunches on trays in the combination sleeping-sitting room.

"Always her bed fascinated me—it was so huge and high that she used a step to reach it," said Carrie's reader, Virginia Kay, a bespectacled, lean woman quite dedicated to Carrie. "Carrie looked about her often; as if it were the last time she'd ever see her familiar possessions, but always with a kind of smiling complacency that made me admire the resiliency of the woman. When reading, I made a supreme effort to keep my voice calm and pleasant with her voluminous mail. I was astonished and a little horrified to find how many letters came from strangers, asking, asking, and asking. They asked for everything from autographs to financial aid, to help in publishing songs, and to positions available."

"What was that?" Carrie would ask, almost bewildered.

"It is puzzling, isn't it," Kay said reassuringly, but with resentment at the lack of simple courtesy reflected in the requests, which were crass enough to unhinge the elderly Carrie.

***

Kay recalls the summer day when they drove to the Hollywood Bowl to hear Grace Moore rehearse—for the composer and the diva were old friends.

"It was the only time I ever knew Carrie to *use* the power of her name. We were barred from the Bowl amphitheatre—"No Visitors Allowed," until Mrs. Bond said very quietly, "I am Carrie Jacobs-Bond." Whereupon, a stuttering young man hastily lifted ropes, all but scraped the ground, and beamed like the mid-day sun.

"Carrie gave a nod of satisfaction, and her smile deepened," Kay added. "I must have looked awestruck, the last emotion Carrie expected from anyone.

"She quickly responded. 'The tribute I would treasure most is just to be remembered in the hearts of those who loved me.'

"She'd been looking down at her shoes," said Kay, "but her bright blue eyes rose to meet mine in complete guilelessness. To be disallowed a visit with Moore would have been a disappointment akin to a thousand shards of glass in Carrie's heart."

***

In the spring of 1946, a Hollywood director visited with Monica Irvine in Iron River, and a buzz of conversation began. He wanted to plan a movie about Carrie's life, but the movie company could not seem to agree on a lead. Monica went to Hollywood in March where conferences were held at the studio about the movie, the project deeply entrenched as a positive.

Carrie was down and out ill with nurses around the clock, but she asked to see Monica.

"There was mostly silence," said Monica, her eyes the deepest, darkest pools of empathy. "Carrie's heart was in need of prayer and her breath short. She communicated so much by saying so little as if taking full measure of our relationship of many years duration. It was a solemn occasion with Carrie's mouth forming half-smiles as energy ebbed and flowed."

Monica's tall, energetic frame was shook by her thumping heart. She didn't need the sight of an ominous shadow of a great bird flying between her and the sun, or hear the *mea culpas* from the sacristy to know that Carrie's days were numbered. She felt like shouting to the daylight to hang longer, the breeze to lay softer, but the sun setting over the ocean threw dappled shadows against the bedroom walls, across the quilt, highlighting Carrie's silver hair, as if to remind Monica that sanity dictates there are endings to all beginnings.

An eternity passed, but Monica never heard any more of the movie, and did not pursue the proposal. Her visitation was the last one she would have with her dear friend.

A PERFECT DAY

CHAPTER FORTY-THREE

Unusually cool autumn winds blew up the mountainside, causing Carrie to abandon her garden and seek the inner recesses of her home in instinctive protectiveness. It was at this time that she, at eight-four years old, was presented with a bronze statuette of Moses by Michelangelo. The presenters were Dr. Hubert Eaton, Chairman of Forest Lawn Council of Regents and Dr. R. B. Von Kleinsmid, Chancellor of the University of Southern California, and the occasion was the announcement of a four-year scholarship in music established in Carrie's name.

"Ballads are the vocal portraits of the national mind," said Von Kleinsmid, quoting the author, Charles Lamb.

Upon presentation Carrie declared, "I am happy and grateful that whoever receives this scholarship will be saved some of the struggles and heartbreaks that faced me before people knew my songs." She spoke in a thready whisper, the joy simmering through. She survived that honor by four months during which time she wrote, *I Believe.*

> Eighty-four years ago, my spirit was sent
> Into its new home on earth,
> But there was a room for me in my Father's mansion.
> I knew it would always be mine.
> My Book of Life was in this room—
> And every day told.
> I believe God said to the Recording Angel,
> "Balance this book each year.

PEGGY DePUYDT

It shall hold both good and evil
Because to acknowledge both is just.
Write only what you know the motives have been,
Allow no uncertain things to appear on its pages.
I have given her a tender heart,
Never willfully unkind.
She shall have a forgiving sprit, talents to be used as she sees best.
A sincere desire to be good.
I have also given her a quick, impulsive tongue
With which to contend—
A spoken truth may sometimes hurt,
Not always do we know why things are done.
I will give her what the world calls prosperity,
She shall have her heart's desires,
Also crosses to bear and burdens.
She will enjoy greatly.
She will suffer greatly.
She will know that always her room will be waiting—
Waiting just as she left it,
Only now it will be filled
With more than eighty years of worldly experiences.
She will need no earthly honors—
If she has earned them, they will be there."
And thus I face the setting sun,
The same sun that rose for over eighty years
To give me courage for a better life.
The majestic dawn where rose the sun
Through clouds of radiant color,
To give to me a new and perfect day
To mar or beautify.
At last the sunset beckons me

A PERFECT DAY

With rays of brilliant light,
The setting sun fraught with splendor
Ending one more day of strife;
A gorgeous sunset marking out
A path of gold that leads me home.
So shed no tears over the sunshine of my death.
To live is wonderful,
To die is glorious.
And then the full moon silvers my journey's end.

CHAPTER FORTY-FOUR

The late afternoon of December 28 was clear but quickly chilling down. The brown leaves of early winter chased across Carrie's yard tumbled by a brisk afternoon breeze.

A shiver shook Carrie's slender frame. Through a blur, she focused on the Christmas tree twinkling in the living room beyond her bedroom door. The holidays had always been one of her favorite times. Yet, this year her chest was weighty, and it was a struggle to breathe instead of being a bodily function to which one gave no pertinent thought.

She closed her eyes and saw, in virtual color and ambience, the parlor in the farm house in Janesville; her father scooping her into his arms, lifting her high to put the angel atop the tree, her mother complaining about all the fuss when there were so many *other* things demanding their attention.

"Put that child down before you have her spoiled rotten," she grumbled.

Then, here was Fred as a youngster in Iron River, where Dr. Bond showered him with every contrivance imaginable at Christmas. She could again hear the joyous delight of the child as he skipped around the Christmas tree assisting with the trimming rites.

"Do this one," he squealed. "This is the one, Mama," as he held out a special decorative bulb that dazzled with gold glitter. Peals of merry laughter echoed off her mind-walls.

She recalled the many Christmases when little could be purchased for gifts of love to be exchanged. Ribbon candy, peanuts in the shell, and an orange, or two were luxuries seldom allowed. The thought weighed down Carrie's heart as if the poverty were her sin of omission, a foot-dragging insufficiency.

Carrie's chest rose and fell with the labor of breathing. Could she ever have anticipated that Fred would be afflicted with morose depression? Her throat constricted with the thought of his wasted adult life after he left the Bond Shop. Would she forever replay his life, his times, his joys, and his deep suffering? Summarily, Fred's life consisted of the exciting emergence of productivity, commingled with the deplorable divergence of complete artlessness, his tangled emotions too complex to unravel. Wouldn't it be miraculous if you could disassemble a body and put that body together again, as a machine? Knowing all this was impossible, she nonetheless agonized to find the gap into which she fell short in rearing the child into the boy, the boy into a man.

Who was crying? She struggled to open her eyes for another glimpse of the glimmering holiday tree. Was that Helen, her bedside nurse crying, or was it Dr. Frank's Nora Nash? Each reminded Carrie of the other: the gentle hands, the compassionate eyes, and the endless vigilance. No one should be crying at such a blessed time of the year. If someone was annoying Helen or Nora, she would get out of this bed and punch him or her out, stunning herself with the thought of such violence, but, yes, she would.

A grimness thinned Carrie's mouth.

"Oh, God, I don't want to lose her." Helen choked on a sob, her farmer's-daughter red cheeks intensifying.

With hardly a heartbeat left in Carrie's chest, Dr. Bond was holding her hand. He rewarded her with a dazzling smile that replicated the sun. She watched him with puzzled eyes. There. There he was in all his youthful handsomeness, noble, kind, and good, with the kindest eyes she had ever seen in a man. He grabbed her up as of old, and swung her wildly in a circle. She was so dizzy.

His dark eyes spoke volumes to her of his love. She knew she was loved, and there is nothing greater.

Where did you go? She mind conveyed. *Fred and I missed you so, and I have so much to tell you.* The words pushed at lazy lips, her body becoming heavier. Carrie's talented piano hands lay unresponsive in Dr. Bond's hands. How she wished to reach up and touch his face.

Helen, a tall woman, bent to look at Carrie. Her jaws clenched; her hand reached for Carrie's pulse.

Carrie struggled to open her eyes, but all she saw were snowflakes coming at her as if in a fierce blizzard.

"Come, Carrie darling, let us go home," Dr. Bond said clearly, erasing any doubt of the direction both their lives were now taking. "We'll leave this darkening room and go into another that is fair and large, luminous and glorious."

Yet, Carrie hesitated, conscious of her doubts about traveling uncharted waters.

The crying had become incessant. Now there were two people crying for heaven's sake. They were Helen Snow and Jaime Palmer, her business manager. They must indeed be in deep and serious straits to be carrying on so. She must help them, but her body was no longer manageable, it was as light as a fuzzy summer cloud. She floated and observed. What a fine looking home she had; her Christmas tree was the prettiest ever. She had so much for which to be thankful. She was filled with the privacy and peace that she had fought all her life to maintain.

Helen and Jaime, a small bird of a woman, tore their glances from each other and sent it slicing to the bed. After all these months and years together, being with Carrie at the hour of her death brought all the more sharply home the way things were, and never could be again.

The light in Carrie's room was becoming bright, lucent bright, and there was Elbert walking toward her with an ethereal glow of goodwill and recognition. She recalled his philanthropic phrase: *Whom the gods love die young no matter how long they live.* Was this then a disillusionment? She looked. She looked beyond and saw Fred with his rascally smile, his eagerness to please. She turned. There was her angel, her own angel!

Outside the wind was prowling, gusting the dry leaves of winter onto the windowpanes as if knocking for permission to enter.

Dr. Bond was yet holding her hand and walking her toward the glorious light. The snowflakes had metamorphosed into a solid bank of white light, the sight filling her with a joy that was bursting.

"Leaves have their time to fall, flowers to wither, and stars to set. It's time to abandon your musical scores to successors." Dr. Bond's message was balm and abetment to Carrie's burdened body. Reason dimmed her desire to linger.

Jaime held her breath, eyes brimming over.

"Don't go, Carrie," Helen sobbed.

But Carrie was not listening. There was stiffness in every line of her body as if in anticipation of an extreme joy, washed free of care and worry, bathed in love. It was not death distressing Carrie; it was the dieing, the unknown, and the thick forest of the unrevealed hereafter.

She quietly slipped away as the copper sun clung to the rim of the Pacific Ocean. A heavy stillness enveloped the house and gardens as if the winter wind had capriciously circumvented the area out of respect to the owner's passing.

In her own bed at End-Of-The-Road, Carrie died

A PERFECT DAY

peacefully, alone, yet known by millions as a poet, a songster, and a primer in benevolence. She inspired love wherever she went with her gracious manners and her retiring attitude. Her music would live forever: simple, melodic and from the heart. The December moon would silver her last journey.

***

A close friend, Mrs. Howard (Betty) Berbeck, a much-in-demand Hollywood designer, arrived just after Carrie died. Consoling Helen and Jaime she said, "Carrie's death merits a canvas only angels could paint. Angels are ever here, forever in attendance," the last words choked under her breath.

"With characteristic faith in a hereafter," Jaime said, "Carrie, after commenting on a presentiment of death, told me last week.

> I don't want you to be unhappy, for I am reconciled. As I have grown older, and have seen presidents, popes and tyrants rise and others fall, and have learned why they did what they did, I have seen how perfectly the law of compensation works out. The reward equals the effort. The deed by itself is not all, but it must be measured by the reason and purpose behind it. It does not matter what people think your reasons are, but in your secret heart, you know them to be; and that is something, which only God and you can know. That is what you are paid for, and you are paid in full measure, according to your true deserts.

With tears streaming down her face, Helen managed to breathe deeply and say, "Carrie was surprised a few weeks ago when she received unsolicited an autographed photograph of

President and Mrs. Truman and their daughter, Margaret. She was delighted at the Chief Executive's remembrance and had the photograph framed and hung in her living room," she gestured. "But her hero, Franklin D. Roosevelt, never acknowledged her work. She would have been so touched."

Helen's hand shook as she presented to Betty Berbeck an essay written in Carrie's last days.

> THOUGHTS THAT COMFORT ME
>
> An essay by: Carrie Jacobs-Bond Glorious sunrise ushered me into the "Valley of Dawn," and I found myself a tiny child in a garden of blossoms. The song of birds gave me the desire to sing and music began to ring in my ears. Loving hands held mine and led me to a path and there began my journey of life. One day of blue skies and scent of new-mown hay, a youth of beauty crossed my path. We looked into each other's eyes, and knew without words that from that hour, we should walk together; and so across the "Valley of Dawn" we wandered on to the "Forest of Dreams." But as the great pines hugged themselves together, we pushed apart, and although we knew the forest when we walked hand in hand, we were lost when separated.
>
> I thought my heart went on with him; I thought I was alone, but a tiny hand, tender responsive fingers, pressed my own, and a voice, dearer than all others, said, "Mother, I am here."
>
> And so I found I was the possessor of two hearts, each filled with each other, two loves separate and apart, hearts full of understanding. No jealous thought could ever enter there for they were filled with pure love.

A PERFECT DAY

We had reached the foot of the "Mountain of Hope." It looked a long way to the top. It was with great joy that we talked of what we should do when we reached the summit.

Often the path was rough. Stones cut our feet—cold winds hushed our voices, but the years rolled by; and always after bruised bodies and speechless hours, we sang again—always sang together, a song of a better tomorrow. We kept music in our souls, as we made our way up the, "Mountain of Hope".

Again, youth crossed my way. The other heart of my son was to be filled. Gladly I loosed his hand, knowing he would always live in my Mother heart. Joy came because of his happiness. No love is ever taken away to make room for another. Pure love expands by giving, and now we three were nearing the top. A few more years and we should be where we could see the other side.

But only a little farther could he walk with us, his work completed. He had left a life filled to overflowing with kind deeds, left precious things for us to carry on down into "Vale of Memories," where I thought again I must walk alone.

But on that lonely road there gleamed three radiant lights—the three loves of my life touched my hands and gave me courage to walk to the end of the blessed path, where all I loved best were waiting for me. And so, from the "Valley of Dawn," through the "Forest of Dreams," up the "Mountain of Hope," cross the "Vale of Memories," I vision the "Gates of Paradise".

A PERFECT DAY

CHAPTER FORTY-FIVE

January 11, 1947 dawned cool and clear in California; a typical Pacific-blue sky greeted early risers who were bustling to attend Carrie Jacobs-Bond's funeral, a ceremonial service matching a monarch's in pomp and protocol.

Seven miles north of the center of Los Angeles lay Glendale nestled in the narrow southeastern tip of the San Fernando Valley. The wooded Verdugo Hills and blue-veiled mountains hem in the city on the west, north, and east. To the south flows the Los Angeles River. Peppertrees and eucalyptus, acacia, and palm trees line the older streets. It was here that Carrie Jacobs-Bond was interred in Forest Lawn Cemetery.

Lulu, (now 59), and Esther Fairbanks, (now 61), having spent the night in Los Angeles, started out for the services by 8:00 a.m., stopping on the way for breakfast.

"I often wonder, Esther, what kind of an adventure it is to die..." Lulu's unruly red hair popped out from under her stylish felt hat, her thick eye-glasses fixing on Esther while lifting small portions of omelet to her mouth.

Esther, whose positive relationship with Lulu was uppermost in her every thought, smiled over her cup of coffee. "I view it as the last and final awakening and not the last sleep into nothingness."

Lulu, her interest in humanities never far removed, paused, and bent her head sideways. "How interesting...*The final awakening*. Yes, the older I get, the more need I have of hanging onto that thought." Her pert nose tilted upward as she sniffed delicately.

Lulu, still a writer and traveler, wished Carrie were yet the companion whom she could take up the Alaskan coastline to any village, any time, any anything. In her grief Lulu had no body, but was just sort of moving energy.

At Forest Lawn, Lulu and Esther's tickets were taken at the door, and they hoped them to be returned as a keepsake, but this did not happen. Some 2000 mourners stood outside to honor the memory of the famous composer, and they saw more celebrities than the Alaskans did and

heard the funeral program through loudspeakers.

The chapel of the Lord's Last Supper was filled with

relatives and friends, including Walter and Cora Gale, Dr. and Monica Irvine, and Col. and Mrs. Ed Fletcher. Lulu and Esther were seated in the fourth row and could see Carrie's bier covered with a heavy velvet pall of a dark red color.

Lulu observed the stained glass, Leonardo da Vinci's *The Last Supper*. It was so well lighted that Christ and His disciples seemed to be almost alive, warm, and touchable. God's own light accompanied by the right time of day made believers out of the most stoic. Lulu and Esther probably understood death for the first time when He put his hand upon their mother, Lucy, one whom they loved dearly, and now that selective hand of God had claimed Carrie.

The program consisted of speeches and songs of Carrie's composition. John Charles Thomas sang *I Love You Truly*, and the Pasadena Boys' Choir sang *The End Of A Perfect Day, and The Hand Of You*. Carrie, proclaimed an Immortal, had the honor of entombment in a crypt beneath the grand stained glass picture. Carrie's ashes are there for all time. Only one other, Gutzon Borglum, sculptor, painter, author, who carved the Mt.

Rushmore Memorial, was declared an Immortal at Forest Lawn. His ashes rest near Carrie's.

As they gathered, the organist played selections from the composer's many songs, some familiar, and some lesser known.

In the section reserved for the family were Mrs. Dorothy Jaehne, and Mrs. Elizabeth Walters Maiden, the composer's granddaughters, and Mr. And Mrs. James Minor, along with other relatives. Minor was a half brother whose lineage is not clear. The memorial program lasted less than an hour. More than an hour before the appointed time, friends, and admirers began to arrive. Impresario L. E. Behymer, Artis Opha Klinker, Novelist Rupert Hughes, Producer Walt Disney, Actor, William Farnum, and Educator, Pearle Aikin-Smith was among them.

In the Memorial Service, Walt Disney, a longtime friend of Carrie's, struggled with his short eulogy. "All our dreams can come true if we have the courage to pursue them, and Carrie did just that with an aplomb that reminded people of fields of flowers and quiet glades."

Dr. Von Kleinsmid, his small, round glasses reflecting light, dwelt on Carrie's many achievements facing adversity with triumph. "Her many successes were resultant of her writing for the people to whom her simple words and melodies are an expression of their own inarticulate sorrows and joys…plain folk form the chorus that shall sing the songs of Carrie. In a sense, she has written her life in music: lullabies, nature songs, and sacred songs, numbering more than three hundred."

Dr. James W. Fifield Jr., of the First Congregational Church, gave the invocation: "Oh God, look down with favor on your daughter, Carrie Jacobs-Bond." His abundance of white hair fluffed as he posed right then left. "Prepare for her a proper place of refreshment, light, and peace. She has had a wise man's heart in her social discourse, which has oftentimes been burdensome. Her tree of life has had many rings, each telling a story of compassion and goodness. I pray You welcome her into Your kingdom."

Dr. Lawrence E. Nelson, a tall, slim man radiating unquestioned honesty, of the University of Redlands, read from the Bible. *"Thou shalt become an astonishment, a proverb, and a byword, among all nations."* (Carrie must have stirred in her bier with the familiar words oftentimes spoken by Grandfather Davis.) "Her charity covered the sins of a multitude. She piped unto millions and they have danced. The desert has rejoiced and blossomed as the rose. Carrie Jacobs-Bond was blessed with a hearing ear, a seeing eye, and an instrumental hand to add joy to the lives of people she never met, never knew, never would know. She has fought the good fight of faith and died in a good old age, full of days, riches, and honor."

Dr. Edgar J. Godspeed robed in white and gold, his pate bald, paid the composer tribute: "'Music is the mediator between the spiritual and the sensual life. Although the spirit be not master of that which it creates through music, yet it is blessed in this creation, which, like every creation of art, is mightier than the artist.' Words by Ludwig Van Beethoven. Did our Carrie think when she composed her heartfelt songs that they would endure forever? I think not. She wrote that which sprung from her soul, from her inner being, that which might not have been easily verbalized in conversation. Our Carrie wrote evergreen poetry, and music resembles poetry; in each are numerous graces, which no methods teach, and which a master hand alone can reach. Our Carrie was truly blessed and a phenomenon living in our lifetime."

New Testament translator, Dr. Rufus B. Von Kleinsmid, University of Southern California read in clipped English bearing German undertones: " 'Music is the art of the prophets, the only art that can calm the agitations of the soul; it is one of the most magnificent and delightful presents God has given us.' Luther. Next to theology I give to music the highest place and honor, and to Carrie Jacobs-Bond my eternal thanks for her contributions of a degree that will live on in history ranking among the mightiest."

While placing a wreath of gold laurel leaves atop the casket, Dr. Hubert Eaton, another Cary Grant, read the Pronouncement of Immortality. He raised his voice in resonating authority. "As the seed dies into a new life, so does man. In the words of Socrates, 'All men's souls are immortal, but the souls of the righteous are both immortal and divine.' No doubts abound that immortality, and that alone, amid Carrie Jacobs-Bond's life's pains, abasements, and heartaches, laid comfort upon her soul, elevated, and filled her with the thought of going home, going to her eternal home of immortality."

Dr Eaton had never delivered on a breath of rushing air, a more stirring benediction, his demeanor suggesting reverence, and his sweeping inclusion of the mourners sober and reflective. The church was hushed; no one dared breathe with the resounding delivery of mighty words, as if from Mt. Sinai.

It took more than an hour for the reluctant crowd to disburse, conversing in closed coveys, gesturing in small sweeps, shuffling as if sedated under the spell of the service.

That which was mortal of Carrie Jacobs-Bond was committed to the grave while that which was immortal of her, the simple songs of love and life and longing, comforted the large gathering of family and friends, who met together to pay final tribute to the composer, universally loved.

The crowd overflowed the hall and scores waited outside the mausoleum until the end of the rites to pass by the bier. The celebrated and rich were there along with the unknown and the poor. They, the people grieved, for it was, *The People for whom Carrie Jacobs-Bond's simple words and melodies were an expression of their own inarticulate sorrow and joys.*

The body of Fred was to be disinterred from its present grave and placed beside that of his mother, in accordance with her wish.

EPILOGUE
A Perfect Day
August 12, 1950

Regents of the University of California accepted the personal property of the late Carrie Jacobs-Bond on the 87th anniversary of the composer's birth.

Materially as well as musically, Carrie had done all right. Her estate—real and personal property and royalties—was to bring more than $15,000 each ($135,000) a year to her two granddaughters, Dorothy Smith Jaehme of Austin, Texas, and Elizabeth Smith Walters Maiden of Massachusetts. Various amounts went to other heirs.

Carrie directed in her will that her effects be presented to the university's Westwood campus. Eighty-two items selected by the university were to furnish a Carrie Jacobs-Bond Memorial room in the Music Building planned for UCLA. Among the effects, in the interim stored in the Clark Memorial Library, was the rosewood melodeon, a wedding gift from Dr. Bond, upon which Carrie composed many of her songs. Other items included desks, table, chairs, bookcases, paintings, autographed books, and a complete file of her scores.

University officials were aided in cataloguing Carrie's effects by Mr. And Mrs. Howard Verbeck, friends of the composer, and Mrs. Jaime Palmer, her business manager. Carrie designated that the color scheme of the memorial room and arrangement of the furnishings be supervised by Verbeck, an interior decorator.

In the year 1949, funds for the projected Music Building were appropriated to erect a $1,000,000, ($7,280,000 in today's dollars), structure at the north end of the campus as a drama-music-art group.

In 1978, The Carrie Jacob-Bond Home in Iron River, Michigan was sold to the Iron County Historical Society for $12,500, and moved to its present site in Caspian, Michigan.

Carrie directed in her Will that a dedication poem to The Little Chapel of Silence, at the University of California Los Angeles be hung in the narthex.

> Through the stress of work and sorrow
> Through the stress of strife and pain
> We must have a place of refuge
> Where we dream our dreams again;
> Where we find the gift of comfort
> Where we find the joy of peace
> In the silence of our Chapel
> Where our heartaches always cease.
> Oh, beloved Little Chapel
> Where I come to kneel and pray
> Asking God to give me courage
> That will help me on my way;
> I can feel your tender blessings
> I can feel the love you give
> In the silence of our Chapel
> Where I learn again to live.

※※※

Lulu Fairbanks (1888 to 1968)

A PERFECT DAY

Lulu Fairbanks was secretary for the International Sourdoughs for 36 years, and they dubbed her "Miss Alaska" for life.

In 1965, the Alaskan legislature honored Lulu in a joint resolution for her years of service to the state.

In 1976, Pioneer Alaska groups in the Pacific Northwest built a monument in Seattle to Lulu to commemorate her accomplishment ties to the 49th State's history. A marble marker was placed at Pier 48 where Alaska ferries moor. The water route traveled by Miss Fairbanks now is served by Alaska ferries from Pier 48, a fitting place for a memorial.

Lulu and Esther were both interred in Seattle near their mother, Lucy.

✻✻✻

Dr. and Mrs. (Monica) Irvine continued serving the city of Iron River, Michigan deep into the 1960's.

UPCOMING BOOKS BY PEGGY DE PUYDT

HAVASU HEAT, fiction.

A Lake Havasu City, Arizona Police Officer struggles to vindicate his wife's death resultant of a drug cartel car bomb.

RUMBELLION, non-fiction.

A small town attorney gains national attention. A vanguard for the Italian populations' right to serve wine with meals during the Prohibition Era, M. S. McDonough faces overwhelming odds from Revenuers.

ALL ABOUT ABE, fiction, a trilogy.

Follow the plodding life of Abe, a one-half Sioux Indian, from handicapped childhood, learning-impaired high school days, to amazing successes as a running back for University of Michigan, to being drafted by the Green Bay Packers as their star running back.

ABOUT THE AUTHOR

Peggy DePuydt was born in Nahma, Michigan in 1932. After taking a degree in Liberal Arts at sixty years old, she became deeply entrenched in composition, resulting in authoring four books, "A Perfect Day" being the fourth. She lives in Lake Havasu City, Arizona with her husband, Richard, a retired Michigan State Police Officer, and is proud of her four children and seven grandchildren.

ABOUT GREATUNPUBLISHED.COM

www.greatunpublished.com is a website that exists to serve writers and readers, and to remove some of the commercial barriers between them. When you purchase a GreatUNpublished title, whether you order it in electronic form or in a paperback volume, the author
is receiving a majority of the post-production revenue.

A GreatUNpublished book is never out of stock, and always available, because each book is printed on-demand, as it is ordered.

A portion of the site's share of profits is channeled into
literacy programs.

So by purchasing this title from GreatUNpublished, you are helping to revolutionize the publishing industry for the benefit of
writers and readers.

And for this we thank you.